Killing Joke

Are You Receiving?

Jyrki "Spider" Hämäläinen

NEW HAVEN PUBLISHING LTD

Published 2020
First Edition
NEW HAVEN PUBLISHING LTD
www.newhavenpublishingltd.com
newhavenpublishing@gmail.com

Front Cover image © Dod Morrison

Cover design © Pete Cunliffe
pcunliffe@blueyonder.co.uk

newhaven
publishing

"You know it's kind of universe's joke really. Futility of our humanity's ego. It is very cleansing and cathartic. Renewing in a kind of nature way. Force of nature."
–   **Martin "Youth" Glover**

Killing Joke
Jaz Coleman - singer
Youth - bassist
Geordie Walker - guitar
"Big Paul" Ferguson - drums

Contributors
Andrew Alekel – engineer
Bill Smith – designer
Dante Bonutto – A&R
Dave Kovacevic – keyboards
Geoff Dugmore – drums
Greg Hunter – producer
Hugh Padgham – engineer/producer
Jah Wobble – bassist (Public Image Limited)
Jerry Kandiah – engineer/producer
Jock McDonald – guitarist (4" Be 2" / the Bollock Brothers)
Mike Coles – designer
Neil Perry – journalist
Nick Launay – engineer/producer
Phil Harding – engineer/producer
Reza Udhin – keyboards
Rob O'Connor – designer
Roi Robertson – keyboards
Shaun Pettigrew – film director
Ted Parsons – drums
Troy Gregory – bass

https://killingjokebook.wordpress.com/

Interviews conducted by Jyrki "Spider" Hämäläinen between 2012 and 2020, unless where otherwise stated.

INTRODUCTION

What you are holding in your hand is the history of post-punk pioneers Killing Joke told by those who were there with the help of archive material. The sound of the Earth vomiting in detail.

The story of Killing Joke is the story of imminent apocalypse, and what better time than the covid pandemic to be reading this.

The members have multiple side projects, from Jaz Coleman's career in classical music and Youth's hit production skills... and so on. Those are merely touched upon at times.

What a journey it was writing this book. I hope you enjoy as much reading it as I did putting the pieces of the puzzle together. Thanks to everyone who gave interviews for the book. It was a great pleasure.

This book is dedicated to the Gatherers.

Jyrki "Spider" Hämäläinen, Porvoo, Finland August 2020

CONTENTS

Acknowledgements

First and foremost, you can thank yourself for buying this book and supporting the industry.

Thanks to *Vive Le Rock*'s editor in chief Eugene Butcher for assigning me to interview Jaz Coleman for a feature in 2012, which led to my first ever cover feature.

Thanks to Teddie Dahlin and New Haven Publishing for making a lifelong dream into a reality. Very impressed: in just around 12 hours from the first point of contact she was ready to offer me a contract, and while bigger publishing companies had expressed interest, they were unable to make a solid offer.

Thank you, Jah Wobble, for the first interview conducted particularly for this book and words of encouragement.

Thanks to Killing Joke: Jaz Coleman, Martin "Youth" Glover, "Big" Paul Ferguson and Geordie Walker for all the interviews over the years. Most of all my gratitude towards Youth for the guest list entries over the years. Killing Joke's publicist Matt Reynolds from Savage Gringo PR for sorting out the initial interviews with the original line up. Most of all passing on the interview requests after the first Jaz Coleman interview, which led to the subsequent interviews at the Roundhouse in London and eventually gave birth to all the material from the original feature being expanded into a cover feature. Hazel Brown for proof-reading chapters 1 and 2 in their earlier stages.

Alphabetical appreciation of interviewees: Andrew Alekel, Benny Calvert (sort of), Dante Bonutto, Jaz Coleman, Mike Coles, Geoff Dugmore, Paul Ferguson, Martin "Youth" Glover, Troy Gregory, Phil Harding, Greg Hunter, Jerry Kandiah, Dave Kovacevic, Jock McDonald, Rob O'Connor, Hugh Padgham, Ted Parsons, Shaun Pettigrew, Bill Smith, Reza Udhin, Kevin "Geordie" Walker and Jah Wobble.

Also, thanks to all the Gatherers who regularly contribute to online communities such as *The Church of Killing Joke* and *The Gatherers* on Facebook.

Parts of this book builds upon foundations laid by other writers, reviewers and interviewers of the press, all of whom I have acknowledged in the main body of the text. Thanks to Paul Hagen and Teddie Dahlin for giving me their interview material to be used in this book.

PART ONE

The formative years

4" Be 2"

Before there was Killing Joke, Martin "Youth" Glover, born on 27th December 1960 in Slough, England, had already experienced the magic of being in a band. That is of course if you include his first performance behind the school shed at the tender age of six. His original nickname was Pig Youth, having named himself after the 70s Jamaican DJ Big Youth (aka Manley Augustus Buchanan), and over time his nickname would be simply shortened to Youth.

In 1977 he joined a punk band called the Rage who went to tour with the Adverts, but most notably he was a founding member in 4" Be 2". 4" Be 2" was a band that featured John Lydon's brother Jimmy Lydon, their father John Christoper Lydon, Jock McDonald and Youth. They released the single 'One Of The Lads' on Island Records in September 1979.

"John Lydon produced the record. He drank a case of lager and fell asleep, which was good because it allowed me to jump on the desk. That was the first proto-punk world record as it has John Lydon playing banjo on it. Disco dub mash up or something like that. It had the disco drums and the disco bass line over it with some edgy guitars and banjo, which made it kind of wordly.

"Top 40 hit! Came out on Island Records, which opened the door for me to a deal with them for Killing Joke. Also the session opened the doors for me into the recording world. Watching Mark Lusardi work the desk, he knew his dub. When it came to us doing our first single we went to him. He did 'Turn to Red' with us. So it was a great experience for me. Very important," says Youth.

John Lydon - formerly known as Johnny Rotten of the Sex Pistols, who had now reverted back to using his real name due to ongoing legal battles with the Sex Pistols manager and svengali Malcolm McLaren - produced the record, guaranteeing the group exposure in the punk rock movement of the late 1970s.

As the band's manager and singer Jock McDonald tells us: "4" Be 2" originally got started over at Gunter Grove in Chelsea in South West

London where John Lydon lived with people such as Shane McGowan, who later became known for The Pogues. Shane McGowan kept saying to Jimmy Lydon, who was to become the singer of the group and his school friend, suggested 'why don't you do an Irish disco paddy record?' Don Letts, the legendary film producer, was there and what happened was Youth popped around and Youth said that would be a good idea, so we all went to Island Studios on Basing Street and we done the first, what everybody reckons, the first Irish disco pop record.

"When we were in the studio producing the record with John Lydon there was something very unusual. When everyone else would fuck off for joints or drinks or booze or eating Youth would remain with John at the [mixing] console. He wouldn't leave it. Everything John had done, like putting loops and the tape backwards Youth paid ultra-attention to that. At the time no one else was interested in doing that sort of a thing. He knew that John was a talent and he wanted to learn everything that John had." John Lydon producing the record was "genius. There is guys who have it and guys who don't. Youth right away knew that John had it."

4" Be 2" signed their record deal with Island Records the very same day that U2 signed theirs. "We were both getting the same champagne from Chris Blackwell," recalls Jock. "If Jimmy hadn't chosen that name we would've busted some records."

Youth had very strongly adopted the look of the bass player Sid Vicious of the Sex Pistols, as Jock recalls. "It was unreal. They were the same height, the same age, they wore the same clothes and they talked in the same manner. Everybody thought he was Sid. So they sent us out to Ireland and Dublin to promote 'One Of The Lads' and when we got to Dublin U2 were playing one of their first gigs down in Howth, it's a fishing village, [where] Bono spotted Youth and he thought he was Sid, so we brought Youth up on stage and introduced him as Sid and played two Sex Pistols numbers and afterwards took him out for a pint and none of us had the heart to tell Bono, 'This is Youth, it's not Sid'. He is getting the drinks in, so we might as well go along with it. Isn't it ironic that in later years in life and Bono would turn around to Youth and say to him 'haven't we met before?' when Youth came over to re-mix U2. Youth still hadn't got the courage to tell him it was me."

4" Be 2" played with U2 at their first ever gig at Howth Community Centre. "Then the fun really began. We went up to Belfast. Terry Hooley brought us up to Belfast." Terry Hooley was the founder of the Good

Vibrations record shop and label. It was home for bands such as The Undertones, Rudi, Protex and The Outcast. BBC national radio DJ John Peel became an important champion of the label after playing the Undertones' 'Teenage Kicks' on his radio show, which came out on Good Vibrations. The band was staying in the Europa hotel when the IRA approached them. "IRA come over to Youth and said 'hi, Sid, can we have your autograph?' The whole of the IRA. Guns and everything. We didn't have the courage ourselves to tell them it wasn't Sid. We were shitting ourselves, because we thought what if they found out it is not Sid. We better go along with it. So he signed for [the] IRA."

Terry Hooley had arranged a gig for 4" Be 2" for the evening at Queens University. "Then it really started happening. The punks who couldn't get into the Queens all jumped through the glass windows and one had a huge bit of glass sticking out of his forehead. The blood went everywhere and he said 'I couldn't give a fuck as long as I meet Sid Vicious.' So, all that happened between Dublin and Belfast because he was identical to Sid. He even ended up playing the part of Sid when he played bass at a show on Studio 21 on 21 Oxford Street on Christmas Day with Steve Jones and Paul Cook from the Sex Pistols and Billy Idol taking the place of Johnny Rotten. The gig had been organised by Jock McDonald and supported by the Bollock Brothers and Bananarama."

Youth didn't think much of the band at the time and the way he describes the situation it could've been one of Malcolm McLaren's swindles.

"It was a bit of a scam band. John Lydon's brother and father and I pretended to be Sid Vicious. John Lydon producing it and Jock McDonald managing it. It was like a big punk scam group," reflects Youth.

The band - scam or not - did end up playing live in Belfast, Northern Ireland, which is notorious for the ongoing conflict between Catholics and Protestants.

"Actually it became real as we did a gig on Christmas Day. Jimmy Lydon bringing out this tricolour Irish flag and started singing rebel songs at this gig we were doing at a Protestant university in Belfast at the time of the troubles. A riot kicked off," Youth recalls.

Youth sensed that it wasn't the right thing to do and decided to part ways with the group.

"We weren't really a band. It was Jimmy and his mates. Jock couldn't play guitar. I was the only one that could play anything apart

12

from John's dad. I don't know how we managed to do that tour. It was just chaos. We came back and did a couple more singles and sessions, but then I had to tell them I was leaving as Killing Joke was taking off. That caused some trouble. I think Jock threatened to chop my fingers off if I left the band. That was a heavy day!" Youth laughs.

Jock McDonald recalls it differently and claims Youth left as he got a big pay off from EG records to join Killing Joke, and walked off from the pub they were in with a massive bag of weed to share with his new band Killing Joke in their headquarters. He admits there might've been some heated words exchanged between them. "I don't remember saying that, but if I did, I apologise," adds Jock, sounding sincere.

Nevertheless, Youth says he was very grateful for the experience. "I'm grateful for Jimmy and Johnny giving me the opportunity at the time."

A music video was made for 'One Of The Lads' showing the band playing in a derelict house in a demolition site. Youth very much still resembles Sid Vicious at this point with this spiky black hair and the R-padlock around his neck. Don Letts directed the video on a building site in North London. "Don Letts is a really good talent and he wanted the real McCoy. He wanted Lydon's dad, who actually worked on an Irish building site. The workmen - he wanted them all real. Even the lorry who drives in to the site. He wanted it bang on and we got it," says Jock.

"We were getting into a lot of trouble," recalls Jock. "It's a real shame. 4" Be 2" at the particular time here in England, 4" Be 2" is Cockney for Jew. Today they say the word yid, it's a football chant. So, what they didn't realise is that Jimmy Lydon had his eye taken out by four be two wood in a building site, so he called the band that after big Irish shamrock, but at that particular time the gutter press in the UK were looking for anything. Anything to wind up any sort of stories, so the band suffered because of that. The Jewish people thought it was very anti-Semitic.

"We got the money from the record company and Youth said to me 'Listen Jock, I'll knock it on the head and move it over to Killing Joke'." He didn't mind as much, but Jimmy Lydon was really upset. Jock appreciated Killing Joke.

Subsequent EP 'All Of The Lads' was released via McDonald and Lydon Records (Shamrock) in 1981. Jock reckons it was "light years ahead of its time. Everyone says that." The A-side only features one track, 'All Of The Lads', which is an instrumental re-recording of 'One

Of The Lads' and doesn't even feature Youth, but Noel 'Wally' Wardon on bass. Youth appears on the songs on the B-side, 'Jimmy Jones' and 'Bitch', from the earlier sessions with John Lydon.

By autumn 1981 the band 4" Be 2" had broken up. Jimmy Lydon had got married and Jock McDonald and the rest of the group had gone on to release two singles, 'Frustration' and 'The Bunker', with his new group the Bollock Brothers. Youth would later, in 1982, guest on the Bollock Brothers' 'The Slow Removal of The Left Ear of Vincent van Gogh' 12 inch single. Anyway, now we're on to Killing Joke…

Getting The Band Together

Lead singer Jeremy "Jaz" Coleman was born on 26th February 1960 to a mixed race couple who were both teachers. His mother was a high-caste Brahmin Indian. He came from a well-educated, musically trained and financially secure background. Jaz explained his upbringing to Phil Sutcliffe for *Sounds* in August 1980: "I'm a complete mixture. I have no culture that's my own. I don't relate to anybody and I'm really proud of that."

He has his roots in the Christian church, as he explained to Angie Baldassarre of now defunct *Toronto Shades* in 1981. "Well, for a start I spent 14 years of my life with the church, intensely. I studied Christian religion, I became it. Because I was so deeply involved I fell out of it. I tried to combine that into music and I did it. Words can destroy a lot, they get misinterpreted, twisted around. It is an instinct to sing."

Jaz told Paul Bursche for another defunct publication, UK's *No. 1* magazine, in April 1984 that he was a choirboy for years and part of the cathedral choir. He was then a member of the National Youth Orchestra and became an accomplished violinist. Apparently, he "was totally straight up to the age of 14, and a very talented musician. Then I discovered rhythm and deviated sharply."

"I'm a very religious person," explained Jaz to Mat Smith of *Melody Maker* in August 1986. "I used to go on a pilgrimage every year. My parents were as pagan as they come, but I chose my own free will and got into church music and sang in the cathedral choir. These Franciscan friars used to take us to a burial mound then on to Wynchcombe Abbey. I did this for about five years without thinking. Then I started taking an interest in pre-Christian religions. I suppose if you want to categorise me I'm a bit of a pagan. I'm looking after number one.

"We didn't even finish basic school. Well it just goes to show that most things are possible. There is a tendency these days in societies we live in to judge people unfit unless they got their basic qualifications. They've written a lot of people off and their sense of self worth by being judged being losers before they have even had a chance to complete their 16th or 17th year on the planet, which is the same feeling that we had and we were really angry. I like to think that people see us and realise that most things are possible through self-education."

Jaz originally met future Killing Joke drummer Paul Ferguson, born 31st March 1958, through a mutual friend he had met in the dole queue. Jaz had been signing on to claim his unemployment benefits at Holland Park in Kensington, on the western edge of central London, where he got talking to Paul's flat-mate in the queue.

Paul Ferguson: "I moved to London in 1978 after my foundation studies in art with the intention of being in a band."

Jaz had told him he came from a provincial town with the intention of getting into a band. They went to the nearby house on Portland Road where Jaz and Paul met for the first time. Jaz had been living in a flat in Ladbroke Grove and Paul suggested he move in with him in Battersea, South London. Bizarrely enough, the story goes that the ceiling fell down on their first night of living together.

Jaz was the keyboard player and Paul the drummer in the Matt Stagger Band, but they were looking for something different. "It was a good band," Jaz said to UK-based weekly music magazine *NME*'s Paul Rambali in their first mainstream press interview in March 1980, "but it was his show, and towards the end it got sickly commercial and we just didn't fit. It wasn't being very honest, and when it comes down to playing, if you lie, it sounds like it."

Paul: "I met Jaz when I was in the Matt Stagger Band, and he and I decided that we wanted our own thing. That was the beginning of Killing Joke 40 years ago!"

Both Jaz and Paul were into magic and the occult and the story goes that they used magic to attract the other two members of the group. On the 26th February 1979 they performed a ritual of dedication in order to reach the other two members they were looking for.

They drew a circle on the floor, drew a pentagram inside it and performed the ritual, which led to a fire starting in the flat. This was later said to have been caused by getting the compass points wrong as they weren't fully rehearsed in the magic they were performing.

They put on ad in British music paper *Melody Maker*, which said the following:

WANT TO BE PART OF THE KILLING JOKE?
We mean it man.

Total exploitation, total publicity, total anonymity.
Bass and lead wanted.

Paul told *The Offense* fanzine writer Blake Gumprecht in 1981 that his musical interests go as far as the rockabilly singer Gene Vincent, but also such artists as The Last Poets. One of Geordie's inspirations was Zal Cleminson from Alex Harvey Band, but he felt that there was much missing as far as rock guitarists were concerned.

Jaz explained the situation regarding the recruitment in 1979 to fanzine *Allied Propaganda #3* as follows:

"We must have had about ninety people ringing up in the first week - we saw about forty of them and they were all tossers, totally the wrong type of people. We wanted people who understood our points of view. Anyway, there was this guy who kept ringing called Geordie, and this guy kept ringing up for about two or three weeks. So we said 'come round to the flat.' Later I was looking in a dustbin for something I'd lost and I was pulling out all this shit from these dustbin bags when I heard a voice: 'Looking for your breakfast, are you?' I looked round and there was this long-haired cunt, some sort of hippy. He asked me where 158 was and I said, 'Here.' So I took him up to the flat. As soon as we sat down we had a good argument and I thought 'this might be the guy' - even though he had long hair - it was just his sarcasm that got me. He suggested we find a bass player and get some music together. Later he phoned up and said, 'I'm being kicked out, I'll have to go back to Milton Keynes', his home town, so we said he might as well move in with us."

As told in *Sounds* in 1980 Kevin "Geordie" Walker was born in County Durham and moved to Milton Keynes as his carpenter father had found work there. They lived on the enormous Lakes Estate, which is still there today, but going through a massive regeneration. The fateful phone call he had made from women's halls of residence at Trent College in Barnet where he was living incognito with his girlfriend. When he rang the group his only prior experience playing guitar was in his mother's flat, but he had a strong attitude. Apart from Youth and his past in what some might call pseudo-group 4" Be 2" the others didn't have all that much experience in playing bands or recording.

Geordie told Max Kay of *Music UK* in June 1984 that his musical career started when he was eight years old when he heard 'Sabre Dance' by Love Sculpture. "It used the guitar as a musical instrument to convey an atmosphere, it wasn't normal guitar playing which people feel they have to play, certain rhythms, certain solos, certain scales. In fact I don't know why he didn't carry on along those lines. A guitar has a lot of musical capability, but it has the rhythm as well." His daily ritual after school was to lock himself in his bedroom and practise with his amp on full volume until his dad came back from work. He got his first guitar at Christmas 1973. His mother, who had seen Jimi Hendrix, helped him to pick a Gibson Les Paul from a shop in Northampton. "I could play about two chords and she said 'we'll take it.'" He states that he is not interested in solos and is more interested in conveying a rhythm. Rather than practice and reading music he is more into making up his own chords and playing melodies.

The band kept publishing the same ad when trying to find the bass player, but a lot of the potential players seemed to have just been interested in making money. At one point Paul went to Egypt to visit his parents, leaving Jaz and Geordie to look after the flat they were living in. The whole band then moved temporarily to Cheltenham to live with Jaz's parents.

Geordie tells how the band found Youth to fanzine *Allied Propaganda #3* as follows:

"There's this prick called Youth who keeps ringing and asking if he can join. We went through all these bassists, they were all shit, and his was the last number. We were just about to pack it all in, so we phoned up and he said, 'Come round.' He lived in this shitty little bedsit on the top of this hotel in Earls Court."

The liner notes of *The Peel Sessions* compilation describe how in May 1979 there had been a knock on the door of the bedsit where Youth and his flatmate Alex Paterson lived and it was long haired Geordie dressed in brothel creepers and full teddy boy outfit. He asked for Youth and Alex woke the bassist who was in the bed in the corner. Youth gave Geordie his acoustic guitar, which only had four strings at the time, to impress him, but was simply told to "fuck off."

In an interview with US fanzine *The Bob* in October 1981, Geordie tells how the bedsit was above Kersland Hotel, where three people were going through sex change operations and there were other interesting characters. Youth had been living with a friend of his who roadied for the band during their early days.

Cheltenham Rehearsals

The singer Jaz Coleman is from Cheltenham, which is a Regency town near the Cotswolds in Gloucestershire. Once upon a time the town became known as a health and holiday spa resort when mineral springs were discovered in 1716.

Geordie tells how the band relocated to Cheltenham to fanzine *Allied Propaganda #3* as follows:

"Anyway, all four of us moved to Cheltenham for four months. We went to play in the studio when we got there and he was fucking shit... Paul said 'the cunt can't play' and there was Youth shouting 'I can, I can, I can play', so we left and went back the next morning. He was shit, so me and Paul left Youth and Geordie in the studio. About an hour later we walked into the studio, really stoned, and Youth and Geordie were playing this one note. All my keyboards were switched on so I went over to play them and Paul went over to his drums and just started playing. I can remember all these people walking in open-mouthed, it was really strange... something happened at our first jam."

Youth: "We spent ten months rehearsing in Cheltenham. We had a cheap place there. Even though I had to hitchhike from London and back to go to Earl's Court to sign on. We spent ten months writing and rehearsing before getting a gig to get that 20 minute set that was killer. For every five or six songs with grit there'd be ten that we'd throw away."

Paul: "We had no money so we stayed at Jaz's parents' house and a friend, Mickey Clarke, gave us a place to rehearse in. We all hitchhiked back and forth to London each week."

Some songs that were included in their early set, 'Animal', 'Nuclear Boy' and 'You're Being Followed', never made it to any of the studio recordings. Others surfaced on the early singles and the debut album such as 'Change', 'The Wait', 'Pssyche', 'Complications', and 'Tomorrow's World'.

Paul: "'Are You Receiving' was the first song we wrote together."
The song is still a fan favourite and has a unique resonance, being their

first creation.

Jaz: "It was a special kind of weird atmosphere. I remember when we first jammed that track. That was the first piece of music we ever wrote. When we finished jamming it there were loads of people in the rehearsal room, we all started laughing after and you could feel it was the destiny. It was tangible you know!"

That song also has its beginnings when Youth auditioned for the band. Jaz and Paul had left Geordie and Youth back at the rehearsal and had headed off to a nearby pub as they weren't initially impressed by Youth or his playing abilities, but once they got back from the pub Geordie and Youth had locked on a note and groove, which set the foundations for 'Are You Receiving?'

One of the band's earliest songs was 'Wardance', which I'd dare to say has been played at their every show. The political nature of the song and the ominous gloom seem to be always relevant to what is happening around the world.

Youth: "We liked the idea of tribal drums, dubby bassline and some brutal guitars. That was the basic template. It's either tribal drums or disco and then dubby distorted bass and slightly discorded guitars. And Jaz's synths! We love Jaz's synths. Little mono synth."

The band has often stated that their music is deeply rooted in the special chemistry between the members of the band.

According to the liner notes of *The Peel Sessions* compilation the band's very first demo was recorded in Jaz's father's garage in Cheltenham. The song in question, 'Pssyche', was then played by Youth to Ivor at Beggars Banquet Records, a British independent record label, which started as a chain of record shops owned by Martin Mills and Nick Austin. The label wanted to sign them just on the basis of the strength of that one song, but the deal didn't materialise.

Mickey Penguin tells in *Kill Your Puppy* that the cassette recording in question was made in the Coleman's garden instead. The band managed to play about three and a half minutes before the police turned up and ordered them to turn off their racket, but they had managed to record an embryonic version of 'Pssyche', which was deliberately spelt with double 's'.

"That's one place we'll never be allowed to go back to," told manager Brian, regarding Cheltenham, to Valac Var Der Veene of *Sounds* in their 31 January issue in 1981. On one of his visits to Cheltenham, he was confronted with the sight of the group under virtual siege. The neighbours were complaining, the Noise Abatement Society had been called in, and the police were knocking on the door every few hours. There was also an unfounded rumour at the time that the band had been sponsored by Led Zeppelin, mainly Jimmy Page, as they shared the same interest in the occult.

The band played their very first gig on 4th August at Witcombe Lodge in Brockworth where they supported Oi group The Ruts and the reggae and ska influenced The Selecter. The venue is now a Premier Inn, but between autumn of 1978 and late 1979 the venue hosted concerts of multiple future stars such as The Cure as well as The Specials and Madness. The prime motor for these concerts was Chris Garland, who had a shop in Cheltenham selling punk clothing. He knew the likes of Malcolm McLaren and Vivienne Westwood from the new punk scene that had sprung up in the capital. He originally set up gigs at the Plough Hotel in the High Street, but then went to try his luck with the middle of nowhere at Witcombe Lodge, where he organised free coach rides for the gig goers to attract the crowd.

The band also covered 'Bodies' by the Sex Pistols, which musically was more traditional rock, but given the morbid theme of a girl bringing an aborted foetus to Johnny Rotten did somehow fit the apocalyptic vision the band has always portrayed. The song appeared on the original release of *The Unperverted Pantomime*, which has the cover as the final track, but has since not appeared on subsequent re-releases. *The Unperverted Pantomime* is an important document as it is the first live recording of the band, rumoured to have taken place at a venue in London on 1st November, but exact confirmation has never been made. Apparently, they also played 'Poptones' by Public Image Limited, the band Johnny Rotten, or John Lydon as he was then known, had started after the Pistols had self-combusted, but the song was never played live during their sets.

Paul: "Our first recording was done in London behind the Marquee Club with an engineer called Mark Lusardi."

Mark Lusardi is the brother of famous glamour model Linda Lusardi and is known for being a pioneer of the UK dub. He perfected his skills working at London's Gooseberry Sound Studios recording the likes of reggae stars Dennis Bovell, Prince Far I and Creation Rebel in the late 1970s. He has worked extensively with bassist Jah Wobble and also worked with Wob's group Public Image Limited. Lusardi had also worked with John Lydon from Public Image Limited while he was

21

known as Johnny Rotten of the Sex Pistols on their famous 'Spunk' demos. In the 1990s he would work with electronic artists such as Radiohead, Massive Attack, Left Field and Daft Punk.

Youth's former flatmate and later the founder of the Orb, Alex Paterson, recalls the recording of the debut EP in the liner notes of *The Peel Sessions* compilation saying that the sessions taking place on Gerrard Street were mostly spent hitting the bong under the mixing desk. At the time Alex and Youth were squatting in Elgin Crescent in Ladbroke Grove where they'd be regularly spinning 'Rapper's Delight' by The Sugarhill Gang, the first rap song to enter *Billboard's* Top 40 Chart, on a huge sound system Youth had bought with the money he got from the 4" Be 2" deal. During the period, Alex Paterson had a band called Bloodsport briefly with Wally Nightingale, who had briefly been in the very early incarnation of the Sex Pistols, on bass, Big Paul on drums and Jaz on OBX synthesiser.

The songs the band had demoed were 'Requiem', 'Wardance', 'Bloodsport', 'The Wait', 'Complications', 'Change', 'Madness', 'Killer Dub (aka Bread & Jam)' and 'Bloodsport'. These would surface on the 2004 *Chaos for Breakfast* 4 CD box set released by Malicious Damage. The songs recorded here are almost identical to the versions appearing on their subsequent albums. Apart from 'Killer Dub' the songs would make it on to the first two albums. Clocking over 19 minutes the 'Killer Dub' instrumental gets very repetitive and not worthy of scoring a place on an album. According to Youth the song might've only been played live a couple of times. The same compilation did include a lot of lesser known early material from the band, but the band playing AC/DC and Deep Purple's 'Smoke on the Water' during soundcheck in 1980 is yet to surface along with dub versions and "Alex Paterson and Paul Ferguson are doing the percussion on broken glass, smashing glasses for the drumbeat. Youth took it away and speeded it up, added voices. Totally mad" as described by Mike Coles in an interview with *Record Collector* in 2004. In the same interview Geordie tells that these recordings appearing on *Chaos for Breakfast* were done at the Roundhouse Studios in Chalk Farm for maybe a week or so before the band did the first album.

Youth: "It wasn't like we were having a lot of commercial success. We did start selling out shows. It was a real band. It wasn't a pretend band [like 4" Be 2"]. A very serious band where everyone wanted to commit to it."

First EP

According to Mickey Penguin in *Kill Your Puppy* the first single was recorded over a weekend. The recording sessions were paid for by money borrowed from Jaz's then girlfriend, Jasmine. Malicious Damage would then handle all the other costs from pressing, designing, advertising and so on. Brian Taylor put most of the money in, Danny Phelan invested some in it and everyone chipped in what they could. Adam Morris borrowed the money from his mum, Milly Mason. The 10" single was pressed at Lyntones on the Holloway Road. The original design of the EP was eleven-inch card and four postcard-type inserts rather than a standard 7-inch single in a picture bag. This turned out to be a costly option. It was a good idea, but it was an expensive and inconvenient idea followed by the problems it caused with the bagging of the release. The release was ready in mid-September and Brian Taylor, Adam Morris and Paul Ferguson went to the BBC building in Portland Place to try and get hold of John Peel, to no avail. They left the EP with the mailer and Brian got a call the following morning at 10am; Peel then repeatedly played songs from the EP on his radio show, which led to interest from Virgin Records. There was a lunch meeting at Richard Branson's boat, but they declined the offer.

In a video interview with *Classic Rock* in May 2013 Jaz Coleman thanks John Lydon for the inspiration that he gave through interviews and his own actions for bands to not use producers and do it themselves instead, which was an idea used in the early Killing Joke records.

This first Killing Joke release was titled 'Turn to Red'. It was originally released on 26th October 1979 by Malicious Damage, which was the record label set up with graphic artist Mike Coles. He is London based and works in print, video and photography. He is also involved in doing live projections at gigs and runs Malicious Damage Records.

Mike Coles: "I met the original members of Malicious Damage as the band were being formed. We all knocked about the same streets, pubs and record shops around Notting Hill and Ladbroke Grove. They wanted to start a record company based around this new band and their music. All I was interested in initially was designing the record sleeves, but when I heard the music I was hooked."

Their well-known clown image surfaced early on in the band's career.

Mike Coles: "Originally it was Mr Punch, I was a big fan and had a lot of photos I'd taken at the annual Mr Punch birthday party in Covent Garden where I was living at the time. Punch and Judy shows from all around the UK turn up and perform every May. We all liked the concept of the evil behind the smile and the smile behind the evil. The clowns turned up later." Today he still regularly works for the band and they always provide him with the albums to get inspiration from. The ideas come "mostly from discussing it with the band, they always have a good feeling for the atmosphere and vibe of an album. Even if they don't agree with each other at first, there's always a germ of consensus that we can build on. Ideas get passed around, bounced back and forth, developed, insulted and rejected until something emerges that probably wasn't intended in the first place, but most of the time it seems to work. It's their music after all. I do fight my corner though and it can be hard work at times, but at the end of the day the band (or at least two of them) have to be happy. And once the dust has settled there's always a treasure chest of imagery left over that gets recycled into videos and remixes."

The EP was hailed by the likes of John Peel and went on heavy rotation on his radio show. Peel was a popular BBC Radio 1 personality who was the first broadcaster to play psychedelic rock and progressive rock records on British radio. He was an early fan of Killing Joke, and the band appeared on his show in 1979 playing 'Pssyche', 'Wardance', 'Nuclear Boy' and 'Malicious Boogie' for his 'Peel Sessions'. He commented on air afterwards "I can't tell you how much pleasure it gives me, even after all of these years, to be able to bring you sessions as good as this one - particularly when it's the band's debut session." The liner notes of *The Peel Sessions* compilation describe how all the songs were recorded and mixed in one day and how Jaz ended up smashing a glass jar with a drum stick and had to go to a hospital because of it. Alex Paterson provided additional backing vocals in the form of the woos on 'Malicious Boogie' and played the cow bell on the song. The first John Peel Sessions were recorded on 17th of October 1979 and were aired not long after on 29th of October.

In fact John Peel was so impressed that he thought that it would be another more established group appearing under a pseudonym. Getting played on his show was an accomplishment in its own right, as he was one of the few disc jockeys to play unsigned and lesser known acts on

24

his show and would constantly be receiving enormous amounts of submissions through the mail. John Peel was widely acknowledged for promoting artists working in a multitude of genres including pop, dub reggae, punk rock and post-punk, electronic music and dance music, indie rock, extreme metal, and British hip hop, and he would have Killing Joke on his show multiple times throughout their career. The first broadcast was repeated as quickly as on the 20th December and would later find its way to a compilation aptly titled *The Peel Sessions 1979-81* released by Virgin Records in 2008. According to *Sounds'* Phil Sutcliffe, Peel had mentioned that Killing Joke sessions were the most requested on his show.

In late 1979 UK fanzine *Rapid Eye Movement* in their first issue reviewed the release, stating that although the band itself was completely unknown to them the album was "Very Lydon-like scratchings, scraping, and things that go bump now and again. A bloody good debut actually."

The EP was later re-released under the moniker 'Almost Red' on 14th December by Island Records. The band had signed a one-single deal with the originally Jamaican label, which had specialised in reggae at that point. 'Almost Red' was basically 'Turn to Red' with less vocals and a more prominent keyboard melody added to the top.

Jaz explained the story behind Island Records in *Allied Propaganda #3*:

"Island had a clause in their contract which stated that they had the option of an album or a single, but we got a solicitor on to that and changed it. So we got a nice fat advance for one single to set up the company and ourselves. They get the money from the sales and we get something like ten percent. All Island are after is money, 'cos they're going broke - they even wanted us to go to America. They always have a clause in their contract stating that if a band aren't big in America after eighteen months, they are automatically dropped. Ultravox and Eddie And The Hot Rods are examples. They send letters to people at known addresses who are paid something like five pounds a month. They get them all to ring up the Capital Hit Line and vote for one of their records. They're all crooks. It's all wrangled and it's only supposed to be a music scene."

The band's first manager was Brian Taylor, who started to manage the band just before the release of their debut EP. He said at the same interview:

"The extra track Island wanted on the twelve-inch was done as a pisstake out of Buggles. They paid us insignificant amounts of money to do the fourth track - we had to argue for two and a half hours to get £180. They thought we were going to sign to Virgin so they dropped all promotion on it and it appears they've pressed relatively few twelve-inch singles anyway. It's a good lesson to us, and we've learnt that everything people say about record companies is absolutely true. They simply took advantage of us 'cos we were skint."

Mike Coles did the artwork for the EP. As described in *Forty Years in the Wilderness* the building in the photo is Centre Point, which is a building in central London, comprising a 33-storey tower and a 9-storey block to the east including shops, offices, retail units and maisonettes. The photo had been taken with Coles' newly acquired Russian Zenit E camera. Mr Punch was drawn using a photo taken at the annual Punk & Judy festival in Covent Garden. The girls originate from an Odol toothpaste advert. The airplane on the poster, but omitted from the EP cover, is a Gloucester Meteor taken from an RAF recruitment ad.

Further live dates in the capital followed with 27th October at Queen Elizabeth College in Greenwich and 13th November at Moonlight Club in West Hampstead with Distribe. Their early shows were all in London.

On November 26th they supported Money at Covent Garden, and on 1st December they played at the 101 Club in Clapham. On 9th December they played in North London at Islington Hope & Anchor with Hardware. According to an interview they gave at the time to a London based fanzine, *Allied Propaganda #3,* the gig hadn't gone too well: "Sometimes we enjoy ourselves, sometimes we don't. It depends on what feedback we get from the audience. As soon as we went on tonight, they were just standing there and we could see what it was going to be like. We should have gone off after the first number," said Jaz. "The audience didn't enjoy it, I didn't enjoy it. None of us enjoyed it," agreed Youth.

The Hope & Anchor would later become well known for being a vital venue for the 80s Two Tone movement fronted by the likes of The Specials and Madness.

It seems that the band didn't have much time for many of their contemporaries in the new punk movement. Youth questioned: "Are you not bored with listening to The Ruts and shit like that? There's shit everywhere. There's only a few bands around worth listening to." In the same fanzine interview he added that "Crass have got the right idea, but

26

their music's bad and they're not real anarchists." In March 1980 he expanded on the notion on the pages of the *NME*: "It's like with the skinheads. They stand there looking around, then they'll decide to start bopping up and down. After about six or seven gigs they'll start to wonder why - and then perhaps they'll start changing, and that'll be worthwhile. But in the meantime you feel like asking them what the fuck are you here for? Why are you doing it? You can see they're not doing it because of the reasons you're doing it." In the *New Musical Express* in June 1980 they expressed their dislike of post-punk band Siouxsie & the Banshees and Oi groups such as Angelic Upstarts and Sham 69. The only band that was to their liking at the time seemed to be John Lydon's Public Image Limited.

"For the first 5 years of our career we used to practise in Notting Hill in the same place that the Clash used to rehearse," Jaz told journalist Teddie Dahlin in 2012. "It's all Youth's fault. Youth went to their studio and they had a huge poster of the Clash, and he put a dollar sign through the S of the word Clash. So every time we saw the Clash during the first 10 years or so, they would be scowling at us and we would be scowling at them. We always thought we were a tighter and better band than them. There was this horrible sort of atmosphere. Then one day I remember being in the pub down the road and Joe Strummer was opposite me and he said 'Jaz, do you want a drink?' And I found him to be this lovely wonderful person. In fact we had this rule, every time we would bump in to each other, which was always in Ladbroke Grove, we would promise to go off on a three-day bender together. And every time I saw Joe from that time it would be 'Let's go !!!' Whatever we were doing in life we would just stop it and go off on a three-day bender. Joe and Paul and so many people recently from my hometown are gone. Before I started Killing Joke there was this heavy metal guitarist called Würzel, and he ended up joining Motorhead two years after I started Killing Joke."

Their manager Brian Taylor saw some connection to the movement in an interview he gave Pete Makowski in April 1980 for the now defunct UK magazine *Zig Zag*:

"Well I don't think punk ever died. I think it's just a way of naming something. It's like the way 'Hippie' was derived, you just fit people in a category. The band are basically into the tenants of punk which was anarchy. They love disrupting anything that is set and criticising conventional attitudes - you'll always have punks as sceptics in a way.

The music is spontaneous, it has all the energy of punk, it's also got a lot of close control. They know absolutely what they are doing. For me Killing Joke have grown organically out of punk, they have got everything that punk promised but record companies never gave an opportunity to come to fruition. I think bands like that and there are a lot of them growing up, like Bauhaus, I really think they have grown out of something and are creating a new sound, they are just going to sweep mod away. There will be probably only be a few bands left from the mod revival thing."

In December they played Music Machine, later known as Koko before it shut down, in Camden Town, North London. The venue is famous for being the place where AC/DC singer Bon Scott headed on his final night out before being found dead in his friend's car the following morning. That gig happily went much better for the band as Jaz recalls in an interview for *Allied Propaganda*:

"After the gig I looked round at the audience. Steve Jones and Paul Cook were standing at the bar, and I was standing there after singing 'Wardance', which means a lot to me. They were just standing there, 'Nice gig, eh!' Our music's destructive - it's not supposed to make people happy. It's supposed to shake them up. I don't remember anything from when I go on stage to when I get off. I suppose I go into a trance, really."

Their last show in London in 1979 was 'Malicious Damage Xmas Party' on Tuesday 18th December with Hardware, held at Moonlight Club in West Hampstead where they'd played a month earlier.

On 30th January 1980 Killing Joke appeared on Capital Radio's Nicky Horne Show performing 'Change', 'Are You Receiving' and 'Complications' - these would later surface on the *Unperverted Pantomime* album.

In February 1980 the band would release 7" single 'Wardance' through Malicious Damage Records, backed by 'Pssyche'. It is worth noting that although the A-side would appear on their debut album later on in the year this version, along with the B-side, come from different sessions. 'Wardance' here is slightly faster and the recording is rougher than the album version. The B-side 'Pssyche' was the first Killing Joke song to be released based on a disco beat and features Big Paul doing vocals on a verse. A limited number of the original pressing included a pre-typed form for signing to the military. The release did not chart in the UK, but made it to number 50 in the US *Billboard* Dance Music charts.

According to Mickey Penguin in *Kill Your Puppy,* Malicious Damage paid for the recording of the second single and it was manufactured and distributed by Geoff Travis at Rough Trade. Scott Piering handled the promotion and later became a well-known radio plugger working for the likes of KLF and The Smiths. Brian Taylor would also play a big part, using his radio DJ friends to get airplay for the release, including in the US.

The cover made by Mike Coles came almost accidentally while flipping through a stash of magazine cuttings. He daubed 'Killing Joke' on a Don McCullin photo and everyone agreed that worked. Through photocopying and retouching Coles ended up with a stark black and white version, which seemed to echo the band's sound and the dystopian feel of the record. He wasn't allowed to be credited on the album, but if you look very carefully you can find 'colesy' scrawled among the rubble on the back cover. The hidden credit went unnoticed for years.

There is strong juxtapositioning in Coles' work, such as Fred Astaire dancing on the 'Wardance' cover. Astaire was an American actor who was widely considered the most influential dancer in the history of film.

"It's the evil behind the smile thing again. Taking something nice and twisting it into something nasty, or taking something evil and making it funny. It's always fascinated me, I think it probably harks back to my Catholic childhood, kneeling down in front of this man on a stick bleeding to death and being told it's wonderful..."

With less than 20 shows played the band got their first major UK concert. On 10th February 1980 the band played at the Lyceum in London, which was bootlegged as *Live at the Venue* released by Square Records as a vinyl LP. Apparently for a short time the album was even available from high street shops such as HMV and Virgin Records before they realised it was a bootleg release and withdrew it from sale. Lyceum operates these days as a 2,100-seat West End theatre located in the City of Westminster, on Wellington Street, just off the Strand. The origins of the theatre date to 1765. In the 60s and 70s, the theatre was used as a pop concert venue and for television broadcasts and featured the likes of Bob Marley and the Wailers, Led Zeppelin, U2 and The Clash.

Not only did the show include the majority of their upcoming debut album, it also included earlier work such as 'Malicious Boogie' and

'Nuclear Boy', which were never recorded in a studio. The encore featured Honey Bane on a song called 'What's the Matter'. It's the only known recording of that song from the band. Today the recording sounds slightly muddy and dated, but as it has been made available as a part of the 3 CD box set released by Candlelight Records USA in 2007 *Vinyl Bootleg Archives, vol.1*, it's worth checking out just for the unreleased material.

Honey Bane, who appeared on the final song, was a 15-year-old teenage runaway who had been in St. Charles Youth Treatment Centre in Essex. She was bizarrely enough managed by Jimmy Pursey from Sham 69 who was doing A&R work for Zonophone at the time. She was lifted from the tabloid pages of British weekly magazines such as *Melody Maker*, *Sounds* and *NME*. She appeared on the chart hit show *Top of the Pops* performing her single 'Turn Me On Turn Me Off' and made an EP 'You Can Be You' backed by none other than the anarcho punk band Crass, but never really made it in the music industry.

The band would make a second appearance on John Peel's show in March of 1980, this time performing 'Change', 'Tomorrow's World' and 'Complications'. The records would surface on the *Bums Rush* bootleg vinyl LP released by A Skid Mark Records and was notable for the fact that the record featured original versions of songs such as 'Follow the Leaders' with alternative lyrics to the finished version. The bootleg had such a great sound quality, even pretty decent by today's standards, that the company releasing it was taken to court by the band. The bootleg was later officially released as a part of the 3 CD box set *Vinyl Bootleg Archives, vol.2* released by Candlelight Records USA in 2007.

In June the band headed off to Spain for their first dates outside the UK. They played at the Metro in Barcelona on 14th June and then promptly returned to play two more dates on 26th and 27th June.

According to Mickey Penguin in *Kill Your Puppy* the band would do a third and final Malicious Damage Killing Joke single, which was 'Tomorrow's World'. It was more of an official bootleg single with red labels and no text featuring 'Change' and 'Tomorrow's World' from the second Peel session. The single was mastered by the vinyl cutter Porky from Porky's Prime Cuts and sold exclusively to fans by mail order and at gigs.

The band told UK pop culture magazine *The Face* in September 1980 that the wizard who occasionally joined the band onstage was a "long-haired madman by all accounts". He was responsible for chalking the seven-pointed star, representing the time of awakening, on a stage when the band was performing. He also breathed fire and did a ritualistic war dance during the concerts. "The gigs we do are like parties. We like to have a party, where there's loads of drugs right, loads of booze, everybody gets completely wasted and gets off on our music," explains Youth in the magazine. He makes a reference towards shebeen parties, which derives from the Irish síbín, meaning 'illicit whiskey', and the party's illicit clubs, which operated and sold alcohol without a licence. They also state that they didn't see the importance of regular concerts although there was pressure from the labels to do them.

A new single 'Requiem' was released on 26th September, and on 2nd October *Smash Hits* reported about the release of their new 12" EP with 'Requiem' as well as 'Change' and Malicious Damage's demo version 2 of 'Requiem', neither of which will be on the upcoming debut album. The 7" version excluded the 'Requiem' demo. Although the single did not chart in the UK it managed to reach number 43 on the US *Billboard* Dance Club Songs chart.

In the October issue of *Smash Hits* the EP is called "an excellent record" with 'Requiem' being seen as the gem, "a real slow burning fuse of a song" with melodic hook and insistent rhythms. 'Change' gets praised for its rawness and funky bass line. The review also points out that the latter two versions won't be on the band's debut album.

'Change' was released on 17th March as a 7" single. The song was lifted from a John Peel session on 5th March 1980 and was issued the same month as a limited-edition promotional single, available at gigs. 'Tomorrow's World' was on the B-side and was also recorded at the same radio session. These two versions would later appear on the 2008 compilation *The Peel Sessions 1979–1981*.

First Album - 1980: *Killing Joke*

The outstanding debut album which captured not only their defining sound, but also the chilling apocalyptic anguish about the world to come. As their central hymn, 'Wardance' proclaimed their angry manifesto and its tight, pulsating, metallic rhythm was music to march to. The majority of the album can still be heard performed in their live sets.

1980 UK Albums Chart #39

"When you think of the first record it got slagged off by everybody and then eight years later we're being told that it was the most groundbreaking record." - Jaz

The self-produced album was recorded at Marquee studios in London in August 1980. Marquee Studios were located on Richmond Mews in Soho, which was also where the legendary live venue the Marquee Club was located originally. The 1960s residences in the Club included everyone from the Rolling Stones, Led Zeppelin, the Yardbirds and even one of Geordie's favourite groups, The Who, as well as Pink Floyd, whom Youth would later go on to produce.

Phil Harding worked as the studio engineer on the album although he remained uncredited on the album. He had started working at the Marquee Studios in 1973 at the age of just sixteen. Before Killing Joke, he had already worked with The Clash in the very same studio.

"It was simply a case of me being one of the young in-house engineers at the Marquee and I don't think I was aware of them as a band before the sessions. The booking was made through EG records. It's a little difficult for people to understand now that when the punk revolution happened part of the philosophy of the bands, and The Clash and Killing Joke are good examples, was when they signed their deals with record companies they pretty much absolutely insisted on not going into a studio with a producer. Although there are some producer credits on some Clash records that certainly was my experience with the Clash. A lot of the bands insisted on producing albums although they had never produced a record in their lives.

"For young engineers like myself that were being schooled as it were, because I had been an assistant engineer for four or five years from 1973, what you learn was that whether it was a band or session musicians backing a singer you'd have the artist in the studio, assistant engineer working with the engineer and a producer generally, certainly at the Marquee, sitting on the left hand side of the engineer at the mixing desk in control of the session. You know that's what you learn and a lot of young engineers like myself suddenly found themselves in sessions like these where that chair on the left of you is empty. That's how you learn to engineer. That's how you've been working up until this kind of revolution when bands are coming in without producers. Having gone through that with the Clash where I had mixed 'White Man in Hammersmith Palais' and recorded four tracks for their 10" album. It was no great surprise when the sessions got booked and the band turned up with Alec from EG Records who was really friendly with the people who ran the studio. I said to him on the first day when we were setting up the studio 'Is there a producer coming in?' and he said 'No' and said 'Here is a crate of beer' and other things he brought with him 'It's you and the band Phil.' From a young engineer's experience it is quite daunting. I had a bit of experience with The Clash, but Killing Joke were booked to do the whole album.

"The sessions were a complete chaos. The band had a certain reputation, which I was unaware of. They got the deal and it was a quite a major deal and we weren't a cheap studio to hire, so there was a lot of respect from everybody at the studio that the band had got themselves into this position.

"We had each band member set up separately. The drums were the only thing making a lot of noise in the studio in terms of volume and that would allow you to set up some room mics, which on 'Wardance', 'Tomorrow's World' and a bit on 'Bloodsport' you can hear those room mics, especially on the tom toms. You've got to bear in mind in 1980 we didn't have digital reverb in terms of me getting the kind of powerful sound that the band wanted, especially for the drums, all we had was two reverb plates, which one would generally be 3 seconds long on the vocals and about 1 second for the drums and the rooms mics and that was about it. You have a few sort of tape delay machines and a few phasers, but compared to today's technology it was fairly limited in 1980.

"Once the sessions were set up and the band had discussed with me what they were going for as a unit that was where the chaos began. Since there was no one sitting to the left of me! We have pretty powerful speakers in the control room in the studio and as an engineer you go out into the studio and see what sort of a sound Geordie has got on his guitars and his amps. Most of the keyboards from Jaz were just plugged direct in, so they weren't a spillage problem, but he would be forever asking them to be louder on his headphones. We had Youth in a separation booth, which he didn't really like, so we ended up sort of pulling him into the studio, but his leads going into the separation booth for his amp. Geordie's guitar amps would've been sectioned off behind separation acoustic panels as much as we could.

"The problems began with getting the headphone balance right so the band felt that they were playing together in a powerful way like they are used to at gigs. And when they'd come into the control room for a playback it was weird, because no one took on the single responsibility of producing, so kind of I had four producers giving me instructions. That was the problem with no producer being there and the layout of the control room at the Marquee was such that the control room was sidelined to the studio and the [mixing] desk had a quite a lot of space between it and the main window where you could stand at the opposite to where I was sitting and listen to stuff coming through the main studio monitors and both sort of look at me and talk to me. One of my main memories was after almost every single playback each member of the band would take turns at standing at the opposite side of the desk to me while the speakers were playing back bloody loud and each one of them individually would scream at me. Jaz was the worst: 'Make the keyboards bigger, make it fatter', but because of the volume of the music playing back was so loud they'd be screaming at me. When I stopped the tape they'd stop screaming and yelling and kind of talking almost.

"You've also got to bear in mind the band are going for it and doing a track a number of times, there is hell of a lot of energy being put out, especially Paul on the drums. He was fantastic. Coming into the control room for a playback was like a little break and a rest for putting their energy into playing. So generally what would happen is they'd come in, assistant would have tea on the go or coffee and they'd either be rolling

34

up some spliffs or my other big memory of the sessions is that they had a bong on the go all the time. It was like a rasta-type bong, Youth would give the best description of this, so rather than something that you held close to you it was a big bowl that would sit on the floor and you'd sit on your feet and you'd have a big pipe coming up to your mouth.

"Generally the sessions, apart from the chaos I've described, went well. They'd come in, have a spliff or have a go on the bong and maybe go out and do another take.

"It took a while to persuade Jaz that we really should overdub the vocals rather than sing at the same time as the band. He would generally be screaming some sort of guide as everything was going down. There was a general sort of feeling that, other than Geordie, they all wanted to be playing together not overdubbing separately like a lot of people would in those days. So it was very much the case of let's get it right and that's it as you can hear on the album there is no extra guitars. There is no doubling the vocals. It's just the main vocal and tracks like 'Wardance' there is some backing vocals. Everything was focused on getting a great take at the time with all the four members in the studio - that's my overriding memory.

"Once we got going it was all flowing. There's eight tracks on the album and I don't think we recorded any more than that. The tracks are pretty long or at least some of them. '$,O,36' is 6.53 and five and half minutes for 'Tomorrow's World'. That's the way it went.

"Although I might have taken a few hits here and there on a spliff to get my psychological and mental process in the same as the band I would never go on the bong as I knew how strong that was and I wasn't really used to that. Obviously I'm getting paid and I'm working! I'm supposed to be holding everything together."

According to Phil Harding it might've taken just as little as two weeks to record the album with a break in the middle.

"At the Marquee we had this studio downstairs and you could play back loud and everything recorded really well down there and the band were happy. As an engineer for the Marquee I sort of had almost an instruction or a commitment to try and persuade clients after everything's recorded to go and mix in the studio upstairs which was signed as a mixing room. It had the same desk, but it was a lot smaller, different speakers and only had a small overdub room.

"By week three, we went upstairs to do some mixing and after a few days I could tell people weren't happy. The problem with it was that it

35

was a smaller studio and in the big studio downstairs it was a big control room, you could have four band members, myself, the studio assistant and people from the record company and everybody had space. The speakers filled the room, it was very comfortable. Whereas upstairs has space for two people behind the desk and a couple people squeezed into corners, so it wasn't a great comfort zone. In retrospect it was a bad suggestion a decision on my part. I think everybody knew 'Requiem' was going to be the first single, you know that way through to the record company, and the record company weren't happy and the band weren't happy. We called it off, those mixing sessions, two or three tracks in."

Phil went to speak to the studio manager Simon White, who was good friends with Alec, and a decision was made to finish the album in the downstairs studio as that was where it had all worked on everyone's behalf. The other alternative was that the rest of the sessions at the Marquee Studios would've been cancelled and the band would've gone elsewhere to mix the album. A decision was made to offer the band one free day in the downstairs studio to mix one song before relocating elsewhere to work with another engineer. The offer of the free studio day convinced the band and the record company on giving it another go. The new mix satisfied everyone and the album was finished at the downstairs studios as planned.

Once the album was ready the band got together at the studio to listen to the final version and decide on the running order before it was sent off to mastering and manufacturing.

"I said to the assistant that make sure you're in control of the tape machine and the monitors as I'm going to sit at the back of the room with the boys and have a go at the bong! That was the only time in the four weeks that I've sat down with them and totally got into their headspace on the bong as my memory is that they were all doing it."

Phil was most impressed by Paul's performance even though he had been smoking the bong. "He is super tight, super powerful. Me and the studio assistant were astonished. He was pretty out of it in terms of how you get when you're communicating, but totally concentrated and together during the recording. I guess that shows how getting your headspace in a sorted area for creativity. As long as you got the fitness, which obviously a drummer needs to have and Paul was super-fit regardless of the drugs and that." The whole album was done under those circumstances and, according to Phil, with only a slight timing discrepancy in the beginning of 'Bloodsport', but otherwise, he assures,

36

it sounds like the drums had been played to a metronome, which hadn't been the case at all.

According to Phil no plan for recording early songs such as 'Nuclear Boy', 'You Are Being Followed', 'Malicious Boogie', 'Today is Forever', 'Animal' or 'What's the Matter?/Dead Dollies' took place. Some of these would surface on bootlegs over the years along with ones mentioned earlier being released as a part of *The Unperverted Pantomime*.

Jaz explained the different ideas behind 'Bloodsport' to Ross Fitzsimons of Irish music paper *Hot Press* in 1981 saying: "Even now man is still the same as he was thousands of years ago. He needs blood, whether it's ritual or war, it's a fact that even now there's something in man that needs blood and if he can understand his own nature maybe instead of bloodshed in fighting, it could be done in pure ritual. If they really knew about the science and the religion - Christianity's just one fucking side of it - call it D.O.G., call it G.O.D., call it what you fucking like, if people had any form of understanding they'd realise for themselves, they'd see themselves fighting and killing, and realise it could be done in pure ritual and achieve the same effect."

According to the September 1980 issue of now defunct *Zig Zag* magazine a song called 'The End' was recorded, but that has most likely surfaced under a different title.

The second single, released in March, was 'Change', which appears on the US pressing of the debut album between the tracks 'Complications' and '$,O,36', but was omitted from the UK release. The song also appeared on the B-side of the 'Requiem' single, which was the last single to be released from the album, in September the same year. In an interview in LA zine *Another Room* in September 1981 Jaz explains that what the band was looking for was "general change." He adds, "take it as you like." The song shares a striking similarity to 'Me and My Brother', a single by War, an American funk band from Long Beach, California. War, originally known as Eric Burdon And War, was extraordinary for the time in the way they transcended racial and cultural barriers with their multi-ethnic line-up. 'Me and My Brother' from their 1973 album *Deliver the Word* had reached #15 on the US pop chart and #18 on the US R&B chart in 1974. How the song came on to Killing Joke's radar was most likely the fact it was re-released as a single in the UK in 1976, where it got to #21 on the UK Singles Chart. There is no denying that the funk beats the band strongly expressed in their music had an influence on Killing Joke.

The song '$,O,36' is referencing a postcode in Berlin, Germany, as well as a direct reference to the SO36 club, a music club on Oranienstrasse near Heinrichplatz in the area of Kreuzberg. The club was frequented by the likes of Iggy Pop and David Bowie in the 70s and the band played there on 10th June as a part of their German tour. The club is still active today putting on punk and new wave concerts along with visual art. The postcode of that area is SO36, in which the SO stands for Südost (South East). The Kreuzberg district has historically been home to the punk rock movement in Berlin along with other alternative subcultures in Germany. This is the first time the band expressed their gravitation towards Berlin.

As on the records previous to the debut album the artwork was done by Mike Coles. The original cutting used for the cover was from *The Sunday Times* magazine on 16th December 1971 during the Troubles, which he then worked on with white gouache. The photo portrays Irish kids running to get away from British troops and the CS gas in Derry, also known as Londonderry, a city on the River Foyle in Northern Ireland. Coles was raised as a Catholic and found that the Catholic versus Protestant religious clashing was the real killing joke hence making an excellent choice for the theme of the debut album. EG Records also obtained the rights for the original photograph to avoid any legal complications.

Mike Coles: "I've always been fascinated by the way religions have caused wars and been used as justification for wars. The photo was taken by Don McCullin in Derry in 1976, it's Irish kids running away from British army tear gas. For some reason I cut the photo from *The Sunday Times* magazine and graffitied the words Killing Joke. There was still a lot of work playing around with photocopies to get that distressed black and white look. The rest is history." The debut album is one of his favourite designs.

As he tells in his book *Forty Years in the Wilderness* the debut album gave Coles an opportunity to chat to a Japanese girl as he was leaving a party on Portobello Road in November 1980. He invited her to a Killing Joke show at the Lyceum the following night. A year and a half later Coles would marry the woman and they've now been married for over 40 years.

The album was released on 5th October 1980 on EG Records. "It got slagged off by everybody and then eight years later we were told it was a ground-breaking record. People are fickle and you have to stand by your own creations," Jaz reflects with a smirk on his face in 2015.

Although some people got it straight away, like Valac Van Der Veene who gave the album full 5 stars in his half page review of the album in *Sounds* in October 1980. He states how he has loved the band ever since their first single and the band "have ripped the flesh off any rock convention with manic, surgical skill – leaving a musical skeleton." He praises the minimalism in the playing of the rhythm section as well as the "stabs of melody" Geordie provides to the sound completing the "figurative figure" Jaz's sometimes paranoid, dreamy and obsessive lyrics and occasional keyboards. He concludes by saying "exit one mentally bruised, highly excited reviewer."

EG Records had been formed in 1969 by David Enthoven and John Gaydon. The name of the label came from their initials. The pair had managed King Crimson before starting the label to release their debut *In the Court of the Crimson King* in October 1969. The label and management company most notably worked in the 1970s and 1980s. The company was sold to Virgin Records in 1992, which continued operating EG. In 1996, after Virgin was sold to EMI, it was absorbed into Virgin. The album debuted at number 41 on the UK Albums Chart on 26 October 1980 and would later peak at number 39. In the first year alone, the album had sold over 30,000 copies.

Bruce Britt highly recommends the album in May in Detroit *Freeb Pres* saying that is on a par with the Sex Pistols' debut *Never mind the Bollocks Here's the Sex Pistols*. The spiteful lyrics and ringing, distorted guitars impress him and he even opens the review with a telling riddle: "What do you get when you mix the teenage angst of the Sex Pistols with the heavy metal bombast of Van Halen? Answer: Killing Joke's debut album."

The band told Mike Nicholls of *Record Mirror* in 1981 that the alternative was signing a ten album deal to another label. The contract with EG was for three albums before the band would have to renegotiate the terms of the contract. The band were extremely worried about the quality of the musical output in a deal that would be as ambitious as ten albums. In an interview with US-based publication *Trouser Press* in December 1981 Geordie stated that EG "were the best of a bad bunch." The band had dealt with Virgin, who later re-issued a lot of their albums, and Chrysalis, but the band wanted as much artistic control as they could possibly get, which proved to be problematic with other labels.

39

The album was re-released in 2005 with additional bonus tracks and Peter Marsh of the BBC described the album as "still powerful and relevant 25 years on, *Killing Joke* is a beautifully scary noise." UK magazine *Mojo* hailed that " 'Wardance' has to be one of post-punk's finest anthems," giving the album four out of five stars. *Uncut* noted that at "their most progressive they kept pace with more lauded contemporaries like Joy Division, Gang of Four and PiL," rating the album only three out of five. Online music database *All Music*'s Bradley Torreano gave the album four and half stars out of five and noted that "Certain parts of the album have not dated well; the vocals and drums are mixed in such a way that they lose some of their effectiveness, and the fact that so many other bands have used this same formula does take some of the visceral feeling away." The producer and engineer Phil Harding also noted that the album doesn't sound as big and massive as he remembered it being during the making of it. In hindsight the only song that Geordie stated that he liked on the first album is 'Bloodsport'.

The album would eventually become a landmark argument in defining post-punk and later heavy metal as well. Notable covers from the album include 'The Wait', which was covered by Metallica on 'The $5.98 E.P. - Garage Days Re-Revisited' EP in 1987 and 'Requiem' which would be covered by Foo Fighters as a B-side to the 'Everlong' single in 1997.

An important concert defining Killing Joke took place at the Campaign for Nuclear Disarmament in Trafalgar Square in London on Sunday 26th October 1980. Jaz introduces the band at the beginning of the set saying "We are the Killing Joke. This is the only honesty here today" followed by a burst of short laughter as the rest of the band tunes up. The songs the band performed during their five song set were 'Pssyche', 'Wardance', 'Change', 'Tomorrow's World' and 'Requiem'. Audience recording of the concert exists, but it sounds very thin and weak by today's standards.

The event got major coverage in all of the main UK papers.

Geordie recalled the concert to *Uncut*'s Peter Watts in 2015: "My favourite gig was the CND rally at Trafalgar Square. 80,000 people and us playing on the steps of the National Gallery in 1980. Jaz told them 'Margaret Thatcher has bought all these cruise missiles and all you can do is stand there with a fucking placard. You deserve what you are going to get. This one's called "Wardance".' It kicked off. It was killer. We never got invited back and I've got my suspicion that's why we never did Glastonbury cos it's the same hippie crowd and they remember."

Campaign for Nuclear Disarmament, also known as CND, began in November 1957 when a committee was formed, including Canon John Collins as chairman, Bertrand Russell as president and Peggy Duff as organising secretary. The organisation advocates unilateral nuclear disarmament by the United Kingdom, international nuclear disarmament and tighter international arms regulation through agreements such as the Nuclear Non-Proliferation Treaty. It opposes the use of nuclear, chemical or biological weapons and the building of nuclear power stations in the UK.

Jaz explained the reason for doing the gig to *No Class* fanzine in early 1981 saying: "the only way to get results with a government like we've got, not wishing to get political, because I'm not interested in politics, the only way to get results is if you've got some nutter like my brother, he's a nuclear physicist, if you get the plans of the nuclear bomb and you sent an anonymous letter to the government, saying that in each of the major capitals there's hidden a nuclear device, we have the plans, show them the plans so that they know you really mean business. Unless your terms are met, the first one goes up, and if they aren't by then, the second goes up, understand? It's the only way you're going to get results out of people like these. They're interested in themselves. You've got to remember, people like Maggie Thatcher, why should they be concerned about 2,000 years onwards from now. They're only going to live another 10 years, what's it to them past the year 2000?"

Jaz tells the *NME* in August 1983 that they used the rally to their advantage and that he was in fact opposed to the CND due to the futility of their cause, but liked the idea how it planted a seed of change.

In November Lynn Hanna described the band's live shows in the *NME* saying that "the only animation on stage is provided by Jaz who crouches behind his synthesiser, making forays like a Neanderthal man gripped by a gesturing, gibbering fury." She also made references that Killing Joke sounded much like early Siouxsie and the Banshees, but "without the thrilling, amoral imagination."

In an interview with London based fanzine *Jamming* in 1981 Youth told of some of his more or less serious ambitions for the group. "Tons of groupies, a pound of grass a week. I want lots of money. I want millions and millions of pound notes." In the same fanzine Jaz talks about their New Year's Eve showcase gig in New York. "There were all these dumb, disco-type Americans standing in front of us with their mouths open. They were out looking for a nice boogie to celebrate New Year's Eve. And we were pretty extreme for them. But it was really funny - one minute they were all just like standing there, and the next minute they were all dancing like puppets. It was really pathetic. And there was that spastic Johnny Thunders. He asked to jam on stage with us. Spastic!" They had just told Thunders to literally fuck off.

The first album proved extremely influential and as expressed in the US zine *Non LP B Side* in 1981 they influenced bands such as Red Beat and Ski Patrol. Both bands were in fact signed to the same Malicious Damage label, but neither made much of a career. "No one believes that Adam Ant was at one of our early gigs," Geordie told the zine and said it was songs such as 'Wardance' that inspired his early music. Listening to Adam & the Ants debut *Dirk Wears White Sox* released on 30th November 1979 one can agree it shares a lot of similarities to early Killing Joke albums.

1981 – What's This For!

Slightly more spacious than their first full length this album builds around the strong backbone Paul Ferguson's drumming creates. If you're ever thinking of going insane this is the album that will help your descent into 'Madness'. Not as flawless as their first born, but still holds some strong gems and makes for some great unsettling listening.

1981 UK Albums Chart   #42

The recording started in late December with Hugh Padgham working as the engineer at Townhouse Studios in London. Town House, which was also known as Townhouse Studios, was a recording studio located at 150 Goldhawk Road in Shepherd's Bush in West London. The studios were built by Richard Branson in 1978, and managed by Barbara Jeffries as part of the Virgin Studios Group. The studios shut down in April 2008, but saw everyone from Elton John and Queen to Jamiroquai and Oasis record there. Probably most important to the band was the connection to Public Image Limited who had at that point had parts of their first three albums recorded there. The studios were chosen as Hugh Padgham was working there as a member of staff along with Nick Launay, who ended up recording most of the album and then mixing it. Hugh Padgham was a fully trained engineer whilst Nick Launay was an assistant engineer. They had both worked at the studios since they opened in 1979. Hugh Padgham had been one of the engineers who had also worked on Public Image Limited's magnum opus *Metal Box* (also known as 'Second Edition') in 1979.

"I knew of the band just because they were sort of reasonably well known on the punk circuit. Well I say the punk circuit I mean the post-punk circuit I suppose and also I worked on Public Image [Limited] as well," recalls Hugh Padgham. He reckons he only worked on the album for four or five days before Nick Launay took the sessions over. "As far as I remember I only did two tracks on the album and then I had to go off and I think I was booked to do work with Phil Collins again or something."

According to Jaz Coleman in *Letters from Cythera*, the sessions with Killing Joke and Hugh Padgham didn't go well and Hugh had later recalled in a BBC interview it was the worst session he ever worked on. Hugh Padgham doesn't recall saying so, but says he might've said so at some point. Padgham points out "to me Public Image were much more difficult to work with. I wonder if that's getting mixed up."

Jaz explains how Youth had gone into the control room one evening heavily under the influence of psychotropic drugs and drawn multi-coloured pictures with chinagraph pencils all over the mixing desk. Apparently even the tape operators at the studio started trying to avoid working with the band. After the incident Nick Launay came in to finish the album. This story is contradicted by Hugh Padgham who says that a similar incident had happened when he was working with Public Image Limited, not with Killing Joke. Hugh Padgham says Jaz's recollection is "all rubbish. The thing is they were so out of it. Nick [Launay] says, he saw Youth recently in LA at one of their gigs, on the sessions he did Youth was hardly ever there. He was basically just out of it on acid the whole time." According to Hugh "there was no fist fights or damage to the controls that was definitely Public Image." Regarding the sessions with Killing Joke he says "I don't think anything terrible happened, because I'm sure I'd remember it.

"I don't remember there being that much of a problem. I seem to remember getting on with them alright. Youth was there on the sessions I did. I think I only literally did two songs. I only did 'Tension' and 'Follow the Leaders' and 'Madness' rings a bell, but I'm not 100 percent sure. And possibly 'You Told You How'. Nick was my young assistant basically who assisted me on various records I did at the Townhouse Studios. He did Killing Joke and then some Public Image [Limited] stuff after that were like the first proper sessions he did on his own. He really kind of remembers it really well. He mixed the whole record and did most of the other songs. We think that the song that opens the album 'The Fall of Because' was done by Phil Harding." Nick Launay added tom tom overdubs to 'Follow the Leaders', but otherwise the song was recorded with Hugh Padgham. 'Brilliant', which surfaced as a bonus track in the 2008 re-issue of the album, doesn't originate from these sessions.

Youth recalled in an interview with *Mix* magazine that he had mixed the album high on acid with Hugh Padgham in a 48-hour session, which he came back for, but according to Hugh this information is incorrect and he wasn't involved in the mixing of the album. "Nick said [Youth] was hardly around and he was just literally taking acid the whole time."

According to Hugh the sessions went ok, but he does state that "they were all mad basically. We did a lot of crazy sessions in those days, with reggae bands and Public Image [Limited]. They weren't just sort of normal people. I mean Killing Joke is a great name for their band, because they have a very sort of sarcastic sense of humour. I remember getting on with them pretty ok. Enough to get those songs more or less finished.

"The reason we believe they didn't give us any credits, because two things really. One, they thought it was funny in their sort of weird sense of humour. Just to sort of not say anything. And second, was actually they adored Public Image [Limited] and they didn't want anyone to think they had stolen the guys who worked on Public Image, which was me and Nick amongst others. That's one big reason why no one has any credits. There was a huge rivalry between Public Image and Killing Joke. I think Killing Joke hero-worshipped Public Image.

"As it is clearly told by Jaz and Youth we didn't produce it. We were just engineers and in a way that is true, but it was my job to get the session together. To get them to play and do overdubs on it. It's a very fine line what you call producing and engineering. As far as my career is concerned, I'm very proud to have worked on that record. And I would say the same about Public Image as well, because they are bands that are still idolised today and very influential on a lot of bands of today and bands of that sort of genre. At the time it was just another session with another band and I was working flat out the whole time. I did two albums with The Police and they were the biggest band in the world. At the time Killing Joke wouldn't have been so important as far as my career was concerned as you know we were selling literally millions and millions of records with The Police, which I was producing. As I said I maybe worked for four or five days with Killing Joke as whereas all the time I worked, for instance, with The Police I'd work for months and months and months. It was a small part of my life, but it wasn't like a cup of tea working with them, but I don't remember it being the worst sessions either. It's difficult to work with people if they're completely out of it you know. When I worked with Public Image, [guitarist] Keith Levene was injecting amphetamines as well as doing heroin. Nick

45

Launay said that Youth was asleep most of the time when he was working with them. They used to wake him up with a fire extinguisher. They used to spray a fire extinguisher over him."

Apparently, Nick Launay, currently living in LA, still gets the majority of his work nowadays thanks to his name being associated with Killing Joke and these particular sessions, along with the connection with Public Image Limited. Hugh recalls that "at the time I was just sort of starting producing myself and I was doing bands like The Police and Phil Collins and stuff. Although I enjoyed working with Killing Joke I got a feeling it was something like four or five days I worked with them, which I sort of slotted in between doing other things."

Hugh Padgham has since won four Grammy awards as a producer, but was left uncredited on the album sleeve notes along with Nick Launay who later took on the sessions. Hugh Padgham became known as the mastermind behind the "gated reverb" sound, which is an effect often associated with the sound of 1980s popular music. Gated reverb, also known as gated ambience, is an audio processing technique that combines strong reverb and a noise gate. The effect, created with producer Steve Lillywhite, first came to be whilst working for artists such as XTC, Peter Gabriel and Phil Collins at Townhouse Studios. One of the best examples of it can be heard in Phil Collins' 1981 debut solo single 'In the Air Tonight'.

Launay had previously worked with Public Image Limited, which surely made him the perfect person to be working with Killing Joke. The songs were first demoed on an 8-track before going to record them on a 24-track in the studio and "fuck it all up" as Paul put it at the time. The album was recorded in the space of a couple of months, six months after the recording of the debut. While the debut album had a year's worth of material the second album was written much more quickly.

Nick Launay, prior to working with the band, had seen them live a couple of times. "I was a fan. I thought they were great. Really, really great band. I didn't meet them until they turned up at Townhouse Studios to work together." Hugh had told the band about Nick and they got interested as he had just produced *Flowers of Romance* for Public Image Limited, which then subsequently got the interest of other similar bands at the time, which was great for Nick as he was just 20, still living with his mum and just starting out in the industry. "Suddenly I was being offered work by all these cool bands that I had been a fan of, so it is really amazing to have [Killing Joke] suddenly walk into the studio.

When I had only seen them up on stage."

Around the time Nick had worked for other quintessential post-punk bands such as Gang of Four and the Birthday Party.

The sessions during Nick's involvement were "hilarious. On reflection they were hilarious. It was like every member of the band is a completely different character and they don't always agree. It can be quite funny I found." The day Nick took over the sessions the band arrived without Youth.

"On day two the receptionist called, or it could've been that first night, got a call from the receptionist saying that 'I think you should come up here 'coz one of your musicians has arrived. And I said 'Just send him down. Tell them to come down to studio two.' And she said 'No, it's a bit more complicated than that.' The other members of the band had to come up and sign for him. And I was like 'what do you mean?' and she said 'you could come up here' and we went up there. And there was Youth in a straightjacket with the medical police who had delivered him to the studio and they needed another member of the band to sign for his release. And so they signed for it and Youth was very drowsy like he was all over the place. His eyes were going all over the place and he didn't look very well. So, we took him back down to the studio so he just laid down, and obviously they took the straightjacket off of him, and he laid down on the couch and fell asleep. So, we continued to do the song without him. The next day came in. We did another song and Youth just stayed asleep. Jaz was probably getting impatient about the whole thing and so they woke him up with a fire extinguisher. You know the dry ice fire extinguishers. So, they sprayed him with that dry ice, so he woke up and was going 'what the fuck is going on?' and they were like 'c'mon you're still in the band. Go fucking play bass.' And this was the most amazing thing. He gets up, plugs in his bass and starts playing to the two songs that were done already and it was fantastic. He played so well. And I was like, 'wow, fucking hell. That was amazing.'

"It's ridiculous. It was an insane way to start an album and it amazed me because Youth was all over the place. He still hadn't come back to earth, but he played bass really great you know. I have very fond memories of that session. It was a bit crazy, because Jaz is a very intense person – and he was angry as well. I remember Geordie almost being like his sidekick, so they were both doing practical jokes all the time. They were kind of being a bit evil to everyone, but it was almost like

47

Jaz was being the main instigator and Geordie would back him up. They had this incredible kind of sarcasm, running joke thing with them and it would kind of make sense that they were called Killing Joke. Then they had Youth who was very, very peaceful and like I said was coming down from this crazy acid trip and Paul was just the loveliest person you could ever meet. Incredible drummer. He was just like the voice of reason. He was the one who kept it all together. He really didn't get involved in these practical jokes. He was on top of things. Trying to keep peace between everyone. I was younger than them and I was just really started making records, but it gave me a great start to my career that it had happened. So, the thing was I wasn't hired to produce their record. I wasn't even hired to engineer. I was just the house engineer that came with the studio. You know, that was the situation, but I ended up contributing a lot of ideas that would be considered production ideas and it has been an ongoing joke with them about that."

Jaz Coleman had a nickname for Nick Launay. He called him Padre as a reference to his clean churchgoing appearance. Once the album was finished and mixed and Nick was very happy with the results Jaz asked him, "So Padre, are you happy with your work on this record?" Prompting Nick to reply: "Yeah I am. I think it turned out really good," to which Jaz apparently replied "That's good, because we're not crediting you. We're not putting your name on the album."

"I mixed the album with the band. I was doing the main mixing on the album, but then there were certain things that were done manually, so Youth would've been up there, and Jaz, pushing buttons. We'd mix it together. That's how we'd done it back in the day. I mixed the whole album apart from 'The Fall of Because'.

"While mixing the record it was Jaz's birthday and they invited a lot of their friends. And their friends were all very real characters. Very odd-looking people. There were what we'd now call gothic looking girls. Different colour hair and all that. Back then the term goth really hadn't come to its full meaning. There was a midget who wore a suit and a top hat and he was hilarious. There was a guy called Wizard with a spiderweb tattooed on his face and he used to go up on stage and throw flames out of his mouth on their gigs. So basically, I'm looking around there are these amazing crazy looking people. You know it was something out of a [Federico] Fellini movie. It was really incredible. Someone brought a chocolate cake. Geordie being Geordie comes up to me and says 'Hey Nick, do you want a piece of cake?' and I go 'yeah.'

'I'll cut you a big piece.' He cut me a big piece of his chocolate cake and I'm just trying to mix and there is all this chaos going on like partying and drinking and God knows what going on, you know. I'm trying to mix this song and I'm just concentrating on that and had a couple of bites out of this cake and I'm sort of noticing that this speaker is sort of coming out at me. Getting closer and closer. Almost coming out and hitting me. What the fuck is going on? I'm looking at the desk and the desk started to wobble and every time I went to touch one of the knobs and turn it the knob would come out of the desk like a snake. I'm like what fuck is going on? I've never experienced anything like this. I remember hearing this laughter behind me that was Jaz and Geordie laughing and they were like going 'Are you alright Nick?' and all I remember is kind of like echoes. 'You alright Nick? You alright Nick?' I'm like what is going on, so I span around on my chair and the whole room just span around like a fucking tornado. And I thought all these crazy people are all looking at me. And because I was young and naïve to all this, I had never taken any drugs in my life, you know, I didn't know what was going on and I thought fucking prankster I thought they'd put something in my drink. I hadn't thought it was the cake - I hadn't put two and two together. So I then try to carry on mixing and realised I couldn't because every time I concentrated on a kick drum or a snare drum or a guitar it got unbearably loud and I couldn't judge whether it was loud or quiet, because then I would concentrate on the next sound and that would get loud and the other thing would be gone. So, I got up and sat down on the couch and just looked at everybody in the room and it was just like chaos. I guess I got kind of worried that I don't know what's happening. They'd obviously spiked my drink and they think it is funny. I got up and left the room and went to the kitchen. On the way to the kitchen there was this long corridor and I saw Cousin It from the Addams Family, that character with the long hair, walking away from me. It's just this hair and I was like 'Oh my God, now I'm fucking imagining a character from a fucking tv show. This is nuts!' So, I follow Cousin It around the corner and it disappears. Could no more find this strange hair thing. Went to the kitchen. Was really hungry. All I could find was cheese. Put the cheese in my mouth and it just overtook my whole head. I thought this is stupid. I can't do anything without it being exaggerated, so I'm just going to bed. So, I went upstairs to these apartments that the Townhouse Studios had, that I don't think most people knew existed. I went up there and crashed out and went to sleep.

What the guys from Killing Joke thought had happened was that they saw me leave and they just probably carried on partying and eventually went on 'hang on where's Nick?', 'Oh fuck! He's left and he is tripping. We better go and find him.' So apparently, they went, as they told me the next day, and sent out a search party around the neighbouring streets to find me. And they couldn't find me, because I was upstairs.

"I thought it was acid in the cake. I knew about acid, because my parents were hippies and all that. I never tried any. I was hallucinating and imagining things that weren't there, but apparently it was a hash cake and it was just very, very strong. I only had a couple of bites.

"Then the record comes out. They didn't credit me. They didn't credit me as an engineer. They didn't credit me as mixing. They didn't credit me as anything. And they thought it was hilarious, because they knew they wound me up. They thought it was funny. I then worked with them again on a single and it came up. They asked me if I was still pissed off that they didn't credit me and I said 'I'm not pissed off, I just thought it was really childish.' What was the point? That was like an ongoing joke for them that they wound me up and they didn't credit me and they credited themselves with everything. And I was like whatever, because it didn't matter as when the record came out and the first big article came out, I think it was *NME* or *Melody Maker*, it said new Killing Joke album produced by Public Image Limited's record producer Nick Launay! I read that and thought that's fucking karma for you.

"The whole thing with Public Image I don't know what happened, but it might've been something where they got compared to each other in the press and Jaz didn't like it. That's a sensitive issue with Jaz. I don't know if that's the reason why he didn't want my name on the record or whether he did it just to wind me up, because he likes winding people up. I wasn't offended by it. I wasn't upset by it. I thought it was a bit stupid. Depending on what articles you read there is no mention of me or Hugh doing the record, or anybody, it just says produced by Killing Joke. Because I wasn't contracted, I was just an in-house engineer there was no legal reason to mention it." More recently when Nick was backstage at a Killing Joke gig Geordie accidentally let it slip to a couple of women backstage and introduced Nick as "the guy who produced our second record." When Jaz, Geordie and Nick all realised what had happened they busted out laughing. "I'm not going to say I produced that record, because I was the in-house engineer and I engineered it, but I definitely put a bit more than just engineering to it."

According to either Nick or Hugh there are no songs left unreleased from the sessions for the second album.

The first song the band worked on with Nick as an engineer was 'Follow the Leaders', which they had already started recording with Hugh. They did tom tom drum overdubs as the basic disco drum track had already been recorded along with vocals followed by the recording of Youth's bass. Some of the guitars for the song had also already been recorded. The second song they worked on in a similar way was 'Tension'. The rest of the album followed. "From my memory there weren't that many takes. Maybe three or four takes of each song. There was quite a bit of editing. I used to edit multi-tracks quite a lot. I was quite good at editing, because I had learned to edit before I went to Townhouse. So a lot of splicing with sticky tape and sometimes I would edit between takes and we would do a couple of overdubs, like making the guitars bigger.

"I do remember that Geordie had this crazy guitar cabinet that was literally a wardrobe. They wheeled in this wardrobe and the wardrobe had the doors cut out and the wood replaced with the speakers in them, but it was a wardrobe and that was pretty amazing. My memory of it was just they were just a killer band and they were just amazing. They were just as amazing in the studio as they are live. They are very tight and Paul is just such a good drummer. He is rock solid and they're just a good band. As much as Youth was a bit out to lunch, he came up with great bass parts and played really well. Jaz had a couple of Oberheim synthesisers. That was his main thing and they had pre-sets that had his kind of sound in them. Jaz is amazing. His takes were first or a second take. There wasn't many takes. I remember doing the vocals to 'Madness' where Geordie and Paul would go out there, and Youth, and they sing 'this is madness, this is madness'. And I think the voice you hear on there is mostly Paul. It's Jaz and then Paul answering. You can really hear his voice - he had a very loud voice.

"There was another incident. There was an assistant who was very new. His name was Steve Tyrell. He was really young. He had a curly hair and he was quite cocky. He was quite self-assured. He played guitar and he played keyboards and he was probably like 19 or something like that. He had been allocated as my assistant engineer on the sessions. He was very curious about the Oberheims and he kept asking Jaz about the pre-sets and all that. We come in one morning and Jaz switches on one of his keyboards and some of the pre-sets have been erased, because someone had been playing with the keyboard. So, Jaz immediately suspected Steve had switched them on after we'd left and played with them and pushed the wrong button and erased some sounds, so Jaz was... to say he was furious was an understatement. There was smoke coming out of his ears. He was pissed off. So he confronted Steve about it and of course Steve denied it and then Jaz grabs Steve by the throat and pushed him up against the wall. He was literally not breathing and Paul had to pull Jaz off of him, because Jaz was going to fucking kill him. It was really violent and it was very, very scary. I'm very thin and I'm not a tough guy, so wasn't going to go and pull Jaz off of him, but Paul was. He is a bigger guy and literally had to pull him away. It was heavy. Steve was choking and left the room – and then it was all sorted. I think Steve did carry on doing the sessions, but Jaz was really fucking pissed off with him. So that was an incident that happened that was a bit ugly.

"There was another practical joke where they heard that there was a secret room under the drum room. If you can imagine a room that's all stone. Like the floor is all stone and the walls are rocks and that's where the drums were done, which is why the drums sound so powerful and big. So I told them there is this room and there is a trap door. What it did it the trap door opened it. Underneath this main recording room there is a small room that used to be like a small pool, like a swimming pool. Very small one. And they used to make films in this building before it was a recording studio. It was left over and it is not very tall. It's probably maybe six foot tall. You had to kind of duck. But it had water in it. It was really musty and smelt of mould. There was a microphone and some speakers there and you could send the sound of things to this room and it was a bit like an echo chamber. They loved that the room was there, so we did some drums with that open, so it echoed and we sent some other things down there.

"There was a midget who came to the sessions maybe two or three times and he was obviously a close friend. Jaz lured him into this room that was underground. He climbed down the stairs down there and Jaz then shut the door. Completely dark and smelt of mould. And Jaz then came into the control room and he then went 'Push fucking record. I wanna hear that guy screaming. Record him screaming.' And I was like 'This is really sick what you are doing' and he was like 'Shut up! Push fucking record.' So, I had a tape rolling and this poor guy was just

52

screaming like 'Let me out! Let me out!' He wasn't crying, but was screaming to be let out. It was all recorded and they then let him out and thought it was hilarious. And then we took the recording of that and we slowed it down to half speed, so it sounded like a man drowning and you can hear that in the background of 'Madness'. I think we might've slowed it on another song. It might be on 'Exit' or 'Butcher'. It was basically this really haunting sound. It sounded like an old man in pain."

Nick didn't see the band until November 2018 when they played at the Roxy in Los Angeles, and he still got on with them like a house on fire. He hadn't seen them for 25 years, so he really enjoyed catching up with them again. "Absolutely love Youth. Very impressed by what he does." According to Nick Launay, some of these incidents the band incorrectly recalls happened during the other later recordings, which he wasn't even part of. "I was definitely shocked by the practical jokes [at the time], but then that's maybe why they're called Killing Joke. That's what it is all about. Taking the piss you know." He goes to point out that the title of the compilation *Laugh? I Nearly Bought One* is a good indication of this.

'The Fall of Because' had been recorded prior to these sessions, quite possibly by Phil Harding, who worked on the debut album, and this was an outtake from the first album. Launay says that "That song was presented to me and I had to edit it into the master and then I went to the mastering room with it." Apart from 'Who Told You How' the songs had been written and well prepared prior to entering the studio. "I just remember it being loads of overdubs, noise and chaos.

"I'm pretty sure they came into the studio with the songs written. It was just a case of them coming into the studio and it was just the case of playing them and me recording them and then you know I'd throw in ideas and they'd go 'no, fuck off' or then 'no, fuck off' and then 'do 'em' and then it ends up on the record. Either one or the other.

"I don't remember it being a very long process. I remember the whole thing maybe taking 6 weeks total, if that. Might've been quicker than that." It has been stated that the sessions would've taken place from late December 1980 to February 1981.

"They're just pranksters. Constantly joking around.

"I had at that stage only really made one other record."

The album has a similar drum sound to the likes of Gang of Four, The Slits and Public Image Limited; they were all recorded at Studio 2 with a particular set up. "They all got a similar sound to them, because of the nature of that room."

As far as Nick Launay's career was concerned he believes working on the album was "very very important. The case of whether I co-produced is never going to be resolved or answered, but if you listen to any record I've produced. If you listen to the Yeah Yeah Yeahs record I've made and listen to Killing Joke the sound is pretty much the same. It's what I do. The thing that I do. The character of what I do is all over that record. I'm really proud of that regardless of what my credit is or could be. I don't think it matters and I don't really care. It didn't bug me then and it doesn't bug me now. It's more of a subject of humour and an ongoing killing joke so to speak. I'm very proud of that record. I'm very proud of being allowed to do it. Being in the right place at the right time. I love 'em and I love them as people. They're just great. They're the type of band I continue to work with. If you look at that I'm working with The Idles now and there's probably a strong point they wanted to work with me is because of Public Image." Nick Launay believes that working with early post-punk bands in and around 1981 "absolutely shaped my career.

"I'm very grateful to the band for asking me to do it and it is fantastic. It doesn't actually matter that there isn't any documentation saying that I was involved."

While the first album presented a year's worth of writing, rehearsing and re-writing the majority of the second album was re-written in the studio, which according to Geordie makes the album "a lot more cohesive." He admitted only liking about three of the songs on the album to *Trouser Press* in 1981, which was an improvement on only liking a single track on the debut album. He states that he gets sick of the songs on the new album due to the intensity of them, saying even that he "gets to hate them sometimes." He notes that "you've got to start somewhere; you've got to make mistakes."

Jaz explained the inspiration behind 'Tension' to Ross Fitzsimons of Irish music paper *Hot Press* in 1981 saying "[in] Ireland - you'll notice that half your pre-Reformation churches are built on stone circles. Look at your ancestors, how they built in circles, how they lined them up with the heavens, they had knowledge of it. So listen, you and me are cold, we're outside. What do we do instinctively? There's a few of us, we light a fire."

In an interview with LA zine *Another Room* in September 1981 further background to the songs is revealed. 'The Fall of Because' turns out to be a song that organically happened and the song is referencing "the collapse of reason. Things have gone beyond reason." 'Who Told You' even featured their on-stage Dave the Wizard's dog barking at the end of the song.

Killing Joke was scheduled to play at Trucks in Wigan on 24th April. With 20-odd gig goers outside the venue it turned out that the venue was unable to provide the band with necessary power for their PA, so the first show of the year got cancelled, prompting Paul to comment to *NME*'s Gavin Martin that "This is one of the killing jokes that follows us everywhere we go."

Youth also ended up being hospitalised in a mental home after reportedly burning five-pound notes outside a bank before he ended up at Chelsea police station only wearing boxing shorts, where the band's publicist came to rescue him. Youth believes he fell victim to a tab of Snoopy acid. "Somebody slipped me the acid. I wouldn't have taken it myself if I'd known what would happen - but the mental home was great. I went crazy, sure, but then I began to see the funny side of life," he commented on the episode to the *NME*.

Youth gave an interview regarding the development of his long lasting acid breakdown in detail to John Higgs, who had an aborted attempt at working on a book about the band. Youth had been doing acid regularly and had got involved with a 21-year-old hairdresser called Heidi on their German tour. She had been financially supporting Youth by helping him stay at nice hotels as well as chauffeuring him to his shows. Jaz had a really bad acid trip once when he was 16 and thought his arm had disappeared, which put him off, and no-one else in the group was too much into it either. Youth had been supplied acid by a friend of his, Ralph, staying at his squat whilst he was away, and a TV had disappeared when Youth was away. Upon running into him in a club Ralph gave him a tab of acid in the form of a Sorcerer's Apprentice trip which had a Mickey Mouse on it. Youth got paranoid, thinking people were out to kill him. Youth's trip was getting worse. He tried to get hold of Ralph, but it turned out he had committed suicide. Youth would even later end up breaking into the Masonic headquarters in Covent Garden as he'd started seeing Masonic conspiracies everywhere all the way to the drain covers. The rest of Killing Joke got concerned about him as he had previously been extremely cynical. He first started burning notes at a bank manager in Clydesdale Bank who was a mason. Later he carried on in a similar vein at a grocery store, wearing just swimming trunks and a kimono, which led to his arrest. Youth was treated at Springfields Hospital near Tooting Bec, where he was given Largactil, which is a medication used to treat various problems such as severe depression or behavioural disturbance, along with Electroconvulsive Therapy. Youth tried escaping and wounded his hand; thinking it was stigmata, this led him to think he was Jesus. He would get daily visits from the wizard who came on stage with the band, who gave him a crystal and advised him to tell the doctors that he was just having a bad LSD trip. This worked and after two weeks at the hospital he was let go and able to go on tour to Wales with the band.

A 15 song outtake bootleg collection appeared with the aptly titled moniker *What This Is For Outtakes* in 1981. The first song on the bootleg was 'Anarchy Dub', which can be seen as an alternative version of 'Turn to Red'. Mainly instrumental and rather chaotic, the somewhat cacophonic song has no other lyrics apart from 'Turn to Red' being sang occasionally over the mesmerising music. 'Nervous Chaos' is as one might expect an alternative version of 'Nervous System'. The song is slower and less together than the version which appeared on the band's EP. On the song it sounds like Jaz hasn't quite found the right rhythm and times for his vocals for the song. The echo seems to be a bit overdone on this version as well. 'Madness' is similar to the finished album version. Also, four different dub versions of the song are presented. Three dub versions of 'Killer' are presented ranging from under three minutes to nearly six minutes. 'Unspeakable' here is very much a work in progress with a running time of 49 seconds. Two untitled songs appear on the record, which seem to be just rough jams which didn't make it further than that. Both are strongly based on Big Paul's tribal beats with Youth's bass trying to find the right pattern on top of them. 'Burner' is the final track on the bootleg and is very dissonant and by the sounds of it later became 'Butcher' on the final album. 'Burner' at this stage is just an instrumental. Overall it's a very shambolic representation of the band and the songs, but gives an interesting insight into the development of the album. Engineer Hugh Padgham doesn't recall these songs being recorded or considered for the album.

On 14th April 1981 the band would record a session for the John Peel show on BBC radio. They recorded powerful versions of 'Tension', 'Butcher' and 'The Fall of Because', all from the upcoming album. The sessions were first broadcast on 27th April 1981. These would later be officially released in 2008 by Virgin Records as a part of *The Peel Sessions 1979-1981* compilation.

In May 1981 the first and only single 'Follow the Leaders' was released. Interestingly enough *Sounds* gave the single full five stars for the music, but only one star for its moral stance. Apparently, they eventually went on to regret the review.

The band would do a session at Langham Studios in London's West End on 29th May for the Richard Skinner Show on BBC Radio 1. Three songs from the brand-new album, 'Tension', Unspeakable' and 'Exit', would be broadcast after the album was released on 10th July. These recordings would appear as the bonus tracks on the 2008 Virgin compilation *The Peel Sessions 1979-1981*.

Giovanni Dadomo goes into detail in an article in UK pop culture magazine *The Face* in May 1981 to explain how the band still live in a once salubrious but now seemingly squat-like flat in West London. The Caribbean painting in their living room would give a strong indication towards their Jamaican imports ranging from everything from rum to grapefruits.

Paul told Dianne Pearson of *Smash Hits* in July 1981 that the band wouldn't ever be using separate producers on their albums stating that "if a band can't get the sound they want themselves then they might as well give up." He also observed that although they had their own ideals they were impractical and they have to keep promoting their products in order to be able to keep recording new albums.

The album artwork was done again by Mike Coles, with the cover image based on a photograph taken at 88 Colegate, Norwich, England.

The album was released in June 1981 by EG Records, reaching No. 42 in the UK Albums Chart. All tracks are credited as being written by Killing Joke (Jaz Coleman, Paul Ferguson, Martin Glover and Geordie Walker). Side one was 'The Fall of Because', 'Tension', 'Unspeakable', 'Butcher' and side two 'Follow the Leaders', 'Madness', 'Who Told You How?' and 'Exit'. The 1981 cassette featured the titles 'This Is Madness' and 'It's Very Nice (Unspeakable!)' instead of 'Madness' and 'Unspeakable'. When the album was re-released in 2005 it had as bonus tracks the dub versions of 'Follow the Leaders' and 'Madness' along with the B-side 'Madness'.

The press wasn't quite sure what to make of it. Adam Sweeting of *Melody Maker* said "This unlistenable record has very little going for it apart from the spaces between the tracks." He added that it was "a tired and very noisy collection of ripoffs." Phil McNeil dedicated half a page of the *NME* saying that it was an excellent record on its own terms and concluding "it's the same wardance as before, slightly better realised. A suitably futile gesture." *Trouser Press* described it as "nearly as terrific, bringing funk to ambient music, implying feeling sublimated in a chaotic world." The album did stand the test of time; for example in 2016 *Paste* magazine's Josh Jackson listed the album on his list of 'The 50 Best Post-Punk Albums' at number 48, commenting that "the real genius here is the human emotion that comes through such spare efficiency."

Probably the most famous review from the time was in the 20 June issue of *Sounds* by John Gill. The full-page review was titled "Jokers Wild" and awards the album a full 5 stars, but then in brackets it says "but * morally". The album is portrayed both as the werewolf attacking its victim as well as the embodiment of evil. The album is strongly compared to the Sex Pistols, with John Gill stating that not since the Sex Pistols had he heard an album with such distinct classics as Killing Joke presents here. He describes the nightmarish visions and champions the way the band has incorporated rhythms from disco to avant-garde to African beats into their sound. Concluding the review he says "Fine music but, like the sorcerer's apprentice, they don't seem to have the ability – let alone the responsibility – to control the monster they've let loose."

In a *Zig Zag* interview in August 1981 Jaz expressed his concerns to Louisa Hennesy about how the band's music got misunderstood. Part of the reason was the decision to exclude lyric sheets from the new album due to it being more cost effective, but it also left the lyrics open to much interpretation. The band felt that it was very vital to communicate via the music and not just the lyrics.

UK magazine *Zig Zag* said in their July 1981 review that the album made "most of its contemporaries seem puny and silly" while complaining that most of the "choruses consist mainly of the song titles repeated."

The band became very wary of what the press wrote about them and often felt completely misunderstood. When talking to the *Sounds* journalist John Gill in July 1981 Jaz expressed how they felt that they were fulfilling a pre-determined destiny with the band. "And we take it beyond music. Music is only one side of it. We like to physically go through the experiences we write about." In a *Cream* interview in

December 1981, with John Neilson, Jaz points out how most journalists, particularly in the *NME*, don't understand the band and see their music as pessimistic, adding that he thinks "it inspires more lust, more vigour, more spirit than most of the escapist nonsense you can buy on the market these days. I like the idea of encouraging lust and raucousness in people as opposed to complacency and apathy."

On July 6th the band played at the legendary Paradiso in Amsterdam, Netherlands. What is also remarkable was the fact it was broadcast on PKP. PKP was a completely autonomous pirate television station which illegally broadcasted in Amsterdam during the summer and autumn of 1981. While apparently most pirate TV stations broadcasted porn, PKP preferred to broadcast music and other entertainment. A lot of groups in those days were very cooperative in having their shows taped and would usually give permission for the broadcast, and the same applied for venues as well. The set is roughly 50 minutes, shot from what appears to be a balcony on stage left with one single camera. "And the next number is called 1984," says Jaz, followed by laughter before exiting the stage to a cheering crowd. The band gives a rather unorganised 10-minute interview where they defend the fact they wanted a major label distribution and deal as opposed to being on an independent label. The interviewer says the band would attract artistic and university types at their shows in the UK, which Geordie completely disagrees with, saying "That's rubbish. There are nutcases at our gigs. They're the only type of honest people out there. They haven't got any pretence about them." He wasn't happy with the audience they had that evening. "Today it was dreadful. They were morons. They didn't know whether to dance or what. I don't know if they considered themselves hip or something." The previous night's show at Rotterdam had been better apparently. Jaz expresses his disrespect for the generic pop groups of the day. The interviewer tries to get Jaz's views on the Dutch women, but he has no interest in replying to questions of that nature.

The band gave an interview to Al, Hud and Pooch of *Flipside* in August 1981 before their first of five shows at the legendary Whiskey A Go Go in Hollywood. The band was pleased that 'Follow the Leaders' had been getting a lot of radio airplay and even broke into the disco charts, which they and Youth in particular were very pleased about. Jaz saw that in the States the band was still seen as a rock and roll band, while in Europe, people had started to perceive it to be more emotional than that. Judging by the live recording that has been making the rounds from the show it wasn't too bad of an affair.

The August 17th show at the East Side Club in Philadelphia, USA was filmed by Michel Polizzi and shot with a single black and white camera, and would surface as the DVD side of *The Original Unperverted Pantomime* released in 2008. As Michel explains in the liner notes the story goes that art fanzine *In the Shatterlight* got in touch with him in early August 1981 to provide recording equipment to film the band's upcoming appearance at the East Side Club. The editor of the fanzine had got the approval from the band with the intention of turning the final product into a Dada-Situationist piece. Due to the camera placed to stage right next to Geordie's amp in the mix Jaz's keyboards are lower, but given the standards and difficulty of recording during the time it serves as an excellent piece of history. There was a disagreement over the quality of the finished recordings, hence the footage being buried for so long. According to the production notes, the club was packed with over 500 people in attendance and the size and amount of people inside the venue set limitations to the recording. The film features almost the full show: 'Wardance', 'Unspeakable', 'The Wait', 'The Fall Of Because', 'Primitive', 'Exit', 'Requiem', 'Follow The Leaders' 'Change', 'Pssyche' and 'Tension'. 'Bloodsport' would later surface online, but was omitted from the DVD due to tape damage. Geordie is playing a Gibson SG at this point rather than the hollow bodied ES that he later became known for. Youth is pumping a Rickenbacker bass in the middle of the stage with a fireman's helmet. Jaz takes the occasional stroll from behind his Oberheim keyboard, but not having a separate keyboard player limits his stage movement.

On 23rd August the band make an appearance at the Police Picnic festival in The Grove, Oakville, Ontario in Canada. The Police Picnic 1 was in an open field in the middle of nowhere and featured a line-up of The Police, who had organised the event, along with The Specials, Iggy Pop, Killing Joke, The Go-Go's, Nash the Slash, John Otway & Wild Willy Barrett, The Payola$, Oingo Boingo, and David Bendeth Band. Killing Joke's set consisted of 'Wardance', 'The Fall of Because', 'Exit', 'The Wait', 'Requiem', 'Unspeakable', 'Bloodsport', 'Change' and 'Pssyche'. By today's standards a rather distorted bootleg recording of the show exists. Angie Baldassarre was there on behalf of now defunct *Toronto Shades* magazine to witness a bit of a shambolic festival and talked to Jaz after the show, who expressed his dislike of the majority of Americans.

60

In November the band expressed their wishes to play more unconventional venues to *The Offense* fanzine writer Blake Gumprecht, but they were financially tied to recording processes.

In October 1981 punk had reached its second wave bands with Scottish punks The Exploited releasing their 'Dead Cities' EP in October, which landed them with an appearance on the BBC TV show *The Top of the Pops*. The brilliant, aggressive, in-your-face EP and the title track made a strange choice for the BBC to have on the show. In an interview with Jaz and Geordie by Chris Burkham for *Sounds* in March 1982 Geordie said that The Exploited "exist as a safe means to keep the rebellious element in the country satisfied. That is because there's no real threat there, and ultimately there's this feeling that 'the kids will grow out of it' or 'they'll settle down soon.'" The Exploited were fronted by the ex-soldier Wattie Buchan, who portrayed, by today's standards, a caricature version of punk with a red mohican, black leather jacket, Ramones-style ripped black jeans and cherry red Doc Marten's boots. The band's bassist Gary McGormack had a Vivienne Westwood white long sleeve T-shirt with an offensive print and red Scottish tartan bondage trousers. Jaz and Geordie said that Killing Joke weren't invited even though their single 'Follow the Leaders' got to number 32 in the official charts, but apparently they wouldn't fit the nice rebel boy category. Neither would they want to go and mime on the show, but would send a music video instead of appearing on the show if they were ever asked. As Geordie put it they "don't want to have to degrade ourselves in front of the amorphous mass. You know, jig and grin on cue."

In fact, a music video, an unofficial one by the looks of things, for 'Follow the Leaders' was made showing newsreel footage of world leaders, British royals, nuclear explosions and pigs waiting for slaughter. It was released on a US VHS music video compilation *Underground Forces #5* by Target Video in 1985. Killing Joke opened the compilation with a music video for 'Exit' and the music video for 'Follow the Leaders'. It featured US bands such as Black Flag, Circle Jerks and X among other lesser known acts that time has since forgotten. The music video for 'Exit' was in a similar vein with footage of tanks, aboriginals and burlesque dancers, and tried to create a menacing atmosphere, which doesn't quite come across in the same way today.

The band made an appearance on Belgium TV show *Generation 80* miming to 'Unspeakable' and 'Exit'. Much as in early music appearances of the time the band is backed with light bulbs portraying various triangular patterns. The band are all dressed in black with the exception of Youth's white-collar shirt. Jaz has his face painted black and he is sat behind his Moog keyboards for the first song. Geordie is playing a Fender Stratocaster rather than a Gibson model this time around. For the second song Jaz stands up and gets more into his stage routine and mannerisms. Fitting to the song, the song fades out with a slow-motion video.

Wearing a mask has always been important to Jaz as it has "incredible importance and my colleagues have noticed it as well from the early days. I've been wearing the mask since then as when I don't, I suffer derangement. I suffer psychological derangement. It's more a psychological thing putting the mask on and then taking it off. Otherwise you live with that personality. It's something I really regret not warning Heath Ledger about."

By the end of the year the band had definitely left their mark in the music scene with Geordie being voted the best guitarist by *NME* readers while another post-punk group The Fall won the best group of the year. While The Fall's guitarist Marc Riley is a very accomplished rock critic and guitarist currently presenting BBC Radio 6 Music he is most definitely overshadowed by Geordie's symphonic soundscape. Yet another post-punk group, Siouxsie & the Banshees, also won the best new group award, so it was clear that in certain terms post-punk had eclipsed punk by the end of 1981 as the most popular and exciting new genre, at least in certain circles.

PART TWO

Commercial Success

1982 – Revelations

Released just prior to singer Jaz Coleman exiling to Iceland, you can sense the band falling apart. While the first side of the album features the eerie power of 'The Pandys Are Coming' and 'Empire Song' the second half falls short. Best enjoyed when heavily immersed in occultism.

Charts 1982

UK Albums Chart #12
France   #33

In late 1981 the band would record four songs from their upcoming album for the Peel Sessions: 'Hum', 'Empire Song', 'We Have Joy' and 'Chop Chop'. These were first broadcast on 16th December 1981 and would later be officially released as a part of *The Peel Sessions 1979-1981* compilation released in 2008 by Virgin Records.

Somewhere between nine and twelve months after the sessions for the second album Nick Launay went to record a version of 'Empire Song' along with 'Brilliant' with the band. His version of 'Empire Song' has remained unreleased, but the B-side 'Brilliant' was released with Conny Plank's version of the A-side. "Back in the day it was all analogue. I might have a copy of it downstairs."

Jaz explains the origins of the song to the *NME* in August 1983 saying that it "was there before the Falklands. I'm a very receptive person, you know. I feel these things every once in a while. But I'm not interested in social observations at the moment." For the record, the Falkland War was a 10-week undeclared war that started on 2nd April between Argentina and the United Kingdom in 1982 over two British dependent territories in the South Atlantic: the Falkland Islands and its territorial dependency, South Georgia and the South Sandwich Islands.

Jaz told Eugene Butcher of *Vive Le Rock* in summer of 2013 that the line "Back to square one, another empire backfires" comes straight from the British tabloid headline in *The Sun* newspaper around the time when the Falklands incident happened. Apparently that brought the band even to the attention of Prime Minister Margaret Thatcher and apparently making things more difficult within the industry.

In a video interview with *Classic Rock* in May 2013 Jaz Coleman says that the song marks his political awakening. He was surprised to see so many people in the music industry behind the leader of the Conservative Party Margaret Thatcher instead of more liberal politics. This also sowed the seed for him to leave the United Kingdom.

When Nick Launay returned to work with the band he had already gained a wealth of experience with other notable artists. "By which point I had done many, many more records. At that point I'd done an album with Kate Bush and The Slits and The Birthday Party. I was more established as a record producer. I also had a manager, so by that point the only way I would work with them was if there was a contract. So, there was a contract and I remember going up to meet up with them at their rehearsal studio. It was somewhere in Notting Hill Gate or Ladbroke Grove or somewhere like that, which is where I lived. It wasn't far I remember. And then we went back into the same studio they had been during their previous sessions. Studio two. One of them was 'Brilliant' and the other song was 'Empire [Song'] I think. It might've been another song, but I can't remember the title, but when I listen to 'Empire Song' it seems very familiar to me."

The single A-side is credited to Conny Plank and Nick Launay believes that the band re-wrote the song and did a new version with him.

Albert Edward writes in *Spiral Scratch* magazine in January 1991 how a bootleg titled *The Bum's Rush* had appeared in the shops early in 1983 and was withdrawn almost immediately following a high court injunction. The LP showed a still from an early slapstick comedy on the cover and consisted of their Peel and Capital Radio sessions along with the original version of 'Follow the Leaders' with alternative lyrics and the original mix of 'Pssyche'. Unlike most bootlegs at the time this release had excellent sound quality hence legal action was taken against it. Since the noughties the material has been officially available.

Their third album was recorded in Cologne, Germany during the first half of 1983. Cologne is a major cultural centre for the Rhineland, the name used for Western Germany, nowadays hosting more than 30 museums and hundreds of galleries. The album was the first one to have an outside producer, or shall we say to give credit to one.

Cologne was the home of the German experimental rock band Can formed in 1968 by the core quartet of bassist Holger Czukay, keyboardist Irmin Schmidt, guitarist Michael Karoli and drummer Jaki Liebezeit.

Konrad 'Conny' Plank, born on 3rd May 1940, was a West German record producer and musician born in Hütschenhausen. Before Killing Joke he had produced influential German bands such as Can and electronic music pioneers Kraftwerk.

"Conny Plank produced us who had produced Can and Kraftwerk who are both major influences of ours," said Youth about the decision to choose him as the producer. The album was recorded at Conny Plank's studio, which was sort of a mountain retreat half an hour outside Cologne.

Unfortunately Conny Plank passed away on 5th December 1987. Plank fell ill while touring South America with Dieter Moebius, Arno Steffen and Detlef Wiederhoeft performing music from an album called *Ludwig's Law*. *Ludwig's Law* was the fourth album recorded by the team of Moebius & Plank, but the only album released by the trio Dieter Moebius, Conny Plank, and Mayo Thompson. He was known for only working with artists that he liked and had a unique vision for the sound of the artists.

Jaz recalls the reason for wanting to work with Conny in *Conny Plank: the Potential of Noise*. It was that he had done a track about Benito Mussolini, an Italian politician and journalist who was the leader of the National Fascist Party. The song was 'Der Mussolini' by D.A.F. (Deutsch Amerikanische Freundschaft) released as a single in 1981. They were an influential German electropunk/Neue Deutsche Welle band from Düsseldorf. "It was the first song I really loved in the German language." The album, which included the song *Alles Ist Gut,* was a massive hit in Germany, charting for 46 weeks as well as ranking at number 8 among the Top Ten Albums of the Year for 1981 in the *NME*. Jaz held Conny in high regard saying "to sum him up I think politically he was a revolutionary and musically it was absolutely revolutionary. Before all the technology and sampling, he was doing it all." Conny had been producing bands for bigger labels, but wasn't happy with the situation and decided to start his own studio in a farmhouse, which was an unusual setting. The remote farmhouse was away from all the distractions. Conny had his wife Christa and son living in the farmhouse as well. He was known for not interfering with the musicians or having any kind of time or money restraints, which surely worked well with

Killing Joke. He was also pushing a certain European approach and wanted bands to find a unique voice. He was in certain ways very anti-commercial and declined to work with commercial artists such as U2 and The Cars. He said he saw himself as the medium between the artist and the tape.

The band tells the *NME* in 1981 that they wouldn't use an outside producer, stating that "if a band can't get the sound they want themselves they might as well give up." They claim that Conny is merely an engineer, much like they claimed Phil Harding to be on their debut album. Jaz explains how they are expanding their sound: "The rhythms on this new album are different, they're more intense than anything. We were experimenting with fourths, because in conventional music, you're never allowed to use intervals of fourths, it produces an undesirable effect, just like in the litanies in church music, y'know, there was a ninth litany they used to use on All Soul's day, and they cut that out, 'cause it inspired naughty things - the actual tones of the notes." There were only a couple of keyboard overdubs on the album and closing track 'Dregs' was completely recorded live.

Youth also says that the times were changing. "What was also great with punk, there were suddenly a lot of women involved in the music. You had The Slits and The Raincoats. Post-punk became more than punk, thank punk really. Ahead of the curve. Bands had the dub influences. Bands like the Bush Tetras and these New York bands like ESG that were all girls and they were doing disco with guitars. If you pick bands like Gang of Four, Killing Joke or one of the other post-punk architects there is the element of disco with abrasive, edgy, dissonant guitars. Especially Joy Division. I think that came from the mash up of Berlin and New York. Can was doing that before and that seemed like a good place to go to. Not only us, but look at Public Image [Limited]. The Public Image template is totally Can. That was close to the source. Can. [John] Lydon really got Can. It seemed like a logical place to go to after punk because it is a bit more organised chaos. There is a chaotic spontaneous element to it. Harnessed in funk and dub as well.

"In fact when we were recording in [Germany] [Jah] Wobble was out there recording with Holger [Czukay from Can]. Wobble was only 21 at the time. He had just left Pil I think. He did these amazing tracks with Jackie Liebezeit and Holger. I was eighteen at the time and I thought 'my God, if I could be as self-realised at 21 and be working with these cats that would be an amazing achievement.'"

The album Youth talks about is collaborative album *Full Circle* recorded in Inner Ear Studios in Cologne and released in 1982 through Virgin Records. With a mere 6 tracks, 3 on each side of the LP, it clocks in at over 40 minutes. The album portrayed heavy krautrock and dub influences and apart from the opening track 'How Much Are They?' has not been on much rotation and completely avoided the charts and mainstream record consumers. Interestingly enough the song was recorded and mixed by Mark Lusardi, who also worked on the first Killing Joke sessions.

Bassist Jah Wobble was one of the founding members of Public Image Limited with Johnny Rotten from the Sex Pistols and Keith Levene who briefly played in the Clash. He played on Pil's most highly rated early albums *Public Image* and *Metal Box*, before departing the band and making a name for himself with the Invaders of the Heart. He also composed the hit 'Visions of You' with Sinead O'Connor and played a big part on Björk's 'Play Dead' on the aptly titled debut *Debut*.

"I knew them early on and I had heard some of the early stuff and liked it. They were all good lads and I was always friendly with Youth. They were very sensible and very committed to each other. They stayed the course, which was something Public Image wouldn't have the sense to do.

"I was puzzled when they started doing heavy metal and that split some of their fans. It wasn't until we supported them with my band a couple of years ago and stayed to listen to their set. I remembered I like this tune and I like that tune. They were well put together. I always liked Geordie's shimmering metal guitar. That's why I told them to get Martin Atkins, because he was someone I wanted to play with from that scene. After a while I realised later on how they moved on into the metal stuff, because it kind of continued to kind of work.

"I played with Youth in his band at the Grosvenor Hotel when he got the lifetime achievement award. I hadn't realised he'd done the Verve! I was like bloody hell. I didn't know that. Youth is a smart guy and he knows how you put records together. He is aesthetically and culturally very aware. Smokes a lot of dope, but doesn't miss a beat!

"So if you're in the studio and you're having a chat about something and you mention something to him even when he is smoking a joint he is always on the ball. He is really on it."

The first single from the album, 'Empire Song', was released in March 1982 backed with 'Brilliant'. The single reached number 43 in the UK Singles Chart later on the same month. The success of the single led to a legendary broadcast on the BBC's *Top of the Pops* programme.

The BBC Riverside television studio received a note on 26th February from the singer just prior to the scheduled recording of the show. The band appeared without the singer, with a doll wearing a beehive helmet as his replacement, performing their latest single 'Empire Song'. The band were still half expecting Jaz to turn up at the studios and according to *Zig Zag* April issue they got merry with Southern Comfort whilst waiting for the singer to turn up. Apparently, there had been sightings of him in Switzerland as well as Iceland near the time. Prior to his disappearance he had voiced concerns of wanting to write a book as well as record a solo album with just drums backing him up.

In the broadcast Paul takes over miming the vocals while a person wearing a beehive mask takes the place behind the keyboard. Youth is wearing a clean white suit and a white scarf, which appears to have oriental writing on it, while Paul and Geordie are dressed in black.

On 23rd February the band had played a sold-out show at the Hammersmith Palais in London, from which six songs were pro shot and broadcast on French TV. The broadcast begins with footage of punks in black leather jackets outside the venue and a short interview with Jaz where he says how the band makes him feel human as well as animal. Also, he ominously gives "the Western civilisation 20 months to survive." 'The Hum', 'The Fall of Because', 'Wardance', 'We Have Joy', 'Empire Song', which are all shown in order from the beginning of the set, then the second to last song of the set 'The Wait', make up the first national live show broadcast of the band. Songs left out from the broadcast were 'Have A Nice Day', 'Tension', 'Chapter III', 'Pssyche', 'Chop Chop', 'Exit', 'Land Of Milk And Honey', 'Change' and 'Unspeakable'.

When Jaz Coleman suddenly disappeared right before the band was due to appear on *Top of the Pops*, the reason was that he thought there'd be more of a chance of surviving the oncoming apocalypse, which he predicted was imminent. Manager Brian Taylor told Steve Sutherland of *Melody Maker* in March 1982 that Jaz had told him he was planning on leaving the band that very year, but he put it down as his "over-active imagination." Jaz's interest in the occult and other sinister signs had been cropping up and he had increasingly got into ritual magic and the teachings of Aleister Crowley. He had seemingly lost interest in the band and had been acting oddly. He later wrote in *An Irrational Domain* that the band would be playing "in areas of abysmal grey matter such as Sheffield and Leeds." And it was important for him to be "spiritually absorbed in all areas of industrial ugliness so that when its antithesis finally arrived, the impact would be overwhelming."

The last show Jaz performed with the band was on 24th February at Top Rank in Brighton. He recalls the events in Killing Joke communique *An Irrational Domain* saying "It had seemed apt to set the date of departure as the evening of Friday 25th so that I would wake up in Reykjavik on the date that four years earlier Big Paul and I had ritually commenced Killing Joke - and more - it was the day I was born." The only person who Jaz informed was his mother whom he called once he had made it to Iceland.

Jaz had experienced a "visitation" whilst in Iceland six months earlier, which prompted him to visit the small island of Iona in the Inner Hebrides off the Ross of Mull on the western coast of Scotland. The name Iona translates as "purple jewel". The main attraction of the island is Iona Abbey, which was a centre of Gaelic monasticism for three centuries. Today the island has less than 200 inhabitants and is mostly known for its relative tranquillity and natural environment.

Geordie later followed the singer to Iceland and at this point Youth parted ways with the group. Youth hadn't been informed about this random move and only came aware of it by reading about it in the music paper the *NME*. Youth was very upset by the way he had not been kept in the loop.

"I left the band after *Revelations*, being a little disappointed in *Revelations* as much as I love working with Connie. It came out a bit dirgy," says Youth. "Then I left the band and they went on and did *Fire Dances* and it was great songwriting and great choruses. Great production and I was like oh shit I would've stayed in the band if I'd known! None the less it was important for me to leave and find my own feet in other areas."

Rob O'Connor was the first designer to be brought in after Mike Coles. Rob O'Connor and his company Stylorouge would go on to work with the likes of Siouxsie and the Banshees and Blur. The company is probably most known for creating the poster for the 1996 British dark heroin-fuelled comedy *Trainspotting*. Rob got involved with the band during the early days of his career.

"Right at the beginning actually I was working for Polydor from 1979 to 1991 and it was one of the projects that came into the art department. Not for us to work on particularly although if I remember correctly we did some press advertising for the first EP. It was one of the most incredible things I've heard at the time. [I was] Very excited about them at the time. Went to see them live a couple of times."

EG was a subsidiary of Polydor and their artwork would go through their art department.

"I was just a youngster starting out as a designer. I was working for Siouxsie and the Banshees when I got there. One of the first projects that came my way and then Killing Joke came along, which was a very special thing to be involved in."

Rob had been good friends with Mike Coles, who had been in charge of the band's artwork up to that moment. They parted company when Rob went on to start his own company Stylorouge.

"I was asked to do things when Mike wasn't available at first."

Rob loved Mike's artwork, in particular the work he had done for the self-titled debut album. "Mike had his own style, kind of collagey and he was ahead of the game really, because he was doing quite a lot of work with computers. A lot of people weren't really doing much of that. He was very much a self-taught artist and loved to do the playful thing Killing Joke did, which was take everyday things and put them into this weird, apocalyptic situation, which I always liked about his work actually."

Rob had actually left Polydor to set up his own company in May 1981 and *Revelations* didn't come out until July 1982. "That was working with the band closer than I had before."

The idea for the artwork for the album came from Jaz. Apparently, according to a *Melody Maker* article in August 1986, the original cover idea was to have the Masonic callipers offset by seven degrees. Following various threats, the idea was ditched by the band.

"Jaz was very into the Freemasons at the time. He was sort of studying it, as he does with everything, in great detail. I never know which side of the fence Jaz really is on when he discovers something that is sinister and dark. The unpleasantness of the human race. Still to this day I don't know if it is something that he appals or admires. Probably a bit of both. I think there was something about the history of the Freemasons that fascinated him and the way that they orchestrated their power in a very mystical way using the occult. And their arrogance they had where people had superiority over others.

"He liked the symbolism. He came in one day with a couple of books talking about some of the imagery that was used and how it was mixing up biblical with magic. He also brought to my attention that imagery was used in the design of money. I'd not really noticed it until then. On the inside of *Revelations* we had sort of a watermark design on each side. One side of a close up of a dollar bill and the other one had a close up of a pound note. Both of which used mythical imagery. Historical mythical imagery. The front cover came from that really. He wanted something that looked like the kind of embroidery that you get in the sort of Freemasons regalia. In those days it was before the Internet obviously, so we had to do all our research from libraries and what not. I went out and researched the Masons and we actually found a company that does embroidery for the Freemasons. That was interesting as they were quite intrigued by why I wanted to have something to do for [Killing Joke]. I told them that it was just a style I really liked. We came out with a design which was sort of a side ribbon. We showed the design in just black and white to the band which we had to get approved beforehand before we could get the embroidery done as it was quite an expensive process. Then we had to wait for this company, who I believe were up in Yorkshire somewhere, to do the work."

Jaz and Geordie turned up to the photoshoot and wanted to get involved in the photograph.

"The lighting was important as we wanted it to look quite moody, not too bright. The record company, as always, were quite concerned about using this imagery, because as they pointed out that a lot of people in the music industry at the time were probably members of the Masons anyway. As it may offend some of them. The people who were the head of their record company were quite possibly Masons themselves."

Rob believes that Mark Fenwick, who was a British businessman, the fifth generation of his family to run the Fenwick department store chain founded in 1882 and behind EG Records, was possibly a Freemason.

"It was either Geordie or Jaz who wanted to have something concealed underneath the silk. You wouldn't know it was there, but they put it underneath it. It was a talisman thing. A very kind of ethnic, maybe something you'd wear around your neck. I think it was Jaz who wanted it underneath, so he knew it was there. I said, 'You know the satin is not very sheer, so you're not going to see through it,' but he said, 'It doesn't matter. I know it's there.'"

No alternative cover suggestions were used. Only the type of satin used was being discussed using the company's catalogue to help to decide which would be their selection.

"At the time they were getting a weird reputation. They were as loved by their fans as they were mistrusted by the industry a little bit, because people didn't know if they were extremely anarchist or whether they were kind of right wing. I knew them not to be right wing. This came up in a conversation [with Jaz] about being nationalistic or in any way sort of right wing and he said 'No, why would I be right wing? I'm a quarter Indian' or something and I didn't realise that at the time. And then we spoke about the song 'The Pandys Are Coming', which was supposedly a Indian tribe kind of thing. I think he said something like his grandfather was one of the last of the Pandys. Whether that is true or not, as what I've read since is that the Pandys are Tamil and I think his mother was part Bengali. That was the only lyric I remember talking to him about while we were doing the cover. I don't remember hearing any demos at the time."

As told in Billy Hell's online Killing Joke perspective in December 2005 on *Perfect Sound Forever* the title 'The Pandys Are Coming' was derived from a song the army of the British Empire sang in India when the 'Pandit' tribe of Hindus invoked 'Kali' before hurtling towards the British to embrace destruction. Kali is a goddess in Hinduism representing creation, destruction and time, and is often presented as dark and violent. It represented a totalitarian state of mind representing Jaz Coleman's own and he also saw no reason why he should not exploit the family name of his Brahmin heritage. Jaz began working on an OBX synthesiser with different effects at Mountain Studios in Wales. He perfected a reproduction of the wailing sound of the Bedouin pipes over time, which created a disturbing vibration with the help of two reeds pitched at quarter tones from one another. The intention was to track about six of them together in a 24-channel studio in order to create a psychologically upsetting ambience in which he would define the irrational interpretation of his current incarnation with Ferguson. He saw that even the personal conflicts of the past had to converge with the present as conflict was seen as timeless.

Brahmin has been defined by British anthropologist Tim Ingold in *Companion Encyclopaedia of Anthropology* as a varna, a Sanskrit word with several meanings including type, order, colour or class, in Hinduism specialising as priests (known as purohit, pandit, or pujari), teachers (acharya) and protectors of sacred learning across generations. In *Merriam-Webster's Encyclopaedia of World Religions* brahmin, also spelled brahman, literally means "one possessing braham" standing for sacred utterance, and is often considered as the highest ranking of the four varnas, also known as social classes, in Hindu India. The belief is that the brahmins are inherently of greater ritual purity compared to members of other castes as well as being capable of performing certain vital religious tasks.

The "Chop Chop" single cover was another that Rob Connor's company did, which originated from an illustration in a medieval book.

"I've always enjoyed, but never really understood, Jaz's lyrics because they're kind of poetry and full of clues, but I've never been able to crack any of them. He has been such a great traveller and always has been. Every bit of money he had was always spent on travelling to New Zealand or Guadalajara. Nearly always to big junctions of ley lines. Wherever there were big historic cities with volcanoes and fault lines. He always seemed to go to the dramatic places in the world. I always admired that about him. He obviously picked up a lot of human interest to put into his songs. I always had to ask them to explain to me what the songs were about and it was always like 'that's not important, this is what we want' and that's generally how it works with them."

The name of the album comes from the Book of Revelation, the final book of the New Testament, and hence also the final book of the Christian Bible. The religious elements on the album are strong lyrically.

'Good Samaritan' is referencing the Samaritans known as guardians, keepers and watchers of the Torah, meaning the first five books (Pentateuch or five books of Moses) of the 24 books of the Hebrew Bible. Samaritans are an ethno-religious group originating from the Israelites (confederation of Iron Age Semitic-speaking tribes) or Hebrews (the Semitic-speaking Israelites) of the Ancient Near East. 'Land of Milk and Honey' refers to the Promised Land of Jewish tradition, as described in Exodus Chapter 3 as "a land flowing with milk and honey." 'Chapter III' is referring to the chapter where the idea of the land of milk and honey comes from. In Chapter 3 of the Exodus Moses is tending to sheep when God appears to him through a burning bush. This is also the first time Jaz refers to his dream, the Island, located at the end of the earth, a lyrical theme that would regularly resurface throughout his career.

The album had ten songs - five on each side. Side one consists of 'The Hum', 'Empire Song', 'We Have Joy', 'Chop-Chop' and 'The Pandys Are Coming'. Side two has 'Chapter III', 'Have a Nice Day', 'Land of Milk and Honey', 'Good Samaritan' and 'Dregs'. Over a minute longer, 'We Have Joy (Alternate Mix)' was released as a bonus track on the 2008 re-release as a sole extra track. This is the first time the producer Conny Plank and sleeve designer Rob O'Connor get credit on the album.

The album suffers from rather monochromatic production, and to some extent lethargy, with the exception of 'Empire Song' and 'The Pandys Are Coming'. It isn't as powerful as their first two albums. It is also quite telling that not many of the songs appear on their live sets either.

Revelations was released in July 1982 by EG Records. It peaked at number 12 in the UK Albums Chart and at number 33 in France. The critics' reception ranged from mixed to favourable. In *Calgary Herald* it was said that "what it reveals is a big disappointment." While "wrenching vocals and doom-laden lyrics" are still there the album "is lacking any meaningful purpose, any spark of emotion or sense of direction." The newspaper doesn't quite impress by stating that the two members left in the band at the time of the release are "Youth Martin" and "Paul du Noyer". It is unclear when Paul du Noyer, the writer for the *NME* and *Q* and later the founder of *Mojo,* joined the band. Nonetheless the review ends by stating that the album "seems to mark a humourless death for Killing Joke."

Paul later states in an interview with *Flaming Pablum* in 2004 that the album "is the overall favourite, but I tend not to listen to it too often, because it really sends me off down memory lane too much."

Tim DiGravina of *Allmusic* says that repeat listens of the album "reveal it to be a most enjoyable departure" for the band, which he rates as one of the best post-punk bands. "*Revelations* sees Killing Joke mangling and discarding the rules of modern rock music with demented, inspired genius." But he points out it sounds "as if it was recorded in some mad, dub chamber, *Revelations* reveals many artsy, staccato pleasures." Jaz "has never sounded more confused and happy. This translates to the listener in the form of dark, fun soundscapes."

When the album was released Kris Needs of *Zig Zag* described it as "sheer honing of the Joke attack into a total over-the-maelstrom of agonised heaving guitars, boomingly different drum figurines and Youth's swall-diving bass underpinning the lot." Jaz's keyboards get referred to as "deadly bomber drones and factory crashes, while his voice comes over with far more melody and injected feel than before."

The *NME* took it upon themselves to run almost a running commentary on Jaz's whereabouts, starting with Shaw Taylor's theory reported on 20th March that he was out visiting ley lines. "In Britain, a number of these lines converge around the Salisbury area and this could be a likely spot for a Jaz spotting." Ley lines refer to straight alignments drawn between prominent landmarks and historic structures. The origins come from early 20th-century Europe, with ley line believers arguing that these alignments were recognised by ancient European societies which then created structures along them. These beliefs are strongly present in esotericism as well as earth mysteries. The ley lines are thought to emit and channel earth energies. As Shaw Taylor points out in the first *NME* article regarding the disappearance Jaz wasn't the first one in the history of rock to disappear in somewhat similar circumstances, in an attempt to clearly ridicule the situation saying how heavy metal guitarist Michael Schender from UFO and the Scorpions had disappeared on a flying saucer hunt and Ted Turner from Wishbone Ash went looking for UFO landing sites in Peru.

Also at the time, according to Taylor's report, the band would carry on as a three piece even if the singer wouldn't return, and were planning on fulfilling the dates they had scheduled for April. A week later Brian Taylor told the *NME* that they "haven't heard from Jaz himself, but someone who's with him called to say he's not interested in coming back." Along with Taylor's statement regarding the future of the band the 27th March issue of the magazine also ran an ad saying "CAN YOU FURTHER THE KILLING JOKE? Chortle Chortle". Taylor stressed to the press that they are "not looking for Jaz clones", though they had been approached by someone claiming to be him in a different form.

When, in April, the *NME* got in touch with Jaz he simply replied "You can wonder all you like. I hate *NME*. You'll see what's gonna happen. Just fuck off, right." Later that month Jaz told the *NME* that Geordie and himself had their own management in Iceland and were planning on opening a new club in the country's capital Reykjavik. The club would specialise in barbaric music and open in about two weeks' time. Also, he said that they were planning on releasing a new EP as well as an LP of what was meant to be the new Killing Joke, featuring Icelandic musicians, by June. Jaz had also completed a book titled *Fortress* due out in less than a month. Their manager Brian Taylor was very unimpressed by this sudden move, saying "they're nuts. They're disturbed, stupid, crazy." Taylor had serious doubts and thought that trying to resurrect the band in Iceland was a very foolish move, but was relieved to see the two gone as they hadn't given him any peace in the two years he had known them. He even said that "they're the biggest bastards under the sun." At this point the band only planned to return to the UK for a couple of gigs, one in London at Hammersmith Palais and possibly another in Manchester, followed by some US dates. The only reason for doing this was purely financial according to Jaz.

It wasn't known at the time, but in an interview with Neil Perry in *Sounds* in November 1986 Jaz would reveal that he was "going mad then, seriously losing my mind." He had decided ten months earlier to leave on February 25th, 1982, the day before his birthday, also noting that they'd started Killing Joke on the 26th. Jaz had made more money up until that point than ever before, and it was important for him to blow it all, get rid of it and go to Iceland with just a single pound to his name. He found the idea of security repulsive. "When Jaz referred to his Iceland adventure and that at the time he was 'going mad', I thought it was funny," recalls Neil Perry. "He was still in the grip of the same madness, whatever it was, four years later. Perhaps even more so. But at least he had enough self-awareness to be able to talk about it."

"At that time, I was intimately involved with Norse mythology, and all the characters - Odin, Thor - had become people to me. They were promiscuous, they liked getting drunk," says Jaz in the interview. "Life in Reykjavik almost became like legend, the boundary between reality and legend was dissolved. It was a remarkable time for me, a big change." Jaz liked the isolation from people and seclusion. The people he likes to be in contact with are very few.

In 1983 Jaz collaborated with an Icelandic new wave band Þeyr. Both bands shared the way they used strange musical intervals in their music rather than just the more traditional major and minor scales. It is quite likely that Jaz had first heard the band on the *Northern Lights Playhouse* compilation LP of Icelandic bands, which was distributed in the UK by Rough Trade. It would've appealed to the singer's interest in the occult and black magic. Þeyr manager Gudni Agnarsson told the *NME* in April 1982 that Jaz Coleman hadn't joined the band, but that he was helping them with a recording project called 'Iceland'. They had a joint gig planned for April 12th in the capital Reykjavik. Jaz and the band had met a year prior and apparently Jaz knew they'd be working together. It seems that Þeyr were aware of Jaz's plans to return to Iceland two or three weeks before it actually happened. According to Agnarsson, Þeyr weren't a regular musical group, rather a number of people dedicated to building their own community, "beyond the system that is forced upon you from birth to death." They were also experimenting with electro-magnetic waves to "create an atmosphere of harmony in concerts and living rooms", and the band had also started to build a studio just outside Reykjavik which was designed to operate underwater. Their manager prophesied that the world was on the brink of natural and human catastrophes and they would survive the Last Wave and be there for the dawning of the New Age. He also emphasised he knew Jaz's reasons for coming to Iceland, but wouldn't want to discuss them and they would be revealed over time.

The group they got together was initially called Iceland before settling with Niceland at the suggestion of their guitarist Guðlaugur Óttarsson. After a couple of weeks of rehearsing the band had composed five originals from which three were recorded in Hljóðriti studios. The songs have never been officially released. It wasn't too long before Jaz's drinking took its toll on the group and they went their separate ways.

Jaz then went to work with guitarist Árni Kristjánsson and drummer Þórarinn Kristjánsson from Vonbrigði. He then reassembled Killing Joke with bassist Birgir Mogensen and Guðlaugur Kristinn Óttarsson playing guitar alongside Geordie. The line up lasted only for a couple of months before Jaz and Geordie returned to the UK.

Apparently Jaz's reasoning behind the sudden move was that Iceland would be the safest place in case of a nuclear war. Also it has been said that at the time he thought he was a re-incarnation of the infamous occultist Aleister Crowley. Jaz believed Iceland might have been the unique island portrayed in the work of Crowley. He had found references to it in Rosicrucian writings.

To dig deeper into this, the Rosicrucian teachings are a combination of occultism and other religious beliefs and practices. Rosicrucianism includes Hermeticism, Jewish mysticism, and Christian gnosticism. The central element of Rosicrucianism is the belief that the members possess secret wisdom that was handed down to them from ancient times.

The beliefs of the Hermetic Order of the Golden Dawn played a part in Jaz's expectations of Iceland. The Hermetic Order of the Golden Dawn during the late 19th and early 20th centuries was a secret society devoted to the study and practice of the occult, metaphysics, and paranormal activities.

In Iceland Jaz underwent the process of individuation (*principium individuationis*). It is a process of transformation whereby the personal and collective unconscious are brought into consciousness through dreams and active imagination as well as free association. These are to be assimilated into the whole personality. It is a completely natural process necessary for the integration of the psyche. It was also during this period Jaz that made contact with what he calls the Universe B, an alternative universe, which was then referenced in Killing Joke's music and lends it name to the B-side of the 'Hosannas from the Basement of Hell' single in 2006. During that time Jaz also heard melodies while going through the process. One of these melodies he heard can be heard in 'Pandys Are Coming' on *Revelations*.

As told to the *NME's* Paul du Noyer in May, Paul and Youth had planned on carrying on with a new vocalist in the UK, which was too much for Geordie, who decided to follow Jaz instead. Upon reflecting on the lyrics of their latest album *Revelations* Paul sensed Jaz's move seemed quite obvious although they didn't really see it whilst making the album. Also, ironically, Youth and Paul found out about the sudden departure from the *NME,* who Jaz claimed he wouldn't be speaking to. The rhythm section didn't waste time, although they were shocked by the move, but started working on new music with the as yet unnamed group.

Richard Cook of the *NME* wasn't too impressed by the new album and the way the band tried to deconstruct the traditional rock structure, claiming that the album was "a real ordeal to get through." He pointed out that "for all its strength, *Revelations* is empty and exhausted." He would end the review saying "I can't see that anyone will miss Killing Joke."

In late May the NME received a letter from Jaz and Geordie in which they denounced their musical partners, Þeyr, as a "vile enterprise" who are no longer associated with Killing Joke, or what remained of the band in Iceland at that point. There were plans to record a single 'The Gathering' backed with 'Spill the Beans' with other Icelandic musicians.

Jaz told the *NME* in August 1983 that he and Geordie "got beaten to fuck with sticks, trying to run me over in Land Rovers, things like that. They didn't like me." This surely prompted them to return back to the UK.

In July, Youth told the *NME* how he got the previously unnamed group up and running although Paul had exited the picture at this point and returned to Killing Joke. Paul was quickly replaced with a friend and session drummer Andy Anderson who had worked on an album by Sham 69 vocalist Jimmy Pursey with Marcus Myers on vocals and Rob Waugh on keyboards. At this point Jaz had appeared back in England and asked Youth to re-join Killing Joke, but he had refused.

Around this time Youth had been having troubles of his own, as he had been taking a lot of acid and begun having a nervous breakdown. He had begun to see conspiracies around him, resulting in him even breaking into the headquarters of the United Grand Lodge of England and the Supreme Grand Chapter of Royal Arch Masons of England in Covent Garden.

Paul was asked to rejoin Killing Joke with Jaz and Geordie. Originally Birgir Mogensen, whom they knew from Iceland, was going to play bass, but he was quickly replaced by Paul Vincent Raven who had previously played with Neon Hearts in late 70s and with Tyla, who later became famous with his group Dogs D'Amour, in a short lived glam rock band Kitsch in 1982. Raven only joined three days before the band headed off for their first US tour in August and spoke to *Melody Maker*'s Steve Sutherland just four or five dates into the affair. According to Jaz, Youth's contribution to Killing Joke only "boils down to a couple of bass-lines" and he claims that the band "frightened him and now he's decided to make some money playing music."

Meanwhile the tour didn't start quite as well as it could've done. According to an *NME* report, at the Whiskey A Go Go in Los Angeles, California, Jaz had been racing from one song to another whilst muddling up his lines as well, thanks to different set lists between the band members. They were even starting different songs at the worst times. The gig ended with Paul throwing a drum stick at Jaz, who was in the middle of 'Complications' coincidentally. It is unclear what the rest of the band were playing. This led to the drummer and the singer not talking for a day and increased tensions among the band. Jaz believed the "spiritual depravity is at its highest" in the US hence it being an excellent breeding ground for Killing Joke. *LA Weekly* included a letter to the editor from someone who had had "the misfortune of being one of those unlucky suckers who spent $7.50" and had left because "their attitude was so intolerably offensive that I left after about four songs… the guitarist and bass player seemed almost to be seething contempt for their audience; their disgust was plainly visible on their glum and disturbing faces, and worst of all, in their mechanical and obviously forced performance." Apparently, they were reminded of the title of the group's new album.

In an interview with Al and Pete for US music magazine *Flipside* in August both Jaz and Geordie express their disdain for the music scene across the pond. Having witnessed the seminal American hardcore band Black Flag Jaz commented that the audience weren't dancing to anything, just moving, prompting him to say "you might as well have a saw mill going." Also, the fact that the band went from playing to roughly five and half thousand people in the UK to smaller venues in the US wasn't satisfactory. Jaz also comments on the importance of drug use saying that "drugs are fucking important, if you know how to use them." What fascinated Jaz about the US was its sacred places of the Indians, along with their curses, between San Francisco and Los Angeles.

The band played two nights at Larry's Hideaway in Toronto, Canada on 9th and 10th August. Described in the *Toronto Sun* by Jonathan Gross as such: "Jaz's atonal synth jabs approach one's equilibrium like the screech of chalk on a blackboard. Only Paul Ferguson's optimistic battle drumming keeps the Joke's death march moving through 'Empire Song', 'The Gathering' and the austere funk of 'Change'." This also resulted in the excellent live EP 'Ha!' Released on 4th November, it marks the first official live release from the band. It was released on cassette and 10-inch vinyl, featuring six tracks, most notably including 'Take Take Take', which was never recorded in the studio. The EP reached number 66 in the UK charts. The album was produced by the band themselves and Conny Plank.

The original artwork planned for 'Ha!' fell through and Rob O'Connor was brought to work on it.

"They wanted to get the tracks out because they were becoming such a fantastic live band, which they were. Incredibly powerful. I think that was an important part of their sound. What they sounded like live and they wanted these four tracks out quickly.

81

"We were pretty much given overnight to put a cover together. We actually created the image just by photocopying two of the guys' faces. It was meant to be an indication of what Jaz was like onstage really. All sort of staring eyes and a wide grin - and the hands. It was autopilot. We had to get the artwork done and delivered by 9 o'clock the next morning. They gave us the brief the afternoon before."

Their show at Channel in Boston, Massachusetts on 19th August was reviewed in *Boston Globe* by Jim Sullivan stating that "Killing Joke is no laughing matter" and that they are "the proper counterweight to all the bubbly, happy-time, rock 'n' roll coming out of England these days." He was impressed by their live attack and saw a resemblance to 60s psychedelic band The Doors in the way that "they confront fear and ugliness". He noted that "it's not pretty. It's pretty compelling," even if they don't offer any joy, but rather stimulation to the audience.

October 1982 saw the band release a new non-album single, 'Birds of A Feather', produced by Conny Plank. It was released as a 7" and 12" single in October 1982 by EG Records in the UK, Polydor in The Netherlands and EG and Passport Records in the US. The 12" release also included the track 'Sun Goes Down'. The single reached No. 64 in the UK Singles Chart. This marked the band's first release featuring the new bassist Raven.

Jaz recalls the recording of the single in *Conny Plank: the Potential of Noise* and how Conny got the song's chorus and took voices from the Nuremberg Rally, which was the annual rally of the Nazi Party in Germany held from 1923 to 1938, and used them as the backing vocals of the song by triggering them at certain times. Conny was drawn to extremes, which appealed to the band themselves.

A tour was arranged according to the press "specially planned at smaller venues in order to restrict admission price to a maximum of £2.50, and the band will be previewing new material for their next album to be recorded in January for spring release." The six-date tour started at Brixton Ace in London, which was broadcast on the short-lived UK music programme *Whatever You Didn't Get*. The show opens with a short interview with Jaz saying that they might be slags for publicity to promote their upcoming album, but now they're really going to make it, and takes a dig at bands wanting to be popular with the journalists. The four songs seen in the broadcast are 'Pssyche', 'The Pandys Are Coming', 'We Have Joy', and 'Wardance'. It's professionally shot, obviously, with extremely good footage and multiple camera angles, excellent sound, and the band giving a great performance.

The appearance on 14th December at Klub Foot, Clarendon Hotel in London is notable for the reason that they perform unreleased 'The Hive' along with 'The Vision', which may have in fact been an alternate version of 'Feast of Blaze'.

1983 – Fire Dances

The original mix apparently suffered due to the excessive use of cocaine while mixing the album which does not provide the primal beat rush expected; although 'Let's All Go' pumps some serotonin into the system and 'Dominator' pounds to the beat of your heart. Serves as a taster of what is to come and brings the new bassist Paul Raven into the picture.

1983   UK Albums Chart   #29

As told to Robin Smith of *Record Mirror* in July 1983, Jaz went to Nascara, Peru in 1982, saying "it was about 110 degrees and the nearest civilisation was four miles away." He much preferred the extremities of the hot and cold weather of the place, clean, unpolluted climate and the company of snakes and scorpions than spending hours in the pub. Jaz would sleep in a tent and survive on a steady diet of porridge and eggs. The clear skies helped Jaz to immerse himself in astrology and study the constellations in extensive detail. He also spent time studying the drawings of birds and spiders on the plains left by ancient civilisations. These experiences became useful when writing songs for their upcoming album and the single 'Let All Go (to the Fire Dances)'. Also, he composed a symphony in which he hoped to describe the magnificent landscape.

"I was always attracted to ritual," explained Jaz to Mat Smith of *Melody Maker* in August 1986. "I used to light fires and sit with the stones in the fields. I was a real opportunist - even then, especially where music's concerned."

The band wrote and rehearsed the album in their rehearsal place in multicultural west London in Shepherd's Bush. The upcoming album *Fire Dances* would celebrate the new dawn of mankind via celebration of festivals and a feast, as Jaz explained to Lynden Barber of *Record Mirror* in late July. He explains how they enjoy fulfilling their needs for pleasure whether through food, wine or women. 'Dominator' is a song about claiming what is rightfully yours rather than domination of other people. At the time Jaz had spent time reading the writings of German existentialist philosopher Friedrich Nietzsche and believes the expression of strong free will is similar to what the band collectively believe in. Jaz also expressed that he would no longer want to live in Iceland and although he saw the future and present stage of the UK as bleak, he enjoyed the British countryside tremendously.

"When I think of the passage of time in my life from 1964 or 1965 when there were just steam trains linking every village in England. The old branch line steam trains. What a different world it was then. The hedgerows were still full and there hadn't been so much development that there has been now. I remember this time and it is a lost world, which is why I hope to go and move to a place of natural beauty, because it has just broke my heart the way they have destroyed this country. They have built over everything. We're meant to have a green belt, but it's being ignored because the building lobbies want to build more houses to make more money and it is the same you got with the arms lobbies and all these other fucking lobbies. It is just systematic human greed and the way I try to combat it is to try not to be greedy. Simple as that. I'm not ambitious, I just cover my basic needs and from beyond that I don't need anything. I don't want to own a big house. I've got a very humble little house on a big area of land. Designed it myself and got someone to put it up, so that makes me an architect I guess. I live very simply, I don't have a refrigerator for example and the reason why is I like my food fresh every day. I go and collect my food every day. I'm not connected to the grid or anything. I got little gas… what I really should do is have my toilet connected and collect the methane and then be completely self-sufficient. Go to the toilet for a cup of tea – we'll get there. On my land there is no pollution. I leave cars nowhere near my property," Jaz reflects in 2012.

The album was recorded in Basing Street Studios in Notting Hill, London, between February and March 1983. The studios were established by Chris Blackwell, the founder of Island Records. The studio is still there today, but is known as Sarm West Studios, SARM being an acronym of Sound and Recording Mobiles. The recording studios were built inside a former deconsecrated church. Chris Blackwell recorded a number of artists there for his label such as heavy metal giants Iron Maiden, reggae originator Bob Marley and when it comes to Killing Joke one of their idols the Sensational Alex Harvey

Band. Also, artists not on Island Records often recorded there, all the way from Madonna to The Clash and the Rolling Stones. The studio was known for being cutting edge. In the mid 1970s the studios were the first 24-track studio in England, and then later on it was the first 48-track recording facility.

Fire Dances was produced by the band themselves with help from English musician and record producer John Porter, who co-produced 'Let's All Go (To the Fire Dances)' and non-album singles, 'Me or You' and 'Wilful Days', which followed later on. Porter made a name for himself first playing bass for Roxy Music on their 1973 album *For Your Pleasure* and subsequently producing their albums as well as Bryan Ferry's solo albums. Porter had made friends with Roxy Music singer Brian Ferry whilst at Newcastle University when he was still fronting his previous band, the Gas Board. Porter went to work with broad ranging artists from blues musicians such as BB King and Buddy Guy to other post-punk inspired artists such as the Smiths. A couple of Porter produced albums have won Grammy Awards, such as 1993 album *Feels Like Rain* by Buddy Guy along with 2003 soundtrack *Martin Scorsese Presents the Blues – Red, White, and Blues*. Niger Mills worked as the recording engineer on the album and assisted with the mixing of it.

The only single released from the album was 'Let's All Go (To the Fire Dances)' as a 12" and 7" vinyl by EG Records in June 1983. The A-side for the 12" single included a live version of 'The Fall of Because', a song originally appearing on their second album. The single B-side 'Dominator' had two different versions, both which are different to the album version. The version on the 7" single is half a minute longer than the album version while the 12" single version titled 'Dominator (Version)' is over a minute longer. The 2008 CD reissue included the latter version as a bonus track, but the original 7" vinyl B-side is unreleased on compact disc. *The Beat* described the single upon its release saying that "the acceptable face of doom boogie fire yet another hefty volley of power and it's a smart blast that should rocket them into the charts."

And it did. The single reached number 51 in the UK Singles Chart and was the band's first single to be promoted with an actual music video. In the video, as one might predict, a bonfire gets lit by what might be perceived to be an aboriginal woman in ceremonial paintings as the opening sequence. Jaz has his face painted white and is wearing a red robe and swinging a black umbrella. The band mimes to the track with

86

Paul sat down beating a single large marching drum in a white wife beater vest and Geordie sat behind him on a box next to Raven who are both playing their guitars and wearing black sleeved shirts. This appears to be inside a soundstage house featuring blue and white rectangular shapes. The child rocking on a toy horse makes an appearance much like on the single cover artwork. Raven occasionally pops into the frame with a Pinocchio nose. Children are dancing with Jaz around the bonfire along with the painted lady. Paul gets to spin a spinning top. It's a very playful video as you might've gathered. For the last third of the video the band appears in the same outfits in the woods near a rock formation. One might get vibes from Pied Piper, *Children of the Corn* and even *Clockwork Orange* watching it.

On 4 July the band recorded a new session for the John Peel show on BBC Radio 1, broadcast on the 12th of that month. They played 'Wilful Days', 'Frenzy', 'Dominator' and 'Harlequin' from the brand new album. These would officially surface on the 2008 expanded re-issue of the album.

The album had 10 songs, 5 on each side of the vinyl. 'The Gathering', 'Fun and Games', 'Rejuvenation', 'Frenzy' and 'Harlequin' were on side one and 'Feast of Blaze', 'Song and Dance', 'Dominator', 'Let's All Go (To the Fire Dances)' and 'Lust Almighty' were on side two. The original versions of 'Dominator' and 'The Gathering' surfaced as bonus tracks on the 2008 re-issue of the album. The original opening track 'The Gathering' is 15 seconds longer whilst the original version of 'Dominator' is over a minute longer than the album version. In the original version of 'The Gathering' the bass is much more prominent in the mix. The bouncy bass line adds to the joyfulness of the song.

The album was released in July 1983 by EG Records. It reached No. 29 in the UK Albums Chart. The critical response to the album was positive. *NME*'s Mat Snow called it "not only their best yet, but also quite likely to be their biggest" when it is released. When in later years *Allmusic*'s David Jeffries reviews the album, he says that "*Fire Dances* bridges Killing Joke's primal past with their more melodic, accessible future and without compromising any of their thunder." He gives it three and half stars out of five.

According to an interview with *Flaming Pablum* in 2004 Paul states that it is his least favourite record and that "It felt a bit jokey to me, pardon the pun. It felt a bit too humorous, and we were all indulging in substances, so the mixing was a bit tinny." This problem was in fact solved in the 2008 re-issues. Not the substances, the mixing.

As Jaz explains to the *NME* in August: "I spent much time in South America last year. Paul spent much time in Egypt. We study the great places. We study the parallels between cultures. Recorded history maintains that these people wore skins, were savages. But my studies, Paul's and Geordie's especially, found that these so-called apes from 5, 6, 7, 8,000 BC were brilliant at geometry, equivalent to our A-level standard syllabus. I find our whole historical concept of man totally up the creek, bullshit. I think that our species, man, is much older than given credit for. And Killing Joke is awakening that element within people, that very primal element within us."

In an interview given at the Prince of Wales Hotel, Melbourne in 1985 he explains his studies of geomancy further. It is "the science of shaping the land, modifying the landscape to enhance the natural forces inherent within it. I have studied holy land. I believe the answer lies in the psychological impact the environment has in its relationship with man. What I perceive in the preliterate civilisations is that man didn't need to use words like god or Allah, everything was there. Have you heard of Sir Alfred Watkins? He found by taking an ordinal survey, that most of the pre-reformation churches in England were on a perfect line with various other stone circles and sacred sites. The line was so accurate it would be out 2 foot after forty miles. And the whole landscape was shaped accordingly. You have this vision, that some time in England, something really great happened there. So, I like to think the answer lies in geomancy combined with geopolitics to orientate our ideals."

As explained to the *NME* in August their first manager Brian Taylor parted ways with the group and a new manager, Tony Bidgood, came into the picture. He was known for bringing the rockabilly revivalist group the Stray Cats to the masses. The theme on the new album is clearly fire along with the purification by fire. To Jaz it symbolises willpower more than anything.

In October the band's second non-album single 'Me or You?' was released by EG Records. The exclusive single was released as a 12", 7", and a limited double vinyl 7" single. The B-side for the 12" and 7" single was 'Feast of Blaze' appearing on their recent album. The 12" version featured the song 'Wilful Days' as a unique B-side. The limited double vinyl 7" single featured 'Wilful Days' as a C-side with a completely blank D-side. 'Wilful Days' and 'Me or You?' both appeared on the 2008 reissue of *Fire Dances*. The single reached No. 57 in the UK Singles Chart the same month it was released.

'Me or You?' was far more poppy than their previous singles and surely had a strong mainstream appeal although it was still in the vein of the latest album stylistically, but due to the pop approach it was justified to be a standalone release. With syrupy lyrics it didn't quite represent what Killing Joke had become known for at the time. 'Wilful Days' was a tribal track starting off with Paul's ominous drumming with Geordie's jittery guitar joining in. The lyrics don't kick in until a minute into the song. It's very much in the vein of the material on *Fire Dances*. Clocking in at just over five minutes the song is quite repetitive and tedious and quite understandably ended up as a B-side rather than an actual album track.

On October 6th the band make an appearance on national Spanish television. La Edad de Oro Estudio 1 de Prado del Rey was shot in Madrid. On The Golden Age they play six songs and give an interview. In the interview, running just under 12 minutes, warpainted Jaz explains how the music of the 1980s should reflect the struggle that people are experiencing at the time, from environmental issues to the tension brought on by supply and demand. He also talks about his interest in classical music and breaking out of the constraints created by categorisation. He believes the band's audience is very tough and capable of adapting to the changing times. "The future of our species inevitably lies in mutation." He adds that Killing Joke reflects the future world.

In December Jaz shared his week in an interesting article in *Flexipop*. On Monday he got up at 10am followed by three cups of Turkish coffee before heading off to a Notting Hill Gate squat where he rendezvoused with Geordie, followed by a meeting with their record company. He also denies any drug use here; particularly you can see his references to amphetamines. He describes how he works on his book *The Fortress*, in which he studies landscape and geomancy. He is planning on uncovering lost secrets of the earth and harmony of the land. At 2pm he strolls off for an afternoon walk to wear off the excessive coffee he has drunk throughout the day. Tuesday started off with him being accused by his former flatmate of stealing his video, which led to Jaz going over to pin his ex-flatmate down to convince him that this hadn't happened. After giving statements at the police station he went to Russell Square to drink coffee followed by a visit to a museum's Egyptology area and buying some papers written by the Cambridge Geomantic Institute. In the evening a couple of his friends came around and they drank wine and played clay pipes he had brought back from Peru. On Wednesday Killing Joke rehearsed and, in the evening, Jaz argued with his, what you might these days call hipster, neighbour. Thursday the band flew to Madrid for a gig and Jaz points out the only thing they like about England is the sense of humour, tea and music. Friday the band had an interview with a radio station, but the questions asked weren't to their liking and when they changed the speed of a Duran Duran record, live on air, they got asked to vacate the premises. The gig was marvellous in the evening. Jaz had covered himself in paint for it. The band drank loads of tequila and stayed up until about 6 o'clock the following morning. Saturday another radio interview, where the interpreter got embarrassed trying to translate their replies to allegedly extremely stupid questions. After the evening's show Geordie got really drunk and punched a bloke who turned out to be a police officer. He got locked up, but after showing his British passport and shouting about the British Consulate he was let go. He returned to the venue, attacked the band's roadie and smashed a lot of bottles. On Sunday the band returned back to the UK after first sleeping until three in the afternoon and having a feast before leaving Spain. Upon arrival Jaz couldn't wait to get out of England again.

In April Jaz and Geordie appeared as guest singles reviewers in *Melody Maker*. They turned up at 10.45am on a Thursday morning to the magazine's office asking for a bottle of whiskey before starting their reviews. English rock singer Roger Chapman's 'How How How' gets a favourable review and they like his rough voice and are impressed by his work with his band Streetwalker. Geordie reckons swapping Jack Daniels to Wild Turkey would "sort his voice right out". Marilyn's 'You Don't Love Me' gets snapped in half, called dreadful and a rip off of David Bowie's 'Sound and Vision'. Even sending to the gas chambers gets indicated. Not many of the singles get good reviews from them and many are by artists which time has since forgotten. Killing Joke's 'Eighties' has been chosen as the single of the week, Jaz saying that "it's a return to roots, going in a new direction" and Geordie describes it as "the most soulful thing to happen for the past 15 years."

The lyrics of this release are vastly different to the original played live during 1983. The "It's hard, it's the Eighties, sitting by the table playing..." lyrics have survived in a live bootleg recording from Squat Rue De Argand in September 1983 in Geneva, Switzerland. Coincidentally this is also Jaz's favourite concert. "When I think of what is Killing Joke's most important concert, which was in 1984 [sic] and it was in a nuclear fallout centre in a squat. We did 2 nights and it was the only time that we set up a gig on our own, did it without the management knowing, and actually made a lot of money out of it. That was in Geneva in Switzerland. And that was amazing. I remember in this squat they hung the Killing Joke banner up for two days, we did two nights, and we just partied day and night for two days and did concerts that were just packed! We had torch lit sessions on stage... and these kinds of things don't happen anymore: squats and illegal gigs... absolutely amazing." The hour long set consisted of 'The Fall of Because', 'Frenzy', 'Pssyche', 'Song and Dance', 'Lust Almighty', 'Sun Goes Down', 'Feast of Blaze', 'Wardance', 'Change', 'Eighties' (the first version of it), 'Empire Song', 'Complications, 'Requiem', 'Primitive', 'We Have Joy', 'The Pandies are Coming' and 'The Gathering'. For those interested in hearing it it's available in its entirety on YouTube in very good sound quality.

Jaz told Paul Bursche of *No. 1* magazine in April 1984 that he wasn't living the supposed punk lifestyle. The complete opposite in fact. He had a very nice house in Portobello Road in Notting Hill, which had a nice balcony as well as a big marble room. He also resided in Geneva in Switzerland where his Swiss girlfriend lived. In London alone Jaz apparently had five girlfriends who all knew each other and were all very possessive.

"Many people have the impression that the western world is a ship that is on the verge of sinking, and fear that it will take them down as it goes. For us this is the start of something new, the possibility of defining a new world," Jaz told French music magazine *Rock & Folk* in 1982, saying that laid the foundations for the ideas in *Fire Dances*.

In 1984 the band first brought an outside keyboard player to the group. According to Paul, Jaz would have rather just been the keyboard player, but the rest of the group persuaded him to be the lead singer. Originally in the 80s Jaz would be playing keyboards as well as singing, but later on the band got a separate keyboard player, so Jaz would be free to roam the stage, which definitely added to their intense live shows. David had been in a band called Cuddly Toys with Raven before, hence the connection to the band. Cuddly Toys were a lesser known new wave band from London formed in 1976 that grew out of the glam rock-influenced punk rock band Raped. Cuddly Toys carried on with various line ups until 1996, with very limited success.

"I first heard of the band in a music newspaper article in about 1982 and thought what an amazing name," says David Kovacevic. "The idea of me playing keys in the band live was so that Jaz could be more free at the front of the stage to perform. At first he showed me exactly what to play. Over time I put a few things of my own in there."

Dave had some prior experience in playing in a band before joining Killing Joke. "I had been in a couple of bands before with Raven and a couple of years after he joined them he called me up and asked if I would like to try out with them on keys. This was just before the release of *Night Time*.

"My first shows were in Spain and Portugal on a mini tour prior to the main tour of the UK and Europe. We did a lot of tours in those days. UK and Europe every year. We did live TV and radio in lots of countries. Festivals, and later I went on three tours of the USA with the line up that had Martin Atkins on drums.

"One time we were in a tour bus high in the Alps," recalls David. "It was being driven by a great bloke with a Mohican haircut. There was a bit of a party going on and I looked out of the window and saw no barriers on the edge of the road and the wheels were actually going over the edge on some of the bends. It was getting a bit *The Italian Job* and we were in Italy. I said 'slow down a bit mate.' Jaz replied 'don't worry my career is not going to end here.' The driver came to his senses and stopped for a comfort break.

"Another time we played a festival on a day that had been sunny and dry. We were playing 'We Watch the Sun Go Down' and indeed the sun was setting big and orange. Then at the very end of the gig it started to rain!"

The band played extensively live in 1984 starting at Hammersmith Palais in London on January 1st followed by dates in The Netherlands, West Germany, Austria and Finland to mid-March. The sole date played in Austria was on 23rd February at U4 Disco in Wien before the tour ending in München was filmed in its entirety. The 45-minute set was shot with multiple cameras for private use, but the sound quality leaves a lot to be desired. Nonetheless it shows the band at a more intimate setting.

On Friday 29th June the band appeared at the prestigious Roskilde festival in Denmark, which was partially broadcast on Dutch TV. The TV broadcast ran just under 20 minutes featuring 'A New Day', 'The Wait', 'Change', 'Requiem' and 'Eighties' from their set. The majority of the show is rather poorly lit as far as the television broadcast is concerned, which means the footage is a bit too dark to get the most out of their performance. Killing Joke also played two shows in Spain in mid-December. The French parts of the tour in May and June were cancelled.

1985 – Night Time

Exploding into the mainstream consciousness with a more approachable, polished sound, which is now deemed stereotypically 1980s. Songs like 'Love Like Blood' will live for eons to come and 'Eighties' was even later re-hashed by Nirvana in 'Come As You Are'. Essential listening while shopping for a Rolex watch on eBay.

UK Album Chart #11

The band embarked on a European tour on 7th March from Rouen in France followed by dates in Italy, Switzerland, Germany and The Netherlands. The last show of the tour was partially broadcast on 11th April on television. Jaz is particularly energised in the footage, where the band play four songs of their most recent work, 'Night Time', 'Kings And Queens', 'Love Like Blood' and 'Eighties', along with older classic 'Pssyche', live at Rijenhal in Arnhem in The Netherlands.

On 5th April 1984 the band went to BBC Maida Vale Studio number 5 to record a session for Kid Jensen's Evening Show. The band recorded four blinding new tracks, which were 'Eighties', 'New Culture', 'Blue Feather' and 'All Play Rebel'. Only the first of the songs would make it to their next album. The songs portrayed a newer, more polished version of the band. These recordings wouldn't be officially released until the excellent expanded re-release of the album by EMI in 2007.

In May 1984 the band entered the studio with Chris Kimsey producing and Brian McGhee engineering. They went to the Hit Factory in New York for a non-album single, 'A New Day'. The cover art drawing was done by Big Paul.

The video released for it begins, as you might imagine, with a sunrise. And of course there are tree branches with speakers hanging off them as always. Geordie is painted blue, as you do, and Jaz holds a tablet of stone while standing on a makeshift mountain. What is worth noting here is that Jaz is wearing a black cloak with a white spider on it. It represents mystery, growth, and power. It represents weaving your own destiny and connecting with the darker aspect of your personality. Lyrically it portrays the struggle and conflict, but also arising opportunism. Quintessential Killing Joke that is. In February 1985 the band explains to Mick Mercer of *Melody Maker* that the video "has some vivisection scenes, a little monkey with plugs in its ears. It turns our stomachs just to see it. You see it on the news but when you see it in a pop promo, so to speak, taken out of the context of a documentary, it becomes far more disturbing."

This was followed by the actual album sessions at Hansa Ton Studios in Berlin, Germany in August and September later that year. Since 1974 the studios were located in a former builders' guild hall in the Kreuzberg district of Berlin. It's important to note that prior to this the Berlin albums by David Bowie and Iggy Pop were recorded here. Later they'd also be the chosen destination for a broad range of artists from Nick Cave and the Bad Seeds to Pet Shop Boys.

As Jaz explained to *The 13th Floor* radio programme in New Zealand in January 2013 they found West Berlin and the subcultural counter-culture of the time very exciting. "Berlin at the time was just amazing." A lot came from people relocating to avoid conscription and going into the army.

Chris Kimsey was originally thankful about being contacted to be interviewed for this book, but later changed his mind very unfortunately. So we're not getting an in depth look here regrettably.

As told in a *Record Production* video interview Chris Kimsey originally got into music production at the age of 16 by persistently going into the Olympic Studios in London. At the time there were about 4 different sessions each day. He spent a year and a half working during the daytime before moving to work with bands in the evening. His first break came working as an assistant engineer on a Johnny Hallyday album in the 1960s. Johnny Hallyday, real name Jean-Philippe Léo Smet, was a French rock and roll and pop singer and actor who has been said to have brought rock and roll to France. Chris Kimsey then got a name for himself working on the Rolling Stones' 1971 *Sticky Fingers* album and this came about due to the engineer not turning up to the sessions occasionally, which gave the opportunity for Chris to take over. Chris also worked with a lot of reggae artists in Jamaica.

Jaz explained how they chose Chris Kimsey in an interview with Fiona Rae in *Rip It Up* in June 1985. The band met Chris on a social level first, at a friend's place, and found him incredibly entertaining.

They were drinking and doing a lot of everything, and after slagging him off about doing the Rolling Stones and really taking the piss out of him, Chris admitted he really loved Killing Joke's music. He was fond of working with live music essentially. "Killing Joke thought the association with Chris Kimsey would be to our advantage in so far as marketing their sound in America. And he thought that working with Killing Joke would be to his advantage. This would bring him associated with more contemporary music and hence would enhance his credibility. The band was very impressed by his talent. He was able to balance the sound and would stop the band from all fighting when they were in the studio. Because the sound is so full and there's so much going on at any one time, the mix is a very difficult thing with Killing Joke. The band's sound is a very unbalanced sound."

In Shaun Pettigrew's *The Death and Resurrection Show* documentary Chris Kimsey admits that he "didn't know who the fuck they were" when he got contacted to work with Killing Joke. EG Records had got in touch with him as they said they had a really awkward band on the label whom they hoped Kimsey would become handy in working with. Kimsey highly rated the band after working with them, particularly praising the extraordinary skills Geordie has as a guitarist and harmonics created by his unique sound from the hollow bodied Gibson.

According to an interview given to UK music and fashion magazine *Buzz* in autumn 1986 Paul would end up climbing the Berlin wall naked on the first night they arrived there, stating that "Berlin is so real that it's addictive. We were staying and rehearsing in this studio that a lot of bands use, and it's right next to the wall. You could see all of the guards rushing about." Raven thinks "Berlin signifies the beginning of the end for the West. Everyone there is just living under pressure. There are a lot of young people who are there just trying to escape conscription. If they stay, they don't have to join up." Both of them believe that Berlin is like a tug that they just have to go back to.

Chris Kimsey told Jay Garrett of *Stereonet* in November 2018 how it was the band that wanted to go to Berlin. Chris was very keen on going over there as well. He made sure that all the gear got there three days in advance. They went there a couple of days before they started the work on the album. Killing Joke had already started spending time with the German assistant engineer, who was the nephew of the owner. He took Killing Joke to a club and subsequently went back to the studio,

96

where they were staying in a flat above the studio. The party started and Geordie was there swirling around and dancing. He picked up a fire extinguisher and sprayed it in an arc in the control room. The powder from the extinguisher landed on the desk and the young assistant freaked out and called the police. Chris was in bed in the hotel at 4am and received a phone call telling him to come to the studio, and that the band had been arrested. When Chris arrived at the studio the band was lined up against the wall by armed police, but they were eventually let go. Chris then had to sweet talk the owner to let the band carry on in the studio. This was even before they had started recording. In later years the powder Geordie had sprayed on the desk would cause a clicking sound as a reminder of the band to anyone using the console. Nonetheless Chris believes they made a great record there. He very much loves everything about the band from their passion to their song writing.

Thomas Stiehler was the engineer on the album. He would go on to work with a broad range of artists from the Psychedelic Furs to Marillion and would be working again with Jaz Coleman and Chris Kimsey when they did the Rolling Stones symphony with the London Symphony Orchestra in the 90s. Unfortunately, he passed away in the summer of 2017, so we weren't able to reach out to him for a comment on the sessions.

Jaz explained how they chose Berlin as the calculated location for the recording in an interview with Fiona Rae in *Rip It Up* in June 1985. Jaz describes it as a place where you can see the absolute insanity of humanity. It's a place where Killing Joke as a band was recognised for their European creative values. "On one side of the wall there's a very dull, mediocre atmosphere - no other adverts but pro-State ones. On the other side there's prostitution of everything I hold sacred, like creative values, blatant consumerism taken to the extreme. We felt aligned with neither of those sides. Berlin's an incredible place. It's a place where we could reflect and it would automatically reflect in the music and the production."

Jaz explained the background of the album in the interview with *Rip It Up* in June 1985, saying that the album was their most focused to date. They decided to mix the guitar to get "that very bell-like quality out of it". They mixed the album with radio play in mind. There was a conscious decision not to use the press to promote the album, but rather rely on airplay and television. The idea was to have people hear the

97

album rather than hear about it. This was to avoid misinterpretations made by the written word and give people the opportunity to make up their own opinions on it.

Jaz revealed the inspirations behind the songs in the interview. 'Tabazan' comes from Jaz's worship of earth. It's an expression of his belief in perceiving the divine in the opposite sex. It is built on his thesis of equilibrium. Sun and moon, and man and woman. It is dating back to a pre-literate era and pre-Christian times when they were distinguished such as Earth Mother and Sky Father. This was later replaced in Christianity with a Virgin Mother and the notion of Father, Son and the Holy Ghost. The song is also a representation of gender equality, which was also lost when Christianity brought forward masculine imbalance. Jaz firmly believes in sexual equality and finds it as the foundations of a working partnership. 'Kings and Queens' is a reflection of their struggle and resorting to living on the dole and poverty, but still thriving in that situation. Also being privileged and fortunate enough to live under such conditions compared to the plight experienced in other countries, such as Ethiopia at the time. Also, it is meant to be an antithesis of 'Do They Know It's Christmas' rubbish. 'Love Like Blood' is about aspiring for perfection. Although vision is imperfect the commitment to an ideal is essential. It is also a critique of rising consumerism and the mediocrity that dominates the society rather than dedication. 'Night Time' is described in the magazine *Buzz* in autumn 1986 by Paul as particularly capturing the atmosphere in Berlin and around the wall. Living in Berlin made Jaz become very introspective, whereas the rest of the band just went apeshit.

Rob O'Connor was brought back in to do the artwork for the *Night Time* album. "That one we did several visuals for. This one I remember the record company saying that you've never been on your album cover and they resisted it really strongly. I think the record company kind of ground them down a little bit and said I want you on the cover. I did my best to try and persuade them that they could be on the cover and look quite cool. If I'm honest I'm not that fond of the cover looking back on it now. What we wanted to do was to make them look a bit distorted and I sold Jaz the idea of being out of focus.

"They didn't enjoy the *Night Time* shoot that much. They had a few other ideas I remember. One was that they'd be in an office with a map of the world behind them." The band dressed as they normally did. "Not looking any different from the way they looked normally. They did dress quite smart for that shoot actually." The main photo was Jaz on the cover, distorted, which was then edited. "We squeezed it and made it look tall and thin. We actually used one special ink when we printed it, which was a different blue to the normal four colour blue. The normal four colour blue is cyan and they wanted it to be really deep, rich blue, so we got the printer to change the cyan blue to reflex blue and of course every other territory in the world wouldn't be bothered to do that! So wherever you go you see different coloured versions of this cover."

Alex Paterson, who later became known for founding the Orb, did two or three intros on *Night Time*. He and Raven were responsible for micing up tunnels as you would with drum kits. "You have mics placed 40 metres away to pick up these noises we were making. They would put a mic in a bucket and then drop all these steel plates on them from 30ft up in the air, and that would be the intro to one of the songs." Alex never received credit for his work, but loved working with his longtime friends.

Jaz told Eugene Butcher of *Vive Le Rock* in summer of 2013 that the song 'Love Like Blood' took about two and half minutes to write. Geordie had the basic chord structure for the song, but Jaz had been pushing him to squeeze in two more chords and one of their biggest hits was born almost as an accident. The unfortunate reality after that was that the record company kept pushing the band to come up with more of the similar money makers in the years to come.

The album was released in late February 1985 by EG Records. Side one consisted of 'Night Time', 'Darkness Before Dawn, 'Love Like Blood' and 'Kings and Queens'. Side two was 'Tabazan', 'Multitudes', 'Europe' and 'Eighties'. 'Blue Feather' was recorded, but excluded from the album. The song would later surface as 'Joke Mix' in a 2007 expanded re-issue of the album. It is unclear whether 'New Culture' or 'All Play Rebel' were ever recorded in the studio. The album was an instant international hit, reaching number 11 in the United Kingdom in its first week on 9th March, number 8 in New Zealand and number 50 in Sweden. The press generally reacted positively to the album. Musically the album also marks the band's venture into more emotional aspects, which hadn't been explored by the band previously.

Paul later states in an interview with *Flaming Pablum* in 2004 that he "thought that was a good, solid step forward in terms of developing our language, encompassing more elements. I thought it was a really good, consistent effort."

On 22nd February Jaz and Raven gave an interview on *The Tube* where they urged people to buy the new 'Love Like Blood' single, which had just come out. They claimed there were golden tickets inside a few of the copies, where you could get a grand's worth of clothes. The brandy drinking duo told the studio audience to shut up, stating that after five albums they finally got famous "because there are too many hairdressers around", adding how they aren't really following fashion and that they're "the most brilliant live band in the world." The interviewer Paula Yates was quite shocked when they talked about their troubled relationship with the press and Jaz jokingly said that he'd take journalists who want to snitch up to the alley and "slap them around a bit." When questioned about the change of their image, possibly towards a sophisticated one, Jaz pointed out that the only difference was that he no longer wore as much warpaint on stage as he used to.

The band had the first commercial success in their career thanks to 'Eighties', released as a single in April 1984. Given the lyrical content of the song it was a very unlikely hit. It reflected the hedonism and greediness created by the economic boom of the 1980s. Musically it had strong power pop elements and was the most mainstream recording the band had done by far. The lyrics even seemed to have portrayed the Falklands War before it happened. Later in 1991 the band took Nirvana to court as on their groundbreaking album *Nevermind* there was a song called 'Come As You Are', which not only had a very similar guitar lead, but also had effects that shared strong similarities to 'Eighties'. In reality 'Life Goes On' released by the Damned on their fifth album *Strawberries* had the same riff beforehand. The band ended the court case with Nirvana when their singer and guitarist Kurt Cobain died in an alleged suicide in 1994, but there has since been talk about restarting the court proceedings.

'Eighties' would stand the test of time and would surface for example among the 50 heavy metal tracks chosen to celebrate the 50 years of heavy metal in *Classic Rock* in October 2019, with the song being described as "Killing Joke put the titanic might of Zeppelin and the riff-propelled metal doom of Sabbath through a hyper-cranked punk'n'funk filter to create a roaring apocalyptic holocaust."

The relative poverty of being in the band was starting to change, but as Geordie explained to Andy Strike in *Record Mirror* in April 1985 the band didn't find it particularly rewarding. "I find it funny because the success of 'Love Like Blood' shows we were right all the time to believe in our music. We've still got no money but the thing is, we've spent five or six years surviving somehow and if we'd had the money we'd have done the exact same things, but we'd just be in a lot worse physical condition."

In February 1985 the band explained to Mick Mercer of *Melody Maker* how the music video for their recent hit single 'Eighties' was shot outside St Paul's Cathedral in London. Paul explained: "We tried it in front of the Bank of England and the police came along. Each video we've done, apart from the first one, we've done several versions."

Geordie told *Vive Le Rock*'s Paul Hagen in 2015: "I think 'Night Time' captured fucking Berlin at its best. Believe me in 198-fucking-5 Berlin was fucking hotter than fucking New York as a place to be. I was nocturnal. I was getting up at nine o'clock at night. The clubs didn't kick off until about 5 a.m. It captured an atmosphere."

'Love Like Blood' gets described by Jaz as "a very moving and disturbing piece of music. It was recorded at a difficult time in my life and it adds an emotional depth to the charts. It's a pleasant change" to Chris Heath of *Smash Hits* UK pop magazine in February 1985. Meanwhile this interview gives a good example of the band's difficult relationship with the press at the time as the interview starts with Jaz asking Chris Heath "Do you want me to smash your face in or something?" before leaning forward to prod him gently on the cheek in warning.

The band laughs in a video interview with *Classic Rock* in May 2013 at how they told the press at the time that the success of 'Love Like Blood' meant they could upgrade their boilers with the money coming in from it. The downside of it was the fact that they had to go on television to mime the song, and it also led the record company to push them for subsequent commercially successful singles, which wasn't what the band was about. The record company also made sure to remind them how much money they owed them. Jaz also reflects on how a hit single falls out that way and you can't really strive to make one. The label also tried to get the band to cover Alice Cooper's 'School's Out', which they turned down. The only time they tried to make a hit was with the earlier song 'Me Or You', which they thought was terrible. The only time the band has had a hit according to them is by sheer accident and it has not happened knowingly.

"'Kings and Queens' is about the necessity of just looking after oneself," Jaz explained to Chris Heath of *Smash Hits* in February 1985.

According to the singer the world would be a better place if the weaker would fall and the strong would get even stronger.

The music video for 'Kings and Queens' was shot at Wembley Arena on March 5th showing a whole new calibre of music video making. The band is seen performing on stage as well as walking through tube station corridors. Smoke machines, cobwebs and the occasional fire are present in the video, which surely did not come cheap. "We all manage to live quite well," Paul says in February 1985 to Mick Mercer of *Melody Maker* regarding 'Kings and Queens'. "We've all lived in squats together but manage to live quite well because we don't mind using people. Don't mind using anything. We don't mind being used, as long as there's mutual advantage."

The song was released as the third single from the album by EG Records on 21st March 1985 as a 7" and 12" single and didn't do quite as well as the previous single 'Love Like Blood', but nonetheless made it to number 58 in the UK charts. The B-side of the 7" single was a dub remix of the song 'Multitudes' also from the same album titled 'The Madding Crowd (Remixed by Killing Joke)'. The 12" single on the other hand featured the dub mix 'Kings and Queens (A Right Royal Mix)' on the A-side while the original version was on the B-side.

Geordie tells *Kerrang* in June 1985 that the band is into rhythms that are "fuckable" and he and Jaz explain that the difference between Killing Joke and a lot of other bands is that they musically summarise the decade they are living in as opposed to just perpetuating the early seventies myth which all these other bands seem to be doing. Their sound is exclusively an eighties sound, there are no solos in it as such, as they don't believe in them, but rather they believe in one glorious rhythm section.

'Love Like Blood' was the main single from *Night Time*. For the cover Rob O'Connor had a full brief and it was based on the writings of Yukio Mishima who was a Japanese multi-talent born in 1925. His first work was classic Japanese Waka poetry, but he quickly moved onto prose. He wrote several novels, some semi-autobiographical, and was considered for the Nobel Prize for Literature three times. He formed Tatenokai, Shield Society, dedicated to traditional Japanese values and veneration of the Emperor. On November 1970 he attempted an unsuccessful coup with other members of the private militant army and then performed seppuku, which is a form of Japanese ritual suicide by disembowelment.

"Someone showed me photographs of Mishima and there was a very haunting black and white photograph where he looked like someone who was seriously into self-harm. There was a photo which was him bare topped holding a knife across his arms and [they] wanted something as powerful as that.

"I know Big Paul was also into his weaponry. When we came to the shoot he said 'don't worry about the sword I can bring my sword.'"

The cover model, who was a fitness enthusiast, was a friend of the photographer's posing with Big Paul's sword.

"There is a tiny, little bit of blood coming on the chest where the sword touches the chest, so it was quite a subtle suggestion of sort of violence if you like.

"It's one of my favourite songs ever, but I still don't quite understand the lyrics if I'm really honest. I tried to read Mishima's books to try and get a little bit of inside knowledge, but didn't quite get it all."

The 'Kings and Queens' cover was made during a shoot where the band had turned up with the map of the world. "That one is quite messy. It was just pasted up and relocated as a photograph."

In the spring of 1985 Jaz talked to music fanzine *Flux*, published by students at Hunter College in New York, whilst over in America trying to secure good distribution for their music. He explains how the band has got very popular in the UK and Europe playing to 3,000 people a night while more heavy metal bands such as Motörhead seem to be less popular. He also tells about the misconceptions the band has gained: "Our music has nothing to do with nationalism, patriotism and all that. It's a mentality in its own right, and when people come to see us, I believe they come to feel sanity." Jaz was heading off to Egypt the following day to work on his book and study preliterate cultures, something he had embarked on earlier in South America.

Jaz Coleman also made an appearance on a TV show in Australia, where he describes how the band is different from other pop groups as there is more to them than just the pleasure principle. He also believes that even though the band has gained popularity with the success of 'Love Like Blood' the core of their audience hasn't changed - it has only grown larger. He talks about the possibility of nuclear war and points out Killing Joke's music closely relates to the 1980s and is resonating with the residue of post-industrial revolution and the paranoia that is taking place in Europe.

1986 – Brighter Than a Thousand Suns

An imminent hangover from their biggest album sounding watered down rather than the nuclear explosion the title suggests. The album has beautiful moments in 'Love of the Masses' and 'Adorations', but the album is still very much an exercise in commercialism. The remastered version with the Chris Kimsey mixes sounds meatier than the original synth heavy release.

UK Album Chart #54

The vast majority of the album was recorded in the same Hansa Ton Studios with Chris Kimsey returning as the producer during October 1985. 'Victory' was recorded later in spring 1986, along with 'Ecstasy', which was the B-side to the 'Adorations' single release, with the help of American producer Stewart Levine, known for his work in pop and R&B. British Grammy-nominated record producer Chris Tsangarides was brought in to produce 'A Southern Sky' in August 1986.

David Kovacec was on keyboards for the album. "I played nearly all the keyboards on the album *Brighter Than a Thousand Suns*. At the time Raven was joking about them being the four horsemen of the apocalypse, so I guess I was the fifth element!

"Living and recording in Berlin at the famous Hansa Ton studio was wild. There was graffiti on the Berlin wall that was like Banksy. I remember we drove all night one time between gigs to do a session in another studio in Germany.

"Musing on our time in Babylon Berlin. Recording music is like trying to take a photo of a moving living thing. This thing being five young men with strong personalities. The famous Hansa Ton studios were only 100 yards from the Berlin wall and had given the world albums like Bowie's *Low*, and The Joke were there for a second album, 1000 suns. The studio really was a magical place at that time. Through the windows of the mixing room you could see the East German soldiers patrolling the wall, and sometimes Raven would light candles in different parts of the music recording area 'to get the vibe right'."

The recording process was very straightforward as Dave recalls: "All the band played live onto tape at the same time! The idea was to get the whole track in one go and it would have a 'living' feel. Boy do you have to go a lot of times for this! And it gets harder as there were regular rounds of vodka or such. Well all work and no play makes Jack a dull boy; so one evening we crossed the checkpoint into East Germany and visited a little restaurant that was stuck in 1958. We went in and there was a Dansette record player on the bar playing a vinyl album of Lily Marlene. That was when the sound engineer told me that he was East German and he had jumped over the wall in 1980. He still lived there in the east on the quiet but crossed into the west everyday as a 'West German' to work in the studio.

"I was housed in a small hotel about a mile from the studio and I used to walk past the ruins of the Reich building each morning. I remember being in a bar after a long day's recording and I asked a guy why they had left this building as rubble for so long. 'It is because we Germans will rebuild it one day when we are reunited'."

The title of the album comes from a Sanskrit writing describing what many believe to be the first ever nuclear explosion, about 7,000BC.

In *Brighter than a Thousand Suns: A Personal History of the Atomic Scientists* by Austrian writer and journalist Robert Jungk published in 1958, the first published account of the Manhattan Project and the German atomic bomb project, he describes how people were transfixed with fright at the power of the explosion during the first atomic bomb which was successfully detonated on July 16th, 1945, in the Trinity test in New Mexico. Oppenheimer was clinging to one of the uprights in the control room, Julius Oppenheimer being a wartime head of the Los Alamos Laboratory and among those who are credited with being the 'father of the atomic bomb' for their role in the Manhattan Project, the World War II undertaking that developed the first nuclear weapons. A passage from the Bhagavad Gita, the sacred epic of the Hindus, flashed into his mind.

'If the radiance of a thousand suns
were to burst into the sky,
that would be like
the splendour of the Mighty One -'

Yet, when the sinister and gigantic cloud rose up in the far distance over Point Zero, he was reminded of another line from the same source:

'I am become Death, the shatterer of worlds.'

'A Southern Sky', as told by Jaz to Neil Perry of *Sounds* in November 1986, was inspired by "a place I've been to, I don't want to say where - I've learned my lesson about that - one of the most beautiful places I've been to in the world. It's an island, a very small island. Geordie and I have been there. I would very much like to see more of this place, to say the least!"

The album's sleeve included a piece called Onion-peelings by Aleister Crowley from his *Book of Lies*. When *SPEX* magazine asked Jaz in December 1986 why it was included in the album artwork he refused to answer, because "Killing Joke don't fit into categories, and if I give the wrong answer to your question you'll pin me down and judge me from just one single angle."

When the album was released Jaz told UK pop music magazine *Smash Hits* in August 1986 that the band endeavour to convey beauty in a contemporary way, make beautiful, profound music and projects that the new album is going to make Killing Joke into a massive, massive international act. He points out he doesn't live a particularly clichéd rock 'n' roll lifestyle. He is married and gets up at six o'clock every morning to write. He is very organised and is currently working on his second symphony and has just finished writing a 110,000 word book on his own philosophy. His philosophy is based on pantheism, which is about seeing the divine in everything.

The second and last photo session Rob O'Connor and his company did was for the album cover, where they were much more comfortable with the situation.

"This was a gift really as Jaz already had a photograph taken of himself. It was an extraordinary striking image and for once he actually agreed it would make a great album cover and the record company were delighted, but what they were worried about, apart from Jaz always being such a strong frontman, was they were always quite a democratic band. They just wanted to make sure that the whole package was representing the band, so we suggested a gatefold and just did four front covers. And at one point there was a suggestion that they'd print four different front covers and just swap everyone around, so each time you saw the album it might have a different members of the band on the front, which was a good idea and everyone liked, but the practicality of that wasn't great. It would've cost a lot of money and also the photographer who had taken the photo of Jaz was abroad and it wasn't that practical to get him to reshoot the people, so we set up his shoot with a lady called Lindy Palmano whose work he liked and so did I. So we did a very simple studio shoot with them to get the close up portraits. To get the solo portraits and then we did a couple of group set ups, which we used for the singles 'Sanity' and 'Adorations'.

"And now we'd gone completely from using the band as the main image, which is not something I'd normally like because it's not so imaginative from a designer's perspective to use the band, but then at the same time it was such an extraordinary image of Jaz. Very powerful. Almost like Che Guevara or Jesus. He looks like one of those fantastic actors from the 1950s. Laurence Olivier or Richard Burton. He has got an extraordinary face."

'Sanity' was done as red on red, black on black and white on white varying according to the format.

"The image of their faces was only there in varnish. We did the four faces in varnish. The white one didn't work very well. Got dirty really quickly."

There was some pressure on behalf of the record company to strive toward commercial success.

"The record company was very, very sensitive to the band's feelings. The guy at the record company who was their main point of contact was Alec Bern. Alec was very much on the band's side strangely even though he worked for EG Records. He championed what the band wanted. He had to keep them on tie a little bit, because they were some issues about some of the things they wanted to do. He was very good at liaising between everybody.

"It was the 80s and everyone was looking gorgeous and wearing their crazy hairdos and they managed to avoid all that. The pictures of the band taken then still look good now. There is no embarrassment about the way they dressed or behaved. Not in those covers at least. Maybe on stage as they've been a bit more theatrical there. Geordie has always been a very dapper looking man. He was always the one who wanted to wear the suit and the boots. I don't think they fell into that trap of being overtly fashionable, so they couldn't be construed on being pop - or falling into the trappings of the music business."

The clown and jester imagery Mike Coles had used was felt to be more his creation and they didn't feel like using his idea for the new artwork and felt sensitive about it although it was still strongly present in the band's merchandise at the time.

"There was sort of reluctance on Jaz's part to be working with a commercial advertising agency. I think he was happier working with Mike [Coles]. Mike was an artist first and foremost. He is almost an equivalent in the 80s of a good street artist. He was quite subversive and that was his main focus and the fact that he got used for a commercial project was a bonus, because he managed to get some money from the establishment to fund his art, which is great.

"There was one time when the record company asked very politely to remove the name Stylorouge from the credit and just put my own name there instead. They didn't want Killing Joke and Stylorouge. They just wanted Killing Joke and Rob O'Connor and I said that was fine. I was very aware of the fact that I was providing a service and I was not a replacement for Mike [Coles] in any way in that respect."

The 80s was the time of Thatcherism and Margaret Thatcher. As told to Mat Smith of *Melody Maker* in August 1986 Jaz absolutely despised it, because she allowed England to be Americanised; he describes her as a hypocrite of the lowest and filthiest form. Jaz identifies as an anti-American and doesn't mind bringing it up although it possesses a problem in the band's career as the rest of the band want to go back there. To him America is the antithesis of the ideal Killing Joke and the creative environment it represents. He says the promise of £50,000 in his bank account means very little and he would not be afraid of sleeping on floors again. He admits liking the open-mindedness of America, but points out that its consciousness is the epitome of mindlessness.

'Adorations' was the first single to be released from the upcoming album in August 1986. All of the releases were mixed by Julian Mendelsohn and Zeus B. Held, who was known for being involved with several artists of the krautrock, disco, and new wave era at the time, and produced by Chris Kimsey and Stewart Levine. The single was released in several versions including remixes. The 7" vinyl single, released in the UK, France, and Spain, was a shorter edit of 'Adorations', with 'Exile' on the B-side. The 12" had an extended mix as its A-side, with 'Exile' and an extended mix of 'Ecstasy' on the B-side. 'Adorations (The Supernatural Mix)' was released on 12" vinyl in the UK and featured 'Love Like Blood (The '86 Remix)' and 'Exile' on the B-side. EG Records released a 7" limited-edition double vinyl single exclusively in the UK featuring the remix of 'Adorations' as the A-side, 'Exile' as the B-side, 'Ecstasy' as the C-side, and 'Adorations

(Instrumental Mix)' as the D-side. A cassette maxi single was also released. The single was accompanied by a music video of the band performing the song in a cathedral. The release would peak at number 42 in the UK single charts.

On 22nd August 1986 the band appeared at the prestigious Reading Festival at Little John's Farm in Reading. The performance was notable as it was nationally broadcast on radio by the BBC. This would make up the majority of the 1995 release *BBC in Concert* with the last three songs, 'Tabazan', 'Tension' and 'Pssyche', having been recorded at Paris Theatre on 6th March back in 1985. It has been often reviewed as just a "better-than-average bootleg" due to the sound quality and would only receive a couple of stars in the reviews.

'Sanity' was the second single from the upcoming album, released on 30th October 1986. The single was released in several versions including remixes. The 7" single was the original album version, backed by 'Goodbye to the Village'. Two 12" vinyl remixes were released, 'Sanity (The Insane Mix)' and 'Sanity (The Roman Mix)'. A cassette maxi single featured an instrumental mix of 'Sanity' with 'Goodbye to the Village' and 'Wardance (Naval Mix)'. It was re-released in America by Virgin Records as a 12" single featuring 'Sanity (The Roman Mix)' on the A-side and 'Sanity (Edited Version)' and 'Eighties' on the B-sides. A 12" promo single of an a cappella mix of the song was also released. The single peaked at number 70 in the UK Singles Chart. All of the releases were mixed by Julian Mendelsohn and Zeus B. Held and produced by Chris Kimsey.

Just prior to the release of the new album, on 31st October, the band appeared on French television TV5 show *Decibels* lip-synching to 'Adorations' and 'Sanity'. In candle light the band go through the motions and surely would regret the caricature of a great band they once used to be. They marvel at the beauty and sound of Geordie's hollow-bodied Gibson in an interview with Paul who can also be seen sipping straight out of a champagne bottle. Jaz explains how they all took time out to travel and now have come back and they've changed the formation and sound of their music. "The sound you hear on *Brighter Than a Thousand Suns* is always what we've dreamed of." He also talks about the inspiration behind the album title, which we've already analysed here. They also talk about the special connection they have with the audience.

Jaz had always been humble when showing appreciation towards the Gatherers as he later stated: "Guess we've been doing the same thing year in year out. I think they know we're completely committed to it. I never lose the sight to the fact that the Gathering puts food to my stomach – on so many occasions. Actually in the last few years on several occasions. I never forget that it is these people that, by the grace of God, keep us alive. And they know that while Walker and myself have two arms and two legs there is gonna be another fucking Killing Joke album coming - and it'll be better than the last one because we have standards. They just know that. You bear interest, you can't get trusting people. You earn the trust."

Brighter Than A Thousand Suns was released on 10th November 1986. But not before Julian Mendelsohn, known for his Top 10 hits, had re-mixed the majority of the album at the request of EG Records. The polished mixes had the guitars and rhythm section generally mixed lower and more prominent reverb. Certain songs were vastly altered. For example, 'Victory' was extended from its original 4 minutes to over 7 in the style of a 12" remix. Only 'Twilight of the Mortal' remained from the original mixes that Chris Kimsey had done, which the band much preferred and has been the mix available since the 2008 reissues.

The vinyl release contained only 8 tracks due to the limited runtime of LP records. Both the cassette and CD versions contained 11, each with a slightly different running order. The album reached number 54 in the UK Albums Chart. In the US *Billboard* 200 Chart the album cropped up at number 194.

The original vinyl release consisted of 'Adorations','Sanity', Chessboards', 'Twilight of the Mortal' on side one and 'Love of the Masses', 'A Southern Sky, 'Wintergardens' and 'Rubicon' on side two. The original CD version had 'Exile', 'Goodbye to the Village' and 'Victory' as additional tracks. The subsequent 2008 expanded remastered and restored version would further include 'Ecstasy', 'Adorations (Supernatural Mix)' and 'Sanity (Insane Mix)'.

"They used to be real hard men once. Now, though, Killing Joke sound as noble and sterling as St. George" opens the review in *Sounds* on 15 November. Richard Cook gives the album 3 out of 5 stars with the "a religious joke?" as the title for the main review of the issue. He finds the album at times "accidentally beautiful". He draws resemblance to "U2 philosophy: Eden is just around the corner". He also ponders whether Killing Joke might be able to forge their own new religion.

It was around this time Paul thought the band was harnessing an energy he had been hoping they would. As he said in an interview with *Flaming Pablum* in September 2004 "I really wanted the band to be huge. Where Metallica are is where I wanted us to be." And he states that rather than money he hoped to have more influence on society.

Jaz didn't hold back when he spoke to Michele Kirsch of the *NME* in August 1986 saying "I actually believe we've materialised perfection on this latest album. I consider it a great work and that's by my standards as an orchestral composer. It's innovative. It's contemporary. The whole school of thought behind it is compatible with the atomic era. It's great." Raven told Nancy Culp of *Record Mirror* in September that they were trying to cover lots of different areas of emotion, reflecting on the different style of the album compared to the earlier ones. "I don't think you can do it all on one album; otherwise, it just sounds a fuckin' mess," he states.

In autumn 1986 Paul points out in an interview with *Buzz* that "the interviews which are full of this mega-thesis about mankind" are from Jaz and "it's not that the rest of the band don't do or say anything; it's just that what we say usually gets left out", which often they don't mind, but sometimes they do, but they don't mind speaking their minds if that's required. They didn't get annoyed by the fact that they were criticised for going more commercial with songs like 'Love Like Blood' as they didn't expect the majority of people to be broad-minded enough for it. "We have more talent in our little fingers than most of the fucking bands around England," said Paul, when talking about the hit bands of the time such as U2 or Simple Minds.

Kirsch of the *NME* went to see the band rehearse on a Saturday morning for their upcoming appearance at the Reading Festival, describing it as: "a veritable wall of sound that Jaz is climbing in sputtering frenzy. He gets himself into a terrible state during each number, as if he's in his own private hell, and rather enjoying it. Every drum break brings on a facial contortion that's half silent scream, half evil leer. The burnt cork eye make-up makes him a look like a maudlin clown, at the moment before he dives into a bucket of water."

At the time the band were rehearsing in Nomis Studios in West London. Located on Sinclair Road it was popular with acts of the 1980s. Nomis Studios was originally owned by pop mogul Simon Napier-Bell, and the building was also used by the likes of the Police, Duran Duran and Dire Straits, proving popular for its secluded location.

The Reading Festival appearance was the first in the UK in over a year and a half. "Jaz Coleman and the boys showed that not all old jokes become uninteresting and dull," writes Nick Robinson in his review of the gig for *Record Mirror*. He is impressed by how the intensely powerful set flowed with aggression and force the band portrays. The older classics like 'Wardance' make the stage shudder while newer songs like 'Adorations' show Killing Joke's controlled rage to a captivated audience. He ends the review saying that "No one can match the band's ability to stir emotions and captivate an audience. It's hard to imagine the punch line of this joke ever becoming stale."

The original 'Adorations' single surprises at how low the ever-prominent guitar is in the mix. As Geordie explains in an interview with Nancy Culp of *Record Mirror* in September: "It doesn't sound so bad in stereo. It is a commercial move, actually, to be honest, because people always like to hear the singer." Jaz points out how the song stands out on the album from the likes 'Rubicon' or 'Twilight Of The Mortals' and is a beautiful piece of music rather than something you listen to with raw energy. "There's a certain amount of idealism in the music. There's higher imagery in there somewhere and that, for me, is romantic. There's a concept of something better," explains Jaz and says there had been hints of this already on *Night Time* and even as far back as *What's This For!*

In October 1986 Jaz gives an interesting interview to *Melody Maker* where he gives credit to his heroes or, as he puts it, "If we're going to have heroes I'd rather go one step further and have gods." We shall delve into his answers and give some more insight to who these people were. Jaz brings up his fellow bandmate Geordie as a hero whom he believes will be a true master if he reaches the age of 35. "The music that he is searching for, the chord structures, are very unorthodox. He always raises my eyebrows when he comes up with a musical sequence that I've just never heard before."

In November 1986 *Sounds* publishes an issue where Jaz is on the cover laughing with the headline "I Am Not A Nutcase!" Journalist Neil Perry is with the band when Jaz goes out to act out revenge regarding an unfavourable *Melody Maker* article. After meeting up with the band at the Virgin Records' headquarters and listening to their new album for a while they head off. Perry describes how the events unfold:

112

"By the time we reach *Melody Maker*, Jaz is energised, possessed, a huge grin stuck on his face. We stroll into reception, where he asks to see various journalists and is refused. When one arrives he asks who wrote the offending piece. He cannot be told, so he turns to the reception desk. He empties the tub of maggots he has been carrying onto the desk then reaches into his pocket and pulls out hunks of liver which swiftly join the maggots. Various people start screaming. And I realise I'm enjoying this afternoon.

"Jaz leaves, grabbing me as he passes, but not before leaving an order that the writer in question apologises over the phone within 12 hours. He did. That afternoon."

Neil Perry recalls the events well years later. "I started writing full-time for *Sounds* in the summer of 1985. I had been studying journalism at college but my only desire was to get into the music press. I applied for a student work placement at *Sounds* for a couple of weeks in April '85, and then just started writing, and that was it, I was in. Killing Joke released *Night Time* in early 1985, so I knew they wouldn't be doing interviews again for a while, until the next LP was released. In the summer of 1986 I went travelling around India for six weeks but I knew a new KJ LP was coming later in the year, so I had left a plea with the *Sounds* editors, saying please do not give the KJ interview to anyone else. When I returned from India in October '86 they had done just that, given it to someone else! So I had to beg the journalist in question to let me do it. Luckily, they knew what it meant to me. And so I ended up on Jaz's infamous liver and maggots raid.

"I remember sitting with the whole band in a small room at the beginning of the interview - it was fairly intimidating, but this was all part of Killing Joke's modus operandi with journalists. I felt like a bug on a pin being examined by mad scientists. I was beginning to panic because it was getting out of hand and the interview was slipping away from me - they were getting very boisterous, shall we say, not really answering questions, making lots of private jokes with each other, all shouting over each other. At least, Jaz, Raven and Geordie were - Paul Ferguson, who was an oasis of calm, was watching his bandmates with detached amusement, but was aware I think that the interview was going nowhere, so he would occasionally try and answer a question seriously. The interesting thing with Killing Joke, and particularly Jaz, is that they didn't care if you were a fan of the band or not - in fact, Jaz probably preferred the antagonistic interviews, because then he could engage in a proper debate. So sitting there and saying, 'Oh, I have all your records, you're amazing...' really didn't cut it. They didn't care about that. You had to up your game as a journalist. In that respect, they were unlike any other band.

"I was relieved when I realised Jaz wanted to continue the interview, because after the group chat I really didn't have enough to write a detailed feature. There was so much I wanted to talk about and I hadn't covered any of it. I would have loved to have sat down with just Paul Ferguson, but that wasn't an option. When Jaz said we were going to the offices of *Melody Maker*, I remember thinking, Oh Christ, what now? So we were in the back of this chauffeur-driven car heading towards central London, and Jaz was smoking large lumps of hash in a pipe. When we made the stops at the butcher's and fishing tackle shop, I still of course had no idea what he was planning.

"The mad few minutes spent in the reception area at the *Melody Maker* office are a bit of a blur, but some images and sounds stand out. One thing left out of my *Sounds* feature (whether on purpose or because of editing I cannot recall) is that after dumping the liver and maggots on the screaming receptionist's desk, Jaz picked up some scissors, held them up open in a 'X' shape, said some words in what sounded like Latin and then stuck the scissors into the liver. I remember there was a security door with a window and various *Melody Maker* journalists were looking through it, open-mouthed. A friend of mine, a fellow Killing Joke fan called Mat Smith who wrote for *Melody Maker*, was on the other side of the glass, and I remember we made eye contact while the madness was going on, both trying not to laugh. Some years later I worked at *Melody Maker* and got to know the receptionist, a great character called Marcia, and she did recall the day with a smile.

"Lots of phone calls went on between *Melody Maker* and *Sounds* during the next few weeks. *Melody Maker* did not want the story of Jaz's attack to appear in the feature. As if! I know that a *Melody Maker* journalist apologised to Jaz about whatever it was that had wound him up - *Melody Maker* had a comedy page where they poked fun at pop stars, but I can't remember what they said. News of 'the liver and maggots incident' spread quickly - the UK music press was a small bubble in those days, and the story grew legs. I certainly never thought I would be talking about it over three decades later, and over the years people have told me all sorts of exaggerated versions of what took place, without realising I was the journalist who was there.

114

"Jaz did not do it for shock value alone, but of course he knew it would add another layer of outrage to the growing Killing Joke mythos. If anything, it was refreshing - Killing Joke played a merry game with the music press during the 1980s, and they really didn't give a shit. It was a sideshow, and amused them, when they were in their prime 'bunch of bastards' phase. They were unconcerned about making friends in the press. So many artists were worried about their public image. Killing Joke were not - or, to put it another way, Killing Joke were happy to maintain the sort of public image that resulted from incidents like the liver and maggots attack. I think Jaz was just sending a message - the press is a bully pulpit, and it was an efficient way of letting people know they couldn't get away with anything where he was concerned. It also made for a great feature. It was certainly my most entertaining day at work."

Not relating to Neil Perry, but Jaz would explain the troubled relationship with the press in general in an interview with Paul Branningan of *Louder than War* in October 2015. "For years, music magazines set out to destroy us. It's different now, people only write about Killing Joke because they like the band, but when we started out magazines felt obliged to cover us, but they'd send out journalists who hated Killing Joke to interview us or review us. And we knew this, because we had spies on the editorial boards, so we'd get a tip off. We had our own ways of dealing with that though. On at least two occasions a member of the band actually shagged the fucking journalists' girlfriends before our interviews: I thought that was genius."

Neil Perry, who was working for *Sounds* at the time, and gave them some great press coverage: "I first heard Killing Joke on John Peel's BBC show when I was 14 years old. He played 'Are You Receiving?', so it must have been around late October/early November 1979, which I believe is when the debut single was released. (I missed the first session KJ did for Peel's show, which was broadcast in October '79, just a few weeks before, so was unaware of their existence.) I remember it clearly, I was lying in bed with the radio pressed up tight to my ear, and that song was like an electric shock to my 14-year-old brain. I was just getting seriously into music then, but listening to punk mostly. But this sounded like something else. I remember the razor-sharp guitar riff, the steady driving beat and the singer proclaiming 'We have orders from the new government to detain these people immediately!' I had no idea what I was hearing. It sounded futuristic to me. As soon as I could get

115

to a record shop, I went and bought it, the 10-inch first and then later the 7-inch and 12-inch of course… good marketing. I loved the artwork, which seemed to match the music. It was inscrutable, and slightly unsettling. There was something there, in both the music and the artwork, that was hard to pin down, but it pulled me in. I managed to see them play for the first time just over a year later, Sunday November 30th 1980, at the Lyceum Ballroom in the Strand, London. By then I had been listening to nothing but their debut album for 6 weeks, which came out in October 1980. I can only describe seeing them play for the first time as a mind-expanding experience. As a teenager at that time, during that era of music in the UK, everything was about genres - even though punk had supposedly been all about breaking down barriers - so it was always, Oh what are you into, are you a punk? A mod? Is this or that band cool or uncool? As a teenager, all this stuff seemed very important. But then I saw Killing Joke, and all of that just went out the window. All that became meaningless. It was just raw, primal music. They had the heaviness of hard rock, the speed of punk, but with danceable beats and rhythms, there was funk and even disco in there, the lyrics were strange and menacing, like much of the music, and the stage presence was intimidating. I could not take my eyes off Jaz. The atmosphere was electric. I remember travelling home and feeling like I had been initiated into something special. After that, if anyone asked what type or genre of music I was into, I just said, Killing Joke. I got to see them again at the same venue the following year, July 1981, and that gig was eventually released on the *Bootleg Vinyl Archive Vol 1 CD* set.

"I spent some more time with Jaz for the purposes of the *Sounds* feature. He is a particularly intense individual and I think at that time, psychological issues were building up. And while it was always fascinating to sit and talk with him - or be talked at, as was often the case - I always felt like I was in the presence of a man with a very short fuse. Less than two years later the band imploded and Raven and Paul left - Jaz's ego was running rampant. The album artwork for *Brighter Than A Thousand Suns* set the alarms ringing - that giant Jaz face on the cover, like a Roman emperor. You could see the way things were going (and it had in fact started with *Night Time*, which also featured Jaz prominently on the artwork). When I sat down and properly listened to that album for the first time, I was hugely disappointed, although it does contain what I think are two of their greatest moments, the songs 'Chessboards' and 'Goodbye To The Village'. Synth-pop! I hated some

116

of it, but then that's why fans are annoying - who's to say whether it was right or wrong for them to make such a fairly radical departure from their traditional sound? A band has to do what it has to do. Listening to it now, I think most of it has held up well, despite the 1980s sound and image. The original Chris Kimsey mixes have gone some way to restoring its reputation. There are moments of beauty on there that I did not appreciate at the time, songs like 'Adorations', 'Sanity' and 'Exile'. There are also songs that I couldn't listen to then and still can't now - like 'A Southern Sky', which was a warning as to what was coming with *Outside The Gate*. I believe *Brighter...* is also the last Killing Joke album on which Geordie had a truly majestic guitar sound.

"Since I was 14 years old I had been wondering what Killing Joke were like as people. I bought every music magazine they appeared in and just devoured the interviews, trying to extract any clues that would help me make sense of their world. I would sit with the lyrics and cross-reference them to what the band said to journalists, trying to get to grips with the Killing Joke belief system. I was the worst sort of fanboy really - I took it all very seriously. And seven years later, when I finally got to spend time with them, all I found was... utter madness! You had to laugh."

Jaz laughed about the maggot incident when talking to Steve Sutherland in an interview for *Melody Maker* in June 1988. "I was having one of those days. I'm not vindictive. Harbouring vengeance in your heart gives you cancer. I like a good laugh. Poor Mat Smith - he took it badly didn't he? I heard he cleaned it all up. Ha! I think people take me too seriously sometimes!"

When interviewed on tour Raven reveals the dynamics of the band to Nancy Culp of *Record Mirror* in December 1986. "Me and Geordie tend to socialise - I see him more than I see Paul and Jaz. There's a distinct split between the thinkers and the doers. Jaz and Paul both like to think and are sort of 'mental', whereas me and Geordie tend to want to get out there and get on with it." Paul also tells how he might show his different side on tour and enjoy drinking. He still is a fitness freak owing to to his profession as a drummer.

In late 1986, in UK magazine *Making Music*, Jaz chooses himself as player of the year and Geordie goes a little more circumspect, picking Killing Joke drummer Raven [sic]. They agree that SSL mixing desks are this year's most helpful bit of technology and that best show of the year was the Berlin Metropole. Jaz informs that the Deutsche

Grammophone Berlin Philharmonic recording of Beethoven's Ninth was his Walkman tape of the year and Herbert von Karajan is his first choice of other musicians to work with, whom we've brought up earlier. Geordie's preferred listening was the two Last Poets' albums *This Is Madness* and *The Last Poets*, both which are spoken word.

The Last Poets, formed in 1968, are several groups of poets and musicians who arose from the late 1960s African-American civil rights movement's black nationalism. The original users of that name were the trio of Felipe Luciano, Gylan Kain, and David Nelson. The name comes from a poem by the South African revolutionary poet Keorapetse Kgositsile, who believed he was in the last era of poetry before guns would take over.

Jaz explains to *SPEX* in December 1986 how bands such as U2 and Simple Minds had got themselves involved with Amnesty International and the Universal Peace Foundation saying "I'm sorry but I don't get it. I don't believe in peace anyway. Peace is the time span between two wars. If there is peace there must be war; with the concept of peace we determine the existence of war. If you want a metaphorical definition of perfection then it's the daily struggle. The way we handle and master it shows intelligence and individuality. Man is aggressive by nature. He's bloodthirsty. He's rapacious."

In January 1987 Jaz speaks to German teenage magazine *Bravo* and is extremely proud of the band's achievements. Killing Joke "have reached a singular level of consciousness. We are so close to the truth, it scares people. In our music you will find enlightenment." Jaz tells journalist Hannsjörg Riemann that his ideas were gained from his adventurous experiences. He lives quite normally with his wife and daughter in an apartment in London, but does however often disappear for months from the picture. Jaz had spent the last summer living in a cliff cave in Iceland, writing about his life experiences, which led other people to set out for similar experiences as well.

Sounds reports in April 1987 that the band has been taking it easy while Jaz waits at home to deliver his baby. Raven had just been in Sri Lanka helping the "Tamil-Nitrates" and was soon heading off to Canada to visit an ex-school friend who became a millionaire by making crossbows. He had been practising in his bedroom balancing apples on his head like William Tell. Problem is he is always drunk, so they fall off.

1988 - Outside the Gate

Although more of a Coleman Walker project the label insisted on releasing the album under the Killing Joke moniker. Synthesisers replace guitars on the album while the title track includes orchestrations that sound out of place and 'Stay One Jump Ahead' even flirts with rap music. Better left outside the gate.

The band recorded *Outside the Gate* in July and August in 1987 at Whitehouse Studios in London. The album was mixed at RAK studios during September and October 1987. The band had also worked on early versions of the songs at Eden Studios in July from which some of the recordings would surface on the 2008 expanded re-issue of the album. The single B-side 'Jihad' had been recorded at Terminal 24 in December 1987.

On 4th April the first single 'America' was released from the upcoming album. The single was first released as a 7" single with 'Jihad' as the exclusive B-side. The 12" single version was released in the UK and Germany with 'America (The Extended Mix)' as the A-side along with 'Jihad' and a remix of 'America' by Glenn Skinner on the B-side. This was also the first single to be released as a CD maxi single, featuring the Glenn Skinner remix of 'America', 'Jihad (Beyrouth Edit)', 'America (the Extended Mix)' and the original 1980 remix of 'Change'. The release was accompanied by a satirical music video depicting Jaz Coleman as a presidential candidate and dressed as Uncle Sam, in a dystopian scene of the United States. The song would peak at number 77 in the UK charts.

In May 1988 *Melody Maker* broke the news that Killing Joke had broken up. What journalist Mat Smith found more distressing than the recent 'America' single from the upcoming album was the news that Paul had been sacked from the group and replaced by Go West's drummer. Bassist Raven had also quit, calling Jaz and Geordie "a pair of ego-strokers", as he slammed the studio door. According to Raven things started to go a bit pear shaped during the last album. He thought the follow up to the *Night Time* LP would be an easy one: "We'd

119

captured a certain feeling in the music that everyone got off on and it seemed to me silly to change track. Jaz kept on trying to get all this other intellectual stuff across. Now, I'm old fashioned in that I believe if you've already got something, you thrash the shit out of it and stuff it down people's throats until they're sick." Jaz and Geordie wanted to do it as a studio project and the rest of the band didn't feel like being too involved. Things dragged on and gradually got worse. 'Tiahuanaco' gets described as "What I Did On My Holidays by Jaz Coleman aged four." Raven thinks that Jaz might think that what he has done is commercial and therefore destined for success, but finds it horrible. As much he likes the music, he thinks the lyrics were done as an afterthought.

'Tihuanaco' is referring to pre-Columbian archaeological site Tiwanaku in western Bolivia near Lake Titicaca, one of the largest sites in South America.

Outside the Gate is vastly different from the previous albums as the band is shifting towards a synth-pop sound and guitars are for the first time going to be buried in the background. Also, it will be the first album to be solely produced by Jaz and Geordie. Although Paul and Raven are no longer in the band, they have been invited to join the recording sessions of the album.

The gematria system Jaz and Geordie are incorporating in their music comes from a collection of papers *777 and Other Qabalistic Writings of Aleister Crowley* first published in 1909. The collection is a reference book based on the Hermetic Qabalah which was edited and introduced by English occultist and ceremonial magician Dr. Israel Regardie.

Paul gives insight into the chaotic situation regarding *Outside the Gate* in an interview with Rahman the Writer for *Louder than War* in October 2016. Paul states that the album was Jaz's solo project, but due to the rising cost of the recording, the record company decided it should be a Killing Joke project, but that himself and Raven should not have been involved in the writing. They were both very unhappy with the arrangement. When Paul acquiesced and went to record the drum tracks with Geordie, personal grievances were getting in the way and acrimony reigned in the studio. Paul couldn't listen to any of Jaz's keyboards when he recorded his drums and also got rid of the click track, which is the metronome drummers use in the studio to help with their time keeping. He played drums to just the guitar and it all seemed to fall into place. Unfortunately, once the keyboards were brought back in the timing was all over the place. Paul suggested re-doing the keyboards to which Jaz replied that they should be getting a new drummer.

English rock drummer Jimmy Copley was brought in to re-do the drums on the album. Copley was mainly a session drummer and worked with a broad range of artists from Black Sabbath's guitarist Tony Iommi, singer Paul Rodgers, who went to front Queen, and the Yardbirds' Jeff Beck. He was known for his open-handed drumming technique. The method dispenses with crossing the hands when playing the hi-hat and snare drum simultaneously, as opposed to the more traditional way of playing drums which features crossed hands as the basic playing position. Copley had been diagnosed with leukaemia in 2015 and relapsed following a bone marrow transplant in May 2017. Jaz told Steve Sutherland in an interview for *Melody Maker* in June 1988 that Jimmy "did the drums perfectly in two days and the guy emanates a very good atmosphere so I thought it was time for a change." Also, Jeff Scantlebury played additional percussion on the album.

Having said that, in 2015 Jaz reflected on the situation saying: "when Paul left us, and it was a long time before he came back, I always knew he would come back. There was never any doubt. I'm not surprised we're still together. It's a very strong bond."

Neil Perry, who had been there during the infamous maggot incident, interviewed the band again, two years later, before the release of *Outside the Gate*. He now recalls it as follows: "I visited the London studio where he and Geordie were finishing off the album. (I do not have this interview, but I think I have tracked down the correct edition of *Sounds*. I can't remember if I knew at that point that the band had split up - I don't remember knowing that, but I do remember it was a strange vibe in the studio.) I do remember Jaz joking with me, saying that with the liver and maggots attack, he gave me the best present a journalist could ever ask for. By then Jaz was a megalomaniac, and *Outside The Gate* is the sound of a man heading towards a nervous breakdown. In the studio, there was a session drummer, and I remember Jaz standing there screaming encouragement at him, and getting frustrated when it wasn't working out. Geordie sat around drinking. Jaz was manic, and loud, and ranted about various topics. They played me some music, some of which sounded quite Killing Joke-like, but nothing I heard ended up on the album. I certainly don't consider *OTG* to be a Killing Joke record. It is a Jaz solo record - Geordie is sidelined massively. It was an occult experiment that Jaz was obsessed with, recording music using the gematria alphanumeric system. Jaz was certainly then an obsessive personality, and I think all these things - his occult explorations, his perfectionism - pushed him over the edge into total paranoia. There was that great quote from Raven after he left - 'If you want a hit album you phone up Stock Aitken & Waterman, not the devil!' I was not surprised to hear that they had split."

Neil Perry is pleased today that the band is still going. "I did not think I would be looking forward to new Killing Joke music and tours in the 2020s, that's for sure, although the thing about Killing Joke is that they just... go away. There was never an announcement that they had split up, that the band was over. So, after the triumph and disappointment of the mid-1990s - *Pandemonium* and *Democracy* - and another long period of silence, I think every fan hoped that they would return. The death of Raven was very sad but that led to where we are now, with three albums featuring the original line-up, a band that has celebrated its 40th anniversary, and what's more a band that is active and creative, not a sad pastiche of its former self. Some of the music they are producing now is phenomenal - it could only be Killing Joke. My musical tastes have changed hugely since I was a young man but my desire to listen to Killing Joke has never faded. I can listen to the first few albums right now and still get excited. They still have moments of genius. We are all older and (hopefully) wiser. Things that were important all those years ago no longer matter. Only the music matters. In the words of a fellow KJ fan, whenever there's a Killing Joke gig, I'm just happy to be in the same room as them."

Two years after the release of *Outside the Gate*, Jaz told *Melody Maker*: "I'll never play any of that stuff live because it isn't Killing Joke. I finished what I set out to do, which was an experiment with melody and complex arrangement, but it wasn't until later that I realised I should have kept all that separate. Everything I touched fell to bits. My life went totally out of control. There is an atmosphere around the band. There always has been. People have said that what we do and what we are as people is essentially evil. But I don't believe in that at all. Any damage that has been done has been done to ourselves." And he states in *Sounds* in December 1990: "In terms of deities, yes, I used to invoke all sorts of forces into my life which created havoc. Nowadays I invoke the human spirit, the life force, the healing force. I am just trying to find peace within myself. You have to be very careful what you bring in through you. There are other outside forces that can wreck your life. For myself, I know that you never ever take intoxicants and practise magic. It's a mistake. When you take intoxicants there are holes in your protective aura, which is where outside influences can get in and attach themselves to you. That's not a concept - that's my experience. I suffered terrible possession."

The original out-of-sync drums are out there as a *Before the Gate* bootleg release; 13 instrumental tracks, three versions of 'Tiuhuanaco', My Love of this Land', two versions of 'Unto the Ends of the Earth', 'America', 'Stay One Jump Ahead' and 'Outside the Gate', but I'd really only seek this out if you're a serious fan. There are no additional songs even, just early versions in slightly different arrangements to what appeared on the final album. Clocking in at just over an hour, the essential early versions appeared on the 2008 expanded re-issue of the album in much superior sound quality compared to what is available here.

Back in 1987 the version of the story given to Mat Smith of *Melody Maker* was Jaz told him that Big Paul had to leave the band because he couldn't drum the exact specifications the singer had laid down for the album. Jaz had written the entire album during times he felt were magically sympathetic. Jaz had been recording using gematria, a cabalistic numerological system which, it is believed, can unlock spiritual forces. According to Jaz, Big Paul was sacked because after much rehearsal time, he still couldn't play to the precise timings needed to exploit the system fully. Raven firmly disagrees with this. Paul and Raven had decided to not participate on the album, so it wouldn't be released under the Killing Joke moniker, but when Raven had been over in Berlin, Paul had gone to do the drums, which then led to Raven to going and recording bass for it, although he didn't receive credit for it on the album sleeve. Raven reckons Jaz "got his head up his arse" and regrets that the band was in such great form with the four of them in the band that Jaz probably hadn't realised how great it was. Meanwhile Raven didn't waste his time and got a new band, The Hellfire Club, together with the Cult drummer Les Warner. He also stated that "Killing Joke will never be the same again, so, if they're not gonna do it then I will, cos I still feel it."

On 19th September 1987 Jaz Coleman gave a lecture at the prestigious Courtauld Institute, a self-governing college of the

University of London specialising in the study of the history of art and conservation. He outlined the thinking behind the band's then-unreleased *Outside the Gate* album, expounding on its origins in gematria and the occult. Geordie Walker accompanied him on acoustic guitar along with session musician Jeff Scantlebury, who also appeared on the album, on percussion, providing a minimal, repetitive musical backing to the lecture. The spoken word performance would surface in 1989 as *The Courtauld Talks* on the band's future drummer Martin Atkins' Invisible Records.

Jaz said in June 1988 to Steve Sutherland in an interview for *Melody Maker* the reason Raven was not credited on the album was because there were none of his bass lines on the finished album. Apparently Raven put his bass lines down, but he wasn't a disciplined musician so they wiped them all off and Geordie re-did them. According to Jaz when Big Paul heard Geordie's bass lines, he suggested firing Raven as he thought he was a crap bass player. Jaz didn't think Raven had the same charisma as Youth had before him. Apparently £15,000 was spent recording Paul's drum parts, but after working for 10 days Jaz decided it wasn't working out as they were "all over the place". Jaz says he rates them both as people, but would rather have trained musicians such as himself and Geordie, saying "I don't want to have a punk rhythm section for the rest of my life." He says that rhythm sections are "10 a penny."

When Raven spoke to Mat Smith of *Melody Maker* in May 1988, he gave the following explanation: "I think that was all a cover up. I think if you try to incorporate some kind of spiritual force in your music, the best way to do it is to come clean. You can't apply those equations to pop music. If you're gonna make pop records, phone Stock, Aitken and Waterman for your system - don't phone the devil!". Raven also reckoned Jaz was guided by the last book he read saying "What it basically came down to was that it didn't sound like they meant it anymore. Jaz was going up to EG Records doing the sensitive artist bit saying he couldn't work with Paul and the pressure and the fights. Really, the band should have split then."

Jaz explained to Steve Sutherland in the June 1988 interview for *Melody Maker* how the recording of the album was vastly different to the approach they had in the past. "We pinpointed the tempo of the songs with a metronome and then related that to cabalistic numerology which gave us, let's say, an imaginative insight into the psychological effect that rhythm has."

When Geordie spoke to Paul Hagen of *Vive Le Rock* in 2015 about the highs and lows of being a band with 15 albums under their belt he brings up *Outside the Gate*. "I think there are a couple of really fucking weak ones. I think we've been really consistent. *Outside the Gate*, well what can you say about that? We accidentally had a hit and were given lots of money. It's lucky we're still alive to be honest. *Outside the Gate* cost £380,000 and I knew it was shit when I started it. You just have that, 'oh, it's going up its own fucking arse'. Forty-eight fucking track studio, crates of fucking wine. Eight days per track to mix. Three hundred and eighty fucking grand."

In June 1988 when Steve Sutherland interviewed Jaz for *Melody Maker*, he was pissed off at the reports he was seeing that the band had broken up. "You see, there is no Killing Joke split because I am Killing Joke and I always have been," states the pissed off singer. Jaz legally holds the name and it therefore goes where he goes. Commenting on sacking the rhythm section he says "I would be sentenced to playing verse-chorus-verse-chorus-development-verse-chorus-outro for the rest of my musical career in 4/4 time. I don't want that. I want a rhythm section capable of going from 4/4 to 7/8 to 13/12 which we have on the new album. I want articulacy, that's what I want. And they were incapable of doing it."

Jaz is self-certain in an interview with *International Musician World* in July 1988 and champions their new line up with Jerome on bass saying that "we've got a very high standard rhythm section." They were happy not to have spent 30 grand to employ a producer and used cabalistic numerology - particularly number 103.

Jaz and Geordie made an appearance on the *Rockin in the UK* TV show in April. They said that they'd moved from a more expensive studio to a cheaper one and started doing their own production. The interviewer wasn't quite following when Jaz tried to explain the gematria system and how it was used in the music, prompting him to comment "Good Lord, sounds quite heady that. Let's pick up the conversation again in a minute when I get over that explanation," and then play the music video for 'Love Like Blood'. They talked about the concern they had with England being dragged down with the US as they were introducing their new single 'America' speculating another market crash. The song has been seen as prophetic.

When they appear on *MTV Europe* the message is similar. They declare that as long as Jaz and Geordie are alive, so is Killing Joke. They don't want to have a punk rhythm section for the next eight years and want a more articulate and funky rhythm section. Jaz talks about playing shows to support the album, but they wouldn't want to do 70 date non-stop touring that they've done in the past. As Geordie points out it is not too good on the kidneys. The plan is to do a couple of special shows to premiere the music rather than anything else. They are hinting at live dates in the summer, but this will not be the case. Jaz believes that the remaining two years of the 1980s will see super-powers drawn into conflict, because of the situation in the Middle East. He also points out that songs such as 'Wardance' are more important now than when written eight years earlier.

Bill Smith Studio were responsible for the sleeve design. This is how Bill Smith himself describes the situation:

"I was art director and studio head for BSS, the designer involved alongside me in this project was Carl Glover. The illustrations were by Andrzeij [Klimowski], I have had no contact with him since that time.

"Never thought about clowns or jesters, I listened to the tracks and decided to go with a very graphic approach based on titles and I liked the idea of using Jaz's portrait but montaged together with Geordie's and then 'heaviness' all around. Really, the single came first and again using the title gave me the idea of American symbols mashed up almost comic book like, but again 'heavy'. I gave my ideas to Andrzeij and let him run with it. Jaz was very open to these ideas.

"I liked the track 'America' but was not a great fan of the band per se. I was called in to do the covers because I'd been doing a lot of work with EG and various other bands including King Crimson, Penguin Cafe and Toyah.

"Not much interaction with Jazzer's, met him at the EG offices a couple of times and that was it. I think everyone was in some sort of legal dispute with EG! Especially Robert Fripp. Certainly the bands weren't happy and subsequently designers like me when bills weren't paid. I always felt the bands/artists and their music were merely 'product' to EG."

The album was released on 27th June with 'America', 'My Love of This Land', 'Stay One Jump Ahead' and 'Unto the Ends of the Earth' on side one. Side two consisted of 'The Calling', 'Obsession', 'Tiahuanaco' and the title track 'Outside the Gate'. In early July the album cropped up at number 92 in the UK charts only to disappear from there after only a week. Martin Rex worked as the recording engineer, previously mentioned Glenn Skinner handled the mixing, while Bill Smith Studio was responsible for the sleeve design and Fil Le Gonidec worked as the crew. Also, for the first time the tracks were credited just to Jaz and Geordie.

'America' is a portrayal of imperialism, extreme capitalism and making riches out of the rat race. There is disdain on Jaz's part regarding how he feels about the American way of living and their politics. 'Unto the Ends of the Earth' was another song in which Jaz expresses his notions of the mythical Island and wishes "to be in the place of beginnings not endings."

The album doesn't impress Sam King of *Sounds* in June 1988; he says that the "splendid, emotionless guitar…has been criminally muted here" having been overshadowed by the keyboards. The band's power had disappeared and things become "an undesirable maze that fails to project Coleman's latest conspiracy theory." Similar treatment is coming from Barbara Ellen of the *NME* in July 1988, referring to Jaz as "talented-as-a-fruitcake" and calling the new album "depicting poor old Jaz wading through quicksand with jeans rolled down yet again."

With Paul being a vital collaborator on the band's lyrics the album lacked on that side and not just musically. He was also then told that he would not only have to re-record his drums, but also pay for the recording of his earlier drum tracks, which he refused to do point blank.

The expanded 2008 release gave more insight into the troubled album by adding the early version of 'My Love of This Land' and 'Obsession', and unreleased song 'May Day', which later evolved into 'Tiahuanaco', to the track list along with the instrumental version 'Unto the Ends of the Earth' and B-side 'Jihad'. Also included were 'America (Extended Mix)' and 'Stay One Jump Ahead (Dub)'.

The second single 'My Love of This Land' was first released on 3rd July as a 7" single with 'Darkness Before Dawn' from *Night Time* serving as the B-side. The 10" single in the UK featured a remix of the song by Glenn Skinner on the A-side, along with 'Darkness Before Dawn', and 'Follow the Leaders (Dub)' and 'Sun Goes Down' on the B-side. The 12" version had the same A-side as the 10" release, with a live version of 'Pssyche' alongside 'Follow the Leaders (Dub)' on the B-side. Unlike the previous single this wasn't released on compact disc. The single made it to number 89 in the UK Single Charts.

There were no gigs to support the album and the album wasn't released in the US. Two months after the release the band was dropped from Virgin. Killing Joke, or what was left of it at this point, were heavily in debt to their record company, Jaz started suffering from depression and the situation seemed doomed on Killing Joke's part. Eventually Jaz ended up in a psychiatric ward and of course the next couple of years saw the band members go completely broke. In an interview with *MTV* in 1991 Jaz explains how they "went through three years of torment and basically we had no contract. We were in litigation, we couldn't record, we couldn't do anything. All avenues of income were cut off and it was a very, very difficult time." This led to intense legal action from their old management and record company, to the extent they even tried to find out who the property Jaz was living at the time belonged to in order to get further financial gain out of the group, which at the time were already, according to Jaz, multi-millionaires.

In December 1988 the band would play three dates in the UK, where none of the songs from *Outside the Gate* would be performed, but they would play new songs such as 'Extremities', 'The Fanatic' and 'The Beautiful Dead'. The first gig was on 17 December at The Leadmill in Sheffield. Adrian Goldberg would be impressed by the band's performance the following evening at Burberries in Birmingham stating in his review in *Sounds* that the audience "were dazed, floored and finally rendered punch-drunk by the new line-up's bonecrushing onslaught." The last show of the three, on 22 December at Portchester Hall in London, was labelled as 'A Midwinter Party', which would also mark the launch of 'Order Of The Distant Island Charter', which would be the band's new way of communicating to their Gatherers. Also, the show would see the release of a 7" flexi disc, which featured the demo recording of 'The Beautiful Dead' featuring just Jaz and Geordie released through ODIC Production. This version wouldn't surface again until 2012's *The Singles Collection 1979-2012*. The price of the event was much higher than your average gig at £15; apparently the cost was brought up due to the Middle Eastern food on offer. Additional dates were played in Europe, the UK and the US through March until August the following year.

"I went to see them play at Kilburn in London in '89, and it was awful," says journalist Neil Perry. "At least, the sound was appalling, which was unusual - throughout the 1980s Killing Joke's live performances were superlative. I don't think anyone could watch them onstage during that era and not be blown away. I think that Kilburn gig was the first time I walked away feeling underwhelmed. Jaz ranted a lot onstage. He did not appear to be in a better place, mentally (although he claimed to be). Yet it is a gig that I've heard fans talking about as if it was a classic. No one knew at that time they were going to disappear for another four years, but when it all went quiet at least the remaining memory was of a band with fire in their bellies, rather than the acrimony and disappointment of *Outside the Gate*."

The band would go on another hiatus as Jaz departed for Egypt to work on *Songs From The Victorious City*, a well-received album blending Western and Arabic classical music in collaboration with Anne Dudley.

PART THREE

Nineties

1990 - Extremities Dirt And Various Repressed Emotions

Their heaviest album to date is a beast compared to their earlier sidetracked venture. Opening with the frenzied anthem 'Money Is Not Our God' and with ex-Public Image Limited/Ministry drummer Martin Atkins they venture to a dark world 'Inside the Termite Mound'. Clearly a cathartic release!

December 1988 sees *Sounds* report that the ex-Smiths bassist Andy Rourke and Martin Atkins from Public Image Limited are to join the band. Andy lasts in the band for a mere three days and is sacked for being too miserable. Later it would emerge he might've had a drug habit. Rourke had first met the band back in 1980 when they were recording the 'Wardance' single. He was then replaced by a Welshman known as Taif who was known for being dangerous, apparently. This revised line up would tour in February and March in Australia and New Zealand. A British tour would commence in April.

Martin Atkins agreed to be interviewed for this book, but unfortunately the interview didn't happen. He is very active in music still and has worked as the music business program coordinator at Millikin University in Decatur, IL. He has published books, such as *Tour Smart*, giving advice on the music industry. He is also a notable drummer when it comes to industrial music having been involved with such bands as Ministry and Nine Inch Nails as well as Pigface.

Martin Atkins recalls in his book *Tour Smart* how he started his label Invisible Records in September 1988 when he received a call from Killing Joke. Although Martin had concerns about returning to the UK as his resident alien paperwork was still being processed he took on the opportunity. He also at the same time became the manager of the band and not only did he embark on multiple tours he also was responsible for t-shirt designs and the artistic direction with the revised line-up.

In an interview with Joel Gausten published in *Pandemonium: Inside Killing Joke,* an interview collection, Martin Atkins says that Geordie had wrestled a guy called Charlie from Washington DC who had auditioned for Killing Joke to get Martin's phone number. Martin had recently formed a construction company with a couple of his mates and was contemplating leaving music behind, but gladly decided to take the leap of faith even if *Outside the Gate* had raised some concerns with him. When Taif left after an American tour and dates in Europe Raven returned to the picture, and his less technical skills, but huge charisma, affected the way Martin played the drums when he joined the band again.

At this point Jaz would start regretting having done the synth heavy *Outside the Gate* album and the new direction the band would be taking would be drastically different.

Reporting in the *Toronto Star* in April 1989 tells how well Martin Atkins has gelled with the band and he seems pleased to be in Killing Joke as apparently Public Image Limited had "become a bloody cabaret" and was in the midst of legal action towards John Lydon. The band was courted by major labels, such as Warner Bros, which added to the momentum they were gaining.

In June 1989 *Alternative Press*' Jason Pettigrew is being told that the band has prepared enough material for their upcoming album with the working title *Extremities*. New songs such as 'Extremities' and 'Intravenous' along with 'Age of Greed' are being offered to the enthusiastic crowds. Jaz expresses how he wanted the new material to be also pleasurable when performed live.

In 1990 keyboard player Kovacec parted ways with the band. "After more than six years playing in the band I wanted to write and record my own music. I took up vocals. Right now I'm recording original 21st century progressive rock. Not in touch with the guys much, but I do get regular visits from Raven on the other side."

Eric reports in NYC-based fanzine *The Village Noize* that the band is in trouble with their former recording label EG Records. They had started recouping recording costs from the band's publishing. In roughly a year Jaz and Geordie made about £40,000 from publishing, but hadn't received any of it due to the situation. Their only source of income would be live concerts. There were companies such as Elektra Records who refused to listen to the band's demo tapes and the band was in a desperate situation, but thankfully Killing Joke would be a band that would thrive through struggle.

George Petros from US-based *Seconds* magazine was told by Jaz that only journalists who hate the band were being sent to review the band's performances. Apparently, they would have already made up their minds even before seeing the gig. Jaz also says the band has been signed to Jem Records then to Virgin for roughly four months. Apparently Virgin America had plans to make the band into the new Cult, which didn't please Jaz or Geordie and they fucked off.

Mark Holan reports in Cleveland-based *Scene* that while the band is touring in America in the spring they are planning on heading to Germany to record their upcoming album. They're also exploring rhythms and song structures outside the regular rock norm. The band is also planning on returning to the studio with Conny Plank, who they believe is able to recreate their live sound, which they believe was also what Chris Kimsey had been able to do. Jaz Coleman says that he wants it to be painful and excruciating, "but beautiful music at the same time."

Steven Wells writes in the *NME* in October 1990 that "Killing Joke are like masturbating with toothache" as he witnesses them onstage in Poland playing their new anthem 'Money is Not Our God' live. Steven is also quick to point out that as much as he likes Jaz he wouldn't want to live with him.

"Extremities is what we've been through," tells Jaz to Trish Jaega of *Sounds* in December 1990, "the world we live in, and trying to make a living doing the kind of music we do." Apparently, the new album nearly didn't happen as he suffered a nervous breakdown. Jaz had travelled to Egypt and stopped doing drugs and got into meditating.

According to a *Melody Maker* article in December 1990 by Mat Smith the new album had been recorded in just two days in London as for some reason the German sessions with Conny Plank were shelved. They had booked two weeks to record it, but it was done in two intense days. The legal hassles that had taken two years of Jaz's life made him explode in the studio as prior to that he was used to making an album a year. Also, Taif left and Raven returned to the group.

"Great music," commented Taif to *The Gathering* website's Alex Wise, "just too much insanity in between the amazingness of the hour on stage every night," regarding his reasons for leaving the band.

This time around they didn't have the backing of a major label and that might've contributed towards returning more to their roots, to a more aggressive and violent form of music. Without a major label pushing them for a commercial sound the band was free to explore harsher realities, embodied perfectly in the lead track, 'Money Is Not Our God', from the new album *Extremities, Dirt and Various Repressed*

Emotions.

It was an era when Tory leader Margaret Thatcher was in power and in the middle of privatising everything from gas to electricity. This was a prevailing theme of the times and clearly reflected throughout the album. The everyday struggle of the working class individual. 'Table wine once a week, if you're lucky,' Jaz declares in 'Age of Greed'.

The album was recorded at the Townhouse Studios in London in August and released on 20th November through heavy metal label Noise. Noise Records was a label formed by Karl-Ulrich Walterbach in Berlin in 1993. The German label was purely a heavy metal label and early on specialised in European thrash bands such as Kreator and Sabbat. In an interview with German *Rock Hard* in 2013 Walterbach stated that he wished he had never signed Killing Joke as they were "a hot potato, no label, big nor small, was willing to work with in the UK. And I was teased into working with a trio of madmen."

Martin Atkins told Joel Gausten in *Pandemonium: Inside Killing Joke* that Martin Rex, who was responsible for producing, engineering and mixing the album, would first map out Martin's drumming at rehearsals, use rehearsal recordings and transfer the DAT tapes to a computer and they'd use the tempo changes in the drumming to create further the atmosphere on the album. John Bechdel also became the band's new keyboard player, replacing someone known as Dave Dave the Keyboard Slave. John was a friend of Martin's from his Brian Brain project. The album was recorded at the Townhouse Studios' Studio B having been booked by Jaz for three to five days. As Martin had been there before with Public Image Limited to record *The Flowers of Romance* he was able to get an excellent deal for the band. Atkins only took ten hours to record all of the drums for the album. During the mixing of the album all the band members took turns in making their contributions louder in the mix. Also the lyrics of 'Age of Greed' brought Martin Rex to tears due to the heavy nature of the content. The spoken intro was recorded by Jessica Villines, who had worked at Chicago Trax. Further disputes over merchandise money between Martin, Killing Joke and Jaz would later pave the way to Atkins exiting the group in 1991.

The album was done very quickly and on a small budget, as Jaz told Eugene Butcher of *Vive Le Rock* in the summer of 2013. The backing tracks were recorded in three days, vocals took only a day and five days were spent mixing the album. Between 1988 and 1992 the band had been very active and had got tight, with only about three or four months off during the whole period, most of it spent on the road.

The album didn't do much damage in the charts and the sole single, 'Money Is Not Our God', failed to chart as well. The music video made to promote the release showed the band performing live and aptly showed Jaz burning a cash register and American dollars along with notes shot out of a shotgun. The message and the single itself is particularly strong, but the rest of the album doesn't quite manage to live up to the same standards. While Martin Atkins had previously drummed in the industrial metal band Ministry he might've inspired the shift towards a more similar sound, which was new to the band. In his book *Tour Smart* Martin recalls how the band went out and bought white parachute suits and screen-printed the dollar bills seen on the video on the suit. The suit also ended up on a couple of magazine covers.

On the album the whole band, along with both Raven and Taif, have been credited for the production. John Bechdel has been credited for programming and sampler. Other credits include Martin Rex (as J.M. Rex) for production, engineering and mixing, Michael Butterworth and Dominic Robson for engineering assistance, Shawn Cymbalisty and Geoff Pryce for technical engineering and recording at Marcus Studios, Malcolm Haywood for photography, and artwork by Birgit Nielsen and Henni Hell, while Paul Raven was at the helm for art direction.

The track listing is 'Money Is Not Our God', 'Age of Greed', 'The Beautiful Dead', 'Extremities', 'Intravenous', 'Inside the Termite Mound', 'Solitude', 'North of the Border', 'Slipstream', 'Kaliyuga' and 'Struggle'. All the songs are extremely long, with the exception of 'Kaliyuga'; they all clock in at over five minutes and tend to have rather unorthodox song structures. The songs are credited to Jaz Coleman, Geordie Walker and Martin Atkins. The majority of the songs were never performed live. Jaz's romanticism is prevalent on the album, as well as his very pro-European views. Apart from the first three songs the album isn't particularly strong.

The 2007 re-issue would add the demos of 'The Party', 'The Fanatic', 'Solitude' and 'Jubilation', which was an early version of 'the Beautiful Dead', along with the live version of 'Age of Greed (Live)'. While Raven played bass on the album Taif is on the additional demo and live songs added in the re-issue, and Dave Kovacevic plays synthesiser on the live song.

Double CD *Inside Extremities, Mixes, Rehearsals And Live* was also released in 2007 by Candelight Records USA. The first disc includes mainly vocal and instrumental takes of 'Money Is Not Our God', 'Struggle', 'Slipstream' and 'Intravenous' and the second disc is a full live set 'Live In Pied – France 7th June 1991'. Oddly enough the double CD is easier to come by than the actual album itself these days.

The eyes on the album belong to German actor Conrad Veidt as featured in the film *The Cabinet of Dr. Caligari* rather than Jaz Coleman as some have believed over the years. The back of the album has two Latin phrases, "hoc volo, sic iubeo, sit pro ratione voluntas", meaning "I wish it, I command it. Let my will take the place of a reason" originating from Roman poet Juvenal; and "semper imitatum nunquam idem" translated as "always imitated, never replicated."

The press was rather favourable towards the album. "It's not so much Killing Joke washing their dirty linen in public, rather ramming the blood, sweat and skid mark stains right under your nose and forcing you to breathe deeply," writes Mat Smith in *Melody Maker* in December 1990. He says that not since *Revelations* has "the band created a cacophony so beautifully ugly. *Extremities...* rages against the financial and consumer gluttony of the ME generation and its resulting cultural and artistic bankruptcy then pushes the knife in on itself, gleefully cutting out and holding up the cancer that, for the last two years, has threatened the band's very existence."

"The new release also welcomes the return of one of the Joke signatures, layers of shimmering guitar," writes Greyson Stoehr in US magazine *Camm* in January 1991. Jaz tells him how the guitars as well as the drums are both very high in the mix, confidently saying that "it's an incredible LP. I play the LP up against the last seven albums and they all pale in intensity in comparison to *Extremities.*"

In a retrospect review Ned Raggett of *Allmusic* champions the way the band has returned to their earlier aggressive sound without trying to replicate the past, incorporating elements of speed and trash metal into the mix. He states that "the end result confirms the core Coleman/Geordie partnership as the strong beast it is."

In an interview with Joel Gausten published in the *Pandemonium: Inside Killing Joke* interview collection Paul Raven says that the atmosphere around the group was different due to the renewed spirit of musical aggression Atkins had brought back into the fold, and also that the band, with the help of the new drummer, were handling their own business better than ever before. Raven's return was partly due to financial reasons, but he also thought that *Extremities* was the album they should have had made after *Night Time* as Geordie had already had some of the ideas developing then. Whilst Big Paul had been a more soulful player according to Raven the former Public Image skinsman "had fire in his balls". Raven thought some of their best work was on that record, such as 'The Beautiful Dead' and 'Age of Greed'.

In December 1990 *Sounds* offered a guide to paganism, in which Jaz talked about his beliefs and also how intoxicants had led him to suffer terrible possession. He then started to steer away from them.

After the release of the album the band embarked on a world tour. Shows began in Dallas in the US on 3 January. The 11 January show at Le Glob in Lyon, France was filmed by TLM, a local television station. The band played 'Extremities', 'Intravenous', 'Wardance' and 'The Beautiful Dead'. The 1 June show in Finsbury Park in London was appraised in the 22 June *Melody Maker*; Killing Joke are "emerging triumphant after managing to summon up the climactic throb of energy that has over the years inspired legions of young groups."

In the spring of 1991 the band tells Al of *Flipside* that they have signed a deal directly with RCA and explain that the hiatus the band have been on can be explained by the litigation that took two and half years of their time. They also say that the band is now based in Chicago, partly due to Martin Atkins being married there, but also because Geordie is married to a woman in Detroit.

After touring Europe and North America the band suddenly once more called it quits, in the middle of the year. Jaz would go to live on a remote island in New Zealand and once more things were over for a while…

In 1991 Martin Atkins parted ways with the group. According to Paul Raven, as told to Joel Gausten in *Pandemonium: Inside Killing Joke,* Martin originally moved the band forward when it came to business related matters, but "as soon as commissions started disappearing from places they shouldn't have been disappearing, and the figure shuffling started, that's when things had to change."

The story of Killing Joke came to a halt when the rest of the group, minus Jaz, formed the industrial music supergroup Murder Inc. in Chicago. The line-up consisted of Chris Connelly, who was known for his involvement with Ministry and the Revolting Cocks, along with Killing Joke members Geordie, Raven, Killing Joke's then keyboardist

John Bechdel and Martin Atkins as well as Big Paul on drums. On 22 June the band would release their eponymous debut album, produced by Steve Albini, through Atkins' Invisible Records, to a mixed response. *AllMusic* critic Tim DiGravina would describe the album as "Killing Joke on a bad day", drawing comparisons to the most recent Killing Joke album.

The few shows planned for 1992 were cancelled as a majority of the line-up was now keeping busy with Murder Inc., and Jaz went to New Zealand and got back to his career in classical music.

Youth rejoined the band, and remixed 'Change' and 'Requiem' in 1992. 'Change: The Youth Mixes' was released in 1992 on CD by EG Records and as a CD maxi single by Virgin Records. Spiral Tribe was released as 'Change (Spiral Tribe Mixes)' in 1992 on CD and 12" vinyl by EG Records. A cassette combining the main Spiral Tribe Mix with three remixes by Youth was also released titled 'Change'. Also, a 7" single with 'Change' on the A-side and 'Tomorrow's World' on the B-side was released.

18 September 1992 in the US and October in the UK and Europe saw the release of the first compilation, aptly titled *Laugh? I Nearly Bought One*. Songs were included from all the studio albums with the exception of *Fire Dances* and *Outside the Gate*. While the exclusion of songs from *Outside the Gate* is understandable as in the end it was more of a Jaz Coleman project, it is rather surprising that no songs from *Fire Dances* made the cut. Three non-album tracks are included as well as with the original Chris Kimsey mix of 'Wintergardens' from *Brighter than a Thousand Suns*, which was previously unreleased at the time. The cover of the compilation was quite controversial with the Nazi salutes. It's worth noting that the priest in the picture was not Pope Pius XII as people thought, but rather German Nazi abbot Alban Schachleiter. Mike Coles tells the story behind it. "That was first used as a poster in 1980, it was a picture that Youth found. It's the 'killing joke' - a high ranking Catholic cardinal saluting the Nazis. The church of goodness blessing the murderers of millions. The evil behind the smile again. Virgin Records actually wimped out when they released the *Laugh? I Nearly Bought One* compilation and I had to change the swastikas to dollar, pound and yen signs." The release also sowed the seed for a re-union as Geordie rang Youth to inquire about possible artwork to be used for the release, leading the bassist to half jokingly suggest a regrouping, and in about a month things started to happen again.

"I felt there was unfinished business," told Youth to Peter Watts of *Uncut* in November 2018. "We hadn't made the great record we could have made. I had leverage, a label imprint and the band were on a low, they'd almost split up. So, I suggested signing them to my label and producing."

Some of the press response was rather interesting. For example, in *Indiecator #1* the reviewer questioned whether "Would anyone really offer them *that* much cash to get it together again?" pointing out that maybe the band had gone their separate ways 'for artistic reasons'. A moment on stage in France is talked about when Geordie had stubbed a lit cigarette intentionally into the singer's face, signalling that the relationship had gone rather pear shaped.

1994 – Pandemonium

Recorded with Youth reinstated inside the Great Pyramid in Egypt the album captures a part of the lost world. Includes pseudo-classics such as ferocious 'Whiteout' and majestic 'Communion' which makes praxis of local Egyptian musicians and grand orchestral backing and materialises as an otherworldly celebration. No need to leave this inside the tomb.

UK Album Chart #14

"I saw Youth when we were working on *Extremities*," explains Jaz to Paul Rees of *Ultrakill!* in 1994. "It was slightly strange at first, because we hadn't spoken for 10 years, but we got talking about the band and basically took it from there." The reformation of the original line up had been on the cards for four years.

Youth told Peter Watts of *Uncut* in November 2018 that a DMT experience had led to him seeing ley lines in different parts of the world and he wanted to go and work in those places, as he was very into Earth energies at the time. The recordings were turned into rituals with three days spent in the pyramid for preparation. Geordie notes that the band just "spent 24 grand for a couple of vocal tracks. That was an expensive holiday."

In August 1994 the band made an unprecedented move by going to the Great Pyramid of Giza to record some of the vocals for their album *Pandemonium*. Before getting permission to record inside the Great Pyramid the band was interviewed by a white witch to determine whether they'd be allowed to proceed with the project. The first session turned out to be a disaster. Jaz had drunk a bit too much and there were a lot of unnecessary people present at the recording. The second day's session had Youth take more responsibility for the sessions and he insisted the band take a more ritualistic approach to it. They only had a few people inside the King's Chamber and a woman appearing dressed in a full Egyptian ceremonial outfit to channel the right energies and vibes for the recording.

According to an interview with Richard Winn of radio station trade magazine *Hits* in October 1994 the band met up with the the Minister of Culture in Egypt and Youth got out 350 US dollars and they were told "You've got two days in the Pyramid." In a later interview with Debbie Jhaj of *Fix* magazine in May 1996 the amount according to Jaz was a thousand dollars and they got three days inside the pyramid.

Greg Hunter worked as the producer on *Pandemonium*. "I first saw Killing Joke live at the Elephant Fair. The audience were throwing pint glasses at the stage, and Jaz just took it with wild eyes. It was chaos. I was impressed at the mayhem. Something was going on. Something I didn't understand."

Greg reckons that "the only way you get into the studio with KJ is if your life is in chaos. Geordie called me our 'wild card'. I didn't care. I really couldn't give a fuck either way, which made me perfect for KJ. I had no axe to grind / nothing to prove. My only concern was the music. I needed to hear music that was a bulldozer trawling my mind, to wash away my pain. Which it did."

The sessions took the band and crew to different parts of the world.

"We started in New Zealand, in Jaz's studio. Me and Jaz had a difficult time, although we made each other laugh. It was like a competition to see who had the darkest humour. He would say something really inappropriate, which I would pick up on and pass back. My father had just died and my best friend who had AIDS was in the studio with us. There was no subject that was taboo. To say the humour was dark, does disjustice to the word. Bleak. About as unPC as you can get. The studio owner hated me because I trashed his brand new studio. I didn't give a fuck. My friend was dying of AIDS. It was Killing Joke for fuck's sake."

The album had strong Arabic musical influences, but rather than it being a conscious decision it all happened organically.

"It was organic. I don't think much of KJ music is conscious, it is all in the moment. Jaz had recorded in Cairo, and often spoke of his connection. I really pushed to go there and do some overdubs once we got to back to UK. Jaz agreed and Youth persuaded the record company. Geordie didn't give a fuck either way."

The majority of the album was recorded in the studio and the band started almost from scratch.

"Everything was written in the studio. Geordie had a few riffs that he wanted to use. But to say the material was prepared, belies a misunderstanding of the creative process of Kiling Joke. This is not a 'normal' band.. politely going in the studio to record their tenth album, with all the tracks nicely demo'd... LOL! NO This is KILLING JOKE. Jaz is the same on or off stage. Jaz is Jaz. Geordie is the greatest living electric guitarist in the world. Make no mistake. When I met Geordie, the first thing he said was that I had to pawn his gold top guitars for £500. Lol. I declined. Look at the way Geordie plays guitar, how his right hand moves. Un-fucking-believable. The real deal."

Vocals for 'Pandemonium', 'Exorcism' and 'Millennium' were recorded in the King's Chamber in the Great Pyramid.

"Jaz had connections in Cairo, one of whom was Bob Clearmountain's ex-wife who owned apogee audio. Anyway she was right into all of the Isis and Osiris crap, there was a scene in Cairo for this Cult. And Jaz booked the pyramid for 'meditation' purposes LOL.

"Me and Jaz and Youth, Geordie didn't give a fuck about all that crap. Me and Youth pointed crystal wands at Jaz while he was singing, And he made this really dismissive 'fucking hippies' gesture kind of thing, which pissed me off, and I went and sat in the corner. While sitting there I saw these 10 metre beings in the shadows, which was odd. But I didn't really give a fuck. Fuck the aliens, and the pyramids as well. This is KJ."

The album was recorded at Townhouse, Metropolis Studios and Butterfly Studios in London and York Street Studio in Auckland, New Zealand, as well as sessions taking place at EMI Studios, Hani Mehana Studios and the King's Chamber of the Great Pyramid in Cairo, Egypt.

"Townhouse we used to re-record the drums with Jeff. Jaz had booked 2 drummers in NZ to do the drums, but Tim at the record company didn't like the drums, so I went into Townhouse with Jeff and rerecorded the drums. There was a big argument, Youth liked the new drums, Jaz the old. They said OK, let's let Greg decide. I was wakened from my depressed sad corner to listen to the takes. I listened and said I preferred the original drums. Jaz immediately changed his mind and said he liked the new drums. Just because I liked the old ones. I stand by my decision by the way.

"Metropolis was used to mix the album with this old engineer who fucked the mixes up imvho. Although his mate was Jamal from the Last Poets, who I got to meet, which made it all worthwhile. Jamal and the engineer (can't remember his name) spoke everything in rhyming couplets which was really cool. Metropolis cost a fucking fortune and was a mistake. Oh well.

"Butterfly was where we did vocals and some overdubs. Geordie only did one overdub on the whole album with a 12 string guitar, which he did in one take. The guitar was out of tune. I didn't bother to ask him to re-do it because there was no fucking way that was going to happen. In retrospect, getting Geordie to do an overdub was actually a real honour, which I only realised much later. I recorded Jaz's vocals on LSD. There was no way Jaz was going to have Yoof telling him what to do. Jaz set up the mic right next to me in the control room and had this interrogation angle-poise light which he would shine in my face after each take and say 'what did you think of that?' I would say something like 'not enough coughing' etc.

"York Street was Jaz's studio in Auckland where we did the backing tracks. There was a bar in the studio, where Geordie hung out. Me and Jaz fought and laughed. Youth held it together.

"EMI - sout el hob is a famous Cairo studio. We started off recording there, but as we were recording really hot +10db Ampex 496, the tape machine had to be realigned before every session, which pissed off the local crew, so we moved to Hani Mehana which had an auto-align multitrack. Cairo was awesome. Full vibe. Full music. Full energy. Nubian hashish. Hot. Perfect for KJ.

"The King's Chamber was a laugh, but honestly we could have just put a big reverb in Jaz's vocal and saved a lot of time. Still it was fun. More like a bit of extra publicity really, if I am being honest."

'Communion' was the first Killing Joke song to incorporate classical instruments. Egyptian violins were recorded in Cairo.

"These were recorded in Olympic studios with an Egyptian violinist called abu-something. Recording violins in Cairo would have been very expensive, so Jaz used this guy and double-tracked him a dozen times. In Cairo we mainly did percussion and few solo instruments. The decision would have been made by Jaz."

'Hallucinations Of A Cynic' was the only track left over from those sessions which didn't make the cut to the album.

"Because it is shit? I think that was the only track which didn't get used. There are a few extra mixes floating around. Ambient versions. LOL ambient KJ!!"

As usual when Killing Joke is around bizarre things happen.

"In NZ we went to this cult which was headed up by this guy who

143

had invented a free-energy machine. All the members wore white robes. We took cactus that was mescaline or something. It was an odd party...

"You cannot speak of *Pandemonium* (I disliked that title btw, and called it Andypandymonium, which made Jaz and Geordie laugh, but not enough to change it) without speaking of CYBERSANK who mixed 'Pandemonium' and 'Millennium'. This guy really beefed up these two tracks and made them into what they are. So much so that Rammstein invited me to Berlin to audition for production, but by then I was a burnt out shell and collapsed in the studio.... oh well.

"*Pandemonium* has the most views of all KJ's albums on Youtube. It is the real deal. I doubt KJ will work with me again because Jaz knows that I am better musician than him. And his pathetic ego cannot handle that. Although I would love to do another KJ album, if you're reading this Jaz, you miserable cunt."

"Paul let us down on *Pandemonium*. He was gonna be in on it. Then, two days before we got to the studio, he tried to blackmail me," explains Youth in *Metallurgy 2 - Reasons To Be Fearful* 1996, a compilation cd-rom interview. "We'd agreed everything, then he said, I want double the money or I'm not coming. He tried to put us in a position where we couldn't say no, but I already had a couple of drummers on hand."

The drums on the album were then done by Geoff Dugmore, Tom Larkin and Larry De Zoete with additional percussion from Hossam Ramzy and Said El Artist. "We used two drummers in New Zealand," explained Jaz to US music magazine *B-Side* in October / November 1994. "And then when we came back to London and scrutinised, we thought we could do a bit better. And we got Geoff Dugmore to replace some of the drums on some of the songs. He just really understood the whole thing."

"I don't know where he came from," comments Jaz in Canadian music magazine *Chart*, Vol. 5 Issue 5, November 1994, "but God can he play! When we play these days, we have the energy we always wanted, and it shows in the crowds that come to see us."

Aboud Abdel Al played the violin on the album and programming was done by Matt Austin and Paddy Free.

"You've got to remember that the guitar is an Arabic instrument, if you trace it back," Geordie explained to *Industrial Nation* Issue #10 in 1995 regarding the more Eastern flavour on the album. "Some of the chords and some of the bends sort of lean that way anyway. Stuff going back to 'Kings & Queens' - just hints of it anyway. We just thought we'd go for it. Jaz loves his studies - Egyptian music - and it just ended up like that."

Recording of the shamanic ritual performed by Jaz and Youth prior to the recording of the vocals at the Great Pyramid of Giza can be found on the super-deluxe version of *The Singles Collection*, only available from Pledge Music in 2012.

On 11 March 1994 'Exorcism' was released as a single in several versions including remixes and live performances.

On 22 May Jaz and Youth promoted the upcoming album on *Metal Express* on French television station M6. Youth says that the band concentrates more on the emotion than the music. They're pleased with the influence they have been to the top artists of the time from Metallica to Soundgarden and Nirvana, but Jaz states that "sooner or later you'll have to come back to the original spirit. And that is not a band, but it is Killing Joke."

The tracks on the final album were 'Pandemonium', 'Exorcism', 'Millennium', 'Communion', 'Black Moon', 'Labyrinth', 'Jana', 'Whiteout', 'Pleasures of the Flesh' and 'Mathematics of Chaos'. The songs were credited to Jaz Coleman, Youth and Geordie Walker. What was unique about the album was that for the first time Jaz combined his classical work with Killing Joke with the strings in 'Communion'. The first half of the album from 'Pandemonium' to 'Communion' are all essential Killing Joke.

Pandemonium was released on 2 August 1994 by Youth's record label Butterfly Records. Unlike the predecessor, the new album made it to number 16 in the UK Charts as well as number 39 in US *Billboard* Heatseekers charts. The singles 'Millennium' and 'Pandemonium' both reached the UK top 20 and the album is the band's best selling work. It was reissued in remastered form in 2005, featuring two additional tracks: a remix of 'Another Cult Goes Down' and an experimental dub remix of 'Pandemonium'. Youth's return to the band can be sensed in the ambient influence on the album and also the interest in Eastern music becomes evident.

The album was generally well received by critics at the time. *Kerrang!* magazine wrote "Gargantuanly heavy, catchy and hilarious at turns, *Pandemonium* yokes pounding slabs of techno-metal to Coleman's cosmic visions, to exhilarating, trance-inducing effect." Kerry Doole of *Impact* called it "arguably the best Killing Joke album in a decade." A similar appraisal came from Richard Winn of *Hits* stating that it is "one of the finest albums they have ever made." *Trouser Press* described it as "a significant upgrade from *Extremities, Dirt and Various Repressed Emotions*." In July 1994 *Melody Maker's* Jonathan Selzer gives the album a rave review saying how 'Exorcism' is "just fucking colossal, a juggernaut putsch rising in fervour, and boiling the blood until Coleman's retching his guts out." He calls the album "hysteria with a mission" and emphasises the ritualistic nature of the new album. Daniel Puckett gives the album 4 out of 5 stars in *Tampa Bay Times* on 4 November saying while there are new Middle Eastern and Egyptian influences on the album it is still recognisable as the same angry band that in 1980 emerged in the scene with 'Wardance'. He concludes with "it's violent, it's hook-packed, it's fascinating and it's wicked danceable – what better farewell for a century as horrifying as this?"

Two music videos were released to promote 'Pandemonium'. The UK version, which is slightly short, revolves around live footage of the band on stage, whilst the US version is more expensive and aimed more towards the MTV generation with footage shot at a desert featuring horn players, exotic dancers and scenes of a new born baby held by the mother. The music video for 'Millennium' was directed by Jon Klein and produced by Juliet Naylor for London based TVP. The video was released on 17 April 1994. The mainly black and white music video consists of a lot of distorted and menacing images from train wrecks to JFK to dancing at what seems to be industrial complexes.

"Forget bungee jumping... this was an emotional washing-machine on full," Youth told Neil Perry of UK magazine *Vox* about the most traumatic experience of his life in 1994. "Killing Joke has always been a philosophy, an approach to life, and all the work I've done before has led to this record. When I saw Killing Joke play four years ago, I realised how much further we could have taken it." In the same publication Jaz thought the album was very special as well as cathartic.

In April the band announces in *Kerrang* that although Paul is playing on the album he won't be joining on the subsequent tour, and the band has been rehearsing with the three original members. As previously noted, Paul's drumming didn't feature on the album in the end.

The band began the tour promoting the album in Belfast, Northern Ireland with more dates in the UK, followed by a tour in the US in November and December, ending with a date in Paris, France and a number of dates in Germany. Most notable of these dates is probably

146

the show on 17 July at the Phoenix Festival in London, which was filmed for television. The band is in top form with great songs from the new album and the energetic live show is complete with dancers and fire breathers.

In 1994 grunge, and Nirvana as the movement's brightest star, became massive. On their magnum opus *Nevermind* there is a song called 'Come As You Are', which shares some resemblance to 'Eighties'. The band was none too pleased about that and Jaz had the following to say to Tim Slater in *Guitarist* in December 1994: "We are very pissed off about that, but it's obvious to everyone. We had two separate musicologists' reports saying it was; our publisher sent their publisher a letter saying it was and they went, Boo, never heard of ya! But the hysterical thing about Nirvana saying they'd never heard of us was that they'd already sent us a Christmas card!" The court case was eventually dropped when Nirvana's lead singer Kurt Cobain died in an apparent suicide; although there had been some talk later on in their career that they might pursue the matter, at the time of writing it seems not to be the case.

"I don't really know what fucking went on at all. There's probably a couple of million dollars lying around, but I don't want it," Geordie told Mike Glader of alternative newspaper *Night Times* in May 1996. "I don't want a dead man's money. Keep it. Spend it on the kid."

In 1995 the band toured in the UK before taking a break to record their next album. The *Wilful Days* compilation was released on 1 May 1995 by Virgin Records. The album consisted mainly of remixes and older material, which weren't readily available on compact disc at the time or hadn't been pulled together into one release before.

1996 – Democracy

Pairing with the earlier release it's a New Age-flavoured release offering big guitars and a more positive view of the times to come. From the tribal urgency of 'Another Bloody Election' to the quintessential guitar sound of the decade and topical content of 'Prozac People' it is a creation of its time.

UK Album Chart #71

After the 1994 *Pandemonium* tour the band reconvened in Cornwall in South West England to write songs for a new album before moving on to Henley-on-Thames, Oxfordshire to record. Production was overseen by Youth and session musician Geoff Dugmore would return to the drum stool. Additional synthesiser and programming was provided by stage keyboardist Nick Holywell-Walker.

"We really connected after not being so much around each other for a few years, and we exchanged a lot of ideas and philosophies. It's been the most optimistic album that we've ever been part of. The ideas we have on this album are those of proportional representation, which is the only true democracy and is something we all believe in," explained Jaz regarding the Cornwall preparations to Debbie Jhaj of *Fix* magazine in May 1996.

The band would remain as a three piece without a full-time drummer, as Jaz would explain to Sheila Rene in March 1994. "I certainly wouldn't like four full-time members in Killing Joke now. I have my own personal reasons for that but we're very comfortable with this particular line-up."

Geoff Dugmore played drums on the albums.

"I knew about Killing Joke back at the start. I had my own band at the time, we were always checking out bands and going to see them play around London. I don't remember seeing them live at the start but I knew who they were and what they were doing. Back then I was sharing a flat in London with another artist singer called Toni Childs and I remember she was friends with big Paul and so I met him a few

148

times when he would come round to see Toni. I liked him right away and I had a good rapport with him."

The songs on the album were 'Savage Freedom', 'Democracy', 'Prozac People', 'Lanterns', 'Aeon', 'Pilgrimage', 'Intellect', 'Medicine Wheel', 'Absent Friends', and 'Another Bloody Election'. The songs were credited as written by Jaz Coleman, Youth and Geordie Walker. The 2005 CD reissue features bonus track 'Democracy (The Russian Tundra Mix)', which clocks in at around an impressive 18 minutes. It's the first album where Geordie can be heard playing acoustic guitar. The title track, 'Intellect' and 'Another Bloody Election' are the highlights from this more personal album.

Early 1996 sees the band tour in the UK and Europe until they play their last show for a number of years on 30 May at Pavillion Penfold in Brest, France.

In 'Lanterns' Jaz expresses his feelings of wanting to escape to the Island and avoid the lunacy and mortgage payments of modern living, and live a green life, embracing the cleanliness of Mother Earth.

Unreleased song 'Four Stations of the Sun' would surface much later in the super-deluxe version of *The Singles Collection*, only available from Pledge Music in 2012. The same box set would also have a version of 'Intellect' in which the violin is very prominent.

Democracy was released on 1 April 1996 by Youth's record label Butterfly Records in conjunction with Big Life, on CD and cassette, peaking at number 71 in the UK Albums Chart.

The title track 'Democracy' was the sole single released from the album, on 11 March 1996. It peaked at number 39 in the UK Singles Chart. Also, a mostly black and white video was released to promote the record, in which the band plays and a protagonist is shown going voting and following the trail of the voting ballots leading him to corrupt officials amending the ballots, resulting in his arrest. The video strongly emphasises the disillusionment regarding the corrupted democratic system.

"Personally, I think Jaz has got a lot of balls to talk about some of the personal things like his experiences with Prozac and stuff like that," Youth told UK music fanzine *Organ* Issue 45, in 1996. "I think he's very brave to sing about some of the things he's gone through, and his state of mind, in such an honest way - and yeah, I think that's very positive. I think people could perceive it as being negative, but then I don't think people really appreciate that within Killing Joke we do talk about ourselves in that way." In the same interview Youth describes the album more generally. "On this album I feel we've kind of gone away from doing what we did on the *Pandemonium* album, which was mixing a lot of techno beats and the more atmospheric ideas. This time I've gone to the more traditional ideas of using pop song arrangements and full guitar, drum and bass instrumentation, which you know I haven't really done since the early days."

Troy Gregory joined the band in 1996 when Youth wasn't able to go on the tour to promote *Democracy*.

He first came aware of Killing Joke through *Cream* magazine, which "had a little blurb thing in the corner about them once and that's why I first heard the name and I used to go to record stores and look at every record in the shop. I'd see the albums, but wouldn't have money to buy them. Friend of mine made me a mix tape when *Night Time* came out and he put 'Tabazan', 'Kings and Queens' and 'Love Like Blood' from that record on a cassette for me on a mix tape."

He heard the *Fire Dances* album at a friend's house around the same time. His first purchase was *Night Time* and right around the same time he was graduating from high school and got *Brighter than a Thousand Suns* as it came out along with 'Adorations'. He then went to get *Revelations* along with the first album and realised he liked the earlier sound even better.

"I really loved the lyrics. They really got me. Like the lyrics to 'Rubicon' and I really had an interest to occult science and theology."

At the time Troy was playing in a band playing "horrible, shitty radio rock" and was digging Killing Joke and their early singles. He would go and see the band live multiple times in places like Chicago and Michigan. He was living in Los Angeles when the band was touring *Extremities, Dirt and Various Other Repressed Emotions* and saw them "a bunch of times" on that tour.

"They were so accessible that band. Even when I was with them, they wouldn't have security backstage, so I would meet them all the time, but as a fan. I was having a conversation with Raven at one of the clubs for a long time. And one time I just wandered backstage and there was this suburban shaman talking with Jaz. That's how I came, I was, for a lack of a better word, a fanboy."

The style of the band had a strong appeal to Troy. He even made a brief appearance in the band's 'Money Is Not Our God' music video for a split second and would not have dreamed of ever playing in the band himself. Killing Joke also didn't fall in with the dumbed down metal, which tried to be socially aware, but didn't quite manage to do it intelligently.

Jaz's persona also appealed to him. "You don't shut off the energy that you're creating or transmitting whether it is yourself, your band mates or your audience. I always found it weird that if a rabbi or a preacher walked out of a synagogue or a church and said 'OK, I'm done with this for the day.' It sticks with them. It is who you are. I like that approach of doing music and I picked up on that."

He liked the band's dub influence as well as the anger in their music along with "incessant need for beauty in the music. They had that as well as the sophistication in the music. Music to take you to a certain place. It's escapism, but more confrontation."

Geordie had married a woman from Michigan and he went to a bar that Troy's wife worked at. Troy went to the bar a few times hoping to run into him. They'd met before in New York when Geordie was on tour with Murder Inc. and Troy was playing in Prong. They ran into each other and Troy and his wife got invited over for dinner at Geordie's. Geordie wanted to play Troy Killing Joke's new record *Democracy*, which they had just recorded.

"I actually heard the original mixes before Youth got to them. Geordie still swears the original mixes were the best ones. I remember him playing me 'Aeon' and 'Savage Freedom'." The original mix had been rawer and had less EDM influence compared to the finished album versions.

They shared the same sense of humour and had a lot to talk about. He complimented Troy saying that what he liked about him was the he was "a real lad. I didn't know what it meant, but when I found out I thought it was a good thing."

Later Troy got the message that Geordie wanted him to call him. It turned out that Youth couldn't do the upcoming tour and Geordie wanted Troy to fill in for him. He was given a thousand dollars a week to go on tour with the band in Europe.

"It was like winning the lottery. All you gotta go and do is playing Killing Joke at night – with Killing Joke! I didn't really even care about the money. They also encouraged me to bring my wife on the tour." Apparently according to Jaz if it was just men they'd "start acting like stupid boys" on tour and having women on tour as well kept everyone in line.

For a moment it seemed as if their drummer Geoff Dugmore couldn't do the tour and that Troy's brother was going to join Killing Joke as well, and they'd rehearsed some songs, such as 'Unspeakable', 'Primitive' and 'Chop Chop' in his basement, but it turned out Geoff was eventually able to go on the tour. Troy was disappointed that his brother couldn't join and share the excitement of joining Killing Joke, but understood their decision to go on tour with someone who was already familiar with the material and had played with them previously.

Before the tour Troy went to England to rehearse and managed to get bronchopneumonia on the way there. Straight from the airport they went to Butterfly studios. "Everyone was just hanging out drinking wine and beer and stuff like that and I was just ready to die."

Jaz didn't remember Troy and wasn't impressed by him at first during the first day of rehearsals. Troy hadn't got the setlist in advance and during the second day they did 'Communion' from 'Pandemonium'. "I really botched it." Geordie reassured Troy, who was having his doubts and was still very ill.

"Jaz was looking at me like I'm not even there and saying to Geordie 'Why did you bring in this Yank? Fuck him.' Because I had played in some metal bands I think he thought I was some dumb metalhead guy. Typical American [type]. It wasn't a fun day.

"I was really lucky that Nick Walker, the keyboardist, was really into herbicidal healing remedies. He brought me this root and told me to boil that and that'll sort ya."

Troy then got an exact setlist from the band and borrowed the CDs and a CD player from their sound man and learned songs from *Pandemonium*. "I didn't know that record at all. And then there were the new songs from *Democracy*, which they weren't sure which they were going to play or not." He then taught himself both of the records that night while simultaneously drinking the unpleasant tasting remedy as well as regularly puking up. Thankfully the remedy worked well and Troy was feeling fine the next day.

"Geordie woke me up in the morning and we were drinking tea and eating digestives. Still listening and playing, even in the cab ride over to the studio."

The band started off with playing 'Millennium' and Troy tells how Jaz "was giving me the stink eye. We start playing it and I'm nailing, but all of a sudden, we get stopped. And I was like 'What?' and Jaz is like 'It doesn't go like that'." Turned out they were meant to do the

152

remix version of the song rather than the regular album version of it. After that the rehearsals went better.

"First couple of days were intimidating. They wanted to see who I was as a person. Got along with Nick [Holywell-Walker] right away. Very sweet guy. And got along with Geoff Dugmore very well too."

Nick Holywell-Walker was a keyboard player from North London who joined the band in 1994 and stayed until 2005, when he decided to go and pursue his own projects, most notably the London rock band 30,000 Days.

At the end of their two weeks of rehearsals Troy felt fine with the band and got along with Jaz as they shared some of the same interest in science. He tried to persuade the band to play older material, but the group was more interested in having the new material in the setlist.

Youth lent some of his basses for Troy to use on the tour, who was also used to using Rickenbacker basses. He managed to smash one of his basses up on stage as he got too into 'Mathematics of Chaos'. He would at times get mistaken for Youth due the fact that they used the same bass and had a similar haircut at the time. Only their age difference gave it away when people got closer to Troy. Troy didn't mind it as a similar thing had happened to him when he joined the American thrash metal and progressive metal band Flotsam and Jetsam to replace Jason Newsted, who later became world known as the bassist for Metallica.

According to Jaz and Geordie the tour had some of the best shows they'd ever played. They were happy to have Troy to be a part of it.

On the tour bus the band would kick back and drink wine that was left over from the shows and listen to Troy's tapes, such as Sparks and Can.

"One time Geordie was really drunk and started throwing bottles out of the window. We had to throw him down, put cushions on top him and sat on him for a while and had a couple of drinks. Then he got out all purple and eyes glowing with a big smile on his face laughing.

"One time we were in France and the bus was stopped and I knew we weren't where we were supposed to go. It was really early in the morning and I see a dog walking outside. Turns out we got pulled out by the police looking for drugs. Geordie gets woken up by the police and he says 'who is the man with the funny hat'. We get all lined up outside and we're supposed to empty our pockets. Meanwhile everyone had been looking for some hash for the last couple of days and we're suspecting Geordie had some hash and he was holding out. He denied it. So we're all lined up, sun is just coming up and everyone had to throw things out of their pockets. People had the strangest things in their pockets. You learn a lot about people by what's in their pockets. Then they got to Geordie and out comes this little packet of hash and everyone stops for a second. And everyone is like 'aah' and after a brief silence Jaz goes 'I knew it was you! I knew you were holding out!' And everyone started laughing, including the cops. So they just took the hash and didn't do anything. I think the reason why we didn't get into any trouble, because the police thought we're dealing here with some real nutters here."

Preparations for the concerts were very ritualistic, including Jaz putting on his war paint. Troy would also express gratitude and other similar feelings in an ancestral worship kind of a way.

"There were parts of the show where everything was just moving in slow motion. I would say to Jaz that the whole section seemed to last a long time and the audience wasn't moving. It was incredible, like lucid dreaming. And he would go 'Oh, it's the white heat. You got it! That's what happens with Killing Joke.' Sure felt it. It was absolutely amazing. Even like when I destroyed my bass it seemed joyful rather than destructive."

Paul Raven also joined Prong after Troy left on his suggestion. Troy and Raven got along great, as did the other members of Prong. Killing Joke had been a major influence on Prong although neither Jaz nor Geordie think much of it.

Troy is still very active in the music scene in Detroit, Michigan. He was in Electric Six, a six piece from Detroit, and played in Dirt Bombs and the Witches among others, along with solo material which he performs under the banner Super Birthday, which takes inspiration from tarot cards he developed.

The band did a short tour in the summer of 1996, which didn't all go according to plan as Youth explains in the *Metallurgy 2 - Reasons To Be Fearful* 1996 compilation cd-rom interview. Jaz had fucked himself up with Prozac and alcohol: "He just really fucked his head. He was really on the edge; he was turning blue on me, ODing and stuff like that. He really didn't wanna tour America and it was fucking hell to go through." Youth had to put a ban on alcohol during the recording sessions as Jaz would become aggressive and threatened Youth with a bottle of whisky during the recording of 'Hollywood Babylon' for the *Showgirls* film. Apparently, he was a bad drunk. He would get drunk rather easily and become obsessive, self-centred and aggressive.

Released on 5 November, *Mortal Kombat: More Kombat*, one of the three soundtrack albums tied to the *Mortal Kombat* action film, which was based on the video game of the same name, included an exclusive Killing Joke track, 'Drug'. This wasn't the actual soundtrack of the film, but rather a tie in with largely exclusive tracks from industrial and electronic bands from Sepultura to Babylon Zoo.

25 November saw the release of electronic compilation *Alchemy - The Remixes* on Rough Trade. The 8 songs on the album were reworked into dub, trance and ambient pieces. The inside cover reads: "The mysteries of sound is revealed in a synthesis of projected intent, tension, release, vision of light, fusion and unity; this is alchemy in its most tribal and intoxication incarnation. The pounding bass of dub, soaring metallic guitars and the melting electronic pulses of trance collude and collide in this bubbling cauldron of magical remixes; a few drops of this potent brew could change your life forever."

Free The West Memphis 3 (A Benefit For Truth & Justice) compilation, released in 2000, featured new Killing Joke song 'Our Last Goodbye'. The West Memphis Three are three men known for being extremely likely wrongfully convicted as teenagers, in 1994, of the 1993 murders of three boys in West Memphis, Arkansas, United States. The song was credited to Walker, Coleman, Raven as well as Chris Vrenna who is best known for having been a drummer in Nine Inch Nails. "We're all opponents of the death penalty. It's as simple as that," Jaz told Joel Gausten of online publication *Compact Disc World* in October 2000. "If I even find somebody who's pro-death penalty in my presence they'll fucking get it! Civilisation must be compassionate and must forgive at the end of the day. I don't believe that man has the right to take life. I just don't believe it, and that's why we contributed."

PART FOUR

Noughties

2003 – Killing Joke

Returning from the hiatus with a very industrial influenced and precise masterpiece with Dave Grohl in the drummer's seat. Containing many of their latter day classics such as 'Loose Cannon' and 'Asteroid' it is one intense ride from the opening guitar chugging of 'The Death and the Resurrection Show'. Unstoppable!

UK Album Chart #43

Big Life management had created a CD-R carrying the plain title 'New Demos – Spring 2001' dating to 18th April 2001 with the songs 'Loose Cannon', 'Future Shock' and 'Silent Rage', which were used to try to get the band a new recording contract. The band landed a deal with Zuma Records. 'Loose Cannon' was the only one of the demos that would survive to the comeback album.

Jaz said in a video interview with *Classic Rock* in May 2013 that there was no record deal ever signed for the album and he was surprised it even managed to come out. Also, the band received no advance for the album. It was all down to the management the band had at the time. "The only way to get through that time was to get blind drunk" is how Jaz recalls promoting the album. Jaz remembers the time as very dark and it would get even darker during the following album.

"Some of the songs on the album started life as hardcore Detroit house tracks, all written in my basement," Geordie explains to Jenny Knight of *Guitar UK* in October 2003. "'Blood On Your Hands' was a fucking 138 bpm slammer, and 'Never Get To Me' was a trance tune - it's now a bit of a ballad, much to 'The Singer's' disgust." Geordie had relocated back to London from Detroit about a year earlier to commence work on the album.

What was different to most recording sessions on this album was that the drums were added last. The original idea was to have three different drummers on the album, but Dave Grohl ended up being the sole drummer. "We got the guy from System Of A Down in for three tracks but we wiped them all because Dave was infinitely superior," Jaz told

Matt Frilingos of the *Daily Telegraph* in August 2003.

Jaz flew over to LA to oversee and approve Grohl's drum tracks. Whether you want to see it as a payback for ripping off 'Eighties', Grohl didn't take payment for his services, and at the time of the release Killing Joke hadn't been getting much exposure in the press, so surely having the former Nirvana drummer and now well established frontman in Foo Fighters did a world of wonders to exposing the mighty Joke to a whole new generation. The recording started in 2002 and was finished in the summer of 2003.

The album turned out to be the second self-titled album, but originally Jaz Coleman and Dave Grohl intended to title the album 'Axis of Evil' as explained in UK metal magazine *Kerrang* in April 2003, in reference to the political lyrical themes: "It's the beginning of the American Empire. They're taking over the world. That's what's happening, and here we are at the heart of the fucking enemy. I never thought I'd see the day." Also 'The Death & Resurrection Show', the title of the opening song on the album, was a working title according to *Rolling Stone*.

Jerry Kandiah worked as a recording engineer on the album: "I was working at Andy Gill's studio, from Gang of Four, and I was assisting him engineer wise and he was producing the album. They came into the studio. Youth was on bass for that one, but so was Raven. He was sending stuff over from the States. Andy went to the States to record drums with Dave Grohl and we mixed it together." Jaz told online publication *Blistering* that Andy Gill was brought to work on the album as he, Geordie and Youth were all producers themselves, so they needed a referee there. Apparently Gill had some extremely good wine to offer as well.

In the interview with *Rolling Stone* Jaz confirmed that three or four songs had been tracked with John Dolmayan, the drummer from System of a Down, but these did not end up on the final album. "Their first album's been one of my favourite albums of all time," told Dave Grohl to *Kerrang* in April 2003. "Killing Joke music is everything I love about music - relevant, melodic, energetic, powerful. Everyone's searching for an album that has meaning and that has melody and that has a power that is different from anything you've heard, and everyone's looking in all the wrong places. The funny thing about meeting Jaz and then hearing the music and the lyrics we're about to record - everything's so relevant, it almost seems prophetic."

158

Jerry Kandiah: "The process was that Andy would get some drum beats together, get some samples up. He'd literally just program some drum ideas, which were supposed to be just ideas, but when Dave Grohl heard Andy's ideas he loved 'em. And he stuck to exactly the same beats Andy had programmed, which was quite cool. We got all the tracks together that way."

Andy Gill was a great choice as a producer as he was a founding member of another English post-punk group, Gang of Four. He was one of the producers on the debut album *Entertainment!* of Gang of Four and has since worked with the likes of the Red Hot Chili Peppers and the Jesus Lizard. Also the sound on Killing Joke's 2003 self-titled album isn't too far off from what he created when Gang of Four re-recorded their songs for 2005's *Return the Gift*. Also you could see how the new more 'metal' sound is in the vein of the band's music and if Killing Joke had been recording their debut album in the Noughties this could've easily been the direction they would've taken from the start. Unfortunately, the great multi-talent that was Andy Gill passed away during the writing of this book, so he can't be here to tell his stories. Gill's death was announced by Gang of Four on 1 February 2020. He was 64. A band's spokesperson told the *New York Times* the cause of death was pneumonia.

The album was recorded at Andy Gill's Beauchamp Building studio in London with the exception of the drums. The studios were located in a condominium complex on Brooke's Market, Holborn in East London. The drums were later recorded at Grand Master Studios on North Cahuenga Boulevard in Los Angeles with Jaz and Geordie flying over to supervise Dave Grohl's drumming.

Grand Master Studios are a legend on their own right. The Hollywood studio has since 1971 had the breakthrough albums of Foo Fighters' 1997 *The Colour and the Shape* and No Doubt's 1995 *Tragic Kingdom* recorded there, along with albums from Bad Religion, Rancid, Red Hot Chili Peppers, Tool and Motörhead recorded there over the decades. Particular care was taken by the acoustic designer Don Davis when it came to the Drum Room. The studio made an ideal location to record drums thanks to the 1973 Neve 8028 Console, which Dave Grohl is known to champion. The sessions were engineered by Nick Raskulinecz, assisted by Andrew Alekel.

As Andrew Alekel would describe it "There were only five 8028s made. It's a little misleading due to no one cared about numbering back then and each console was made to order. What it really means is *Nevermind* was made on Sound City's 8028 and *Colour And The Shape* was made on Grandmaster's 8028. There just happened to be two similar consoles in the LA area at studios that were aesthetically similar. Very 70s vibe, private and stuck in a bygone era that sounded perfectly amazing. If you were tracking on a decently maintained 80 Series Neve with someone that knows what they are doing, you're gonna get timeless sounds."

Jerry Kandiah: "We didn't even know who was going to be doing the drums at the beginning of the album. That's why Andy put down some ruff beats, but they ended up being THE beats."

The other drummers the band had in mind originally for the album were John Dolmayan from System of a Down and Danny Carey from Tool, but Dave insisted on doing all the drum tracks for the album, so no additional musicians were brought in.

Jaz was very proud of Grohl's work on the album, as he told *Blistering*: "Dave played Killing Joke patterns. In trying to become Dave Grohl, he became the drummer for Killing Joke. He worked with us, and those traditional Killing Joke tom-tom patterns that have been in our band and our style since we began. What a fucking great job he's done, a fucking brilliant job. I'm really proud of the man."

Jerry Kandiah: "The band had 11 or 12 tunes. Couple were left out as they interfered with the flow of the album."

The album had 11 songs of which only 'Loose Cannon' from the early demos the band had prior to the album made the cut. The other two songs on the demo 'Future Shock' and 'Silent Rage' did not make it. On top of the regular songs the UK version of the album had the bonus track 'Inferno' and an extra of the 'Loose Cannon' DVD single. The exclusive track on the Japanese version of the album was 'Zennon', which was more mellow than other songs on the album and was largely based on an acoustic guitar.

Also a new version of 'Wardance' was recorded with Dave Grohl on drums, which appeared on the CD single 'Loose Cannon' released in July. It carried the label 'ultimate version' and has the same crunchy dense feeling that the second self-titled album has. It also included a special touch from Gill by adding a special layer of guitar feedback to add to the atmosphere.

Jerry Kandiah: "Remember when there was a classic moment when they were recording a song called 'Asteroid', I remember that one.

Literally that day we were doing the vocals. We went to the local pub, as we did, and there was a big billboard outside the pub and it said in massive letters 'Asteroid on earth collision course'. I think I still got it. I ripped it off the wall. It was just one of those moments were everything kind of came together.

"The album ended up sounding killer as well."

Jerry seems to recall that songs such as 'Future Shock' and 'Silent Rage' were very early demos Jaz and Geordie had done with Youth, but these titles never made it to the main production of the album. "There was a track called 'Chaos Bin' we did, but didn't make it onto the album. I do remember that."

Youth, Raven and Geordie have all been credited with having played bass on the album, but according to Jerry it was Youth who did majority of it, with Raven sending some bass parts over from the States. They "slotted a few in there just to please everybody."

During the mixing stage of 'Loose Cannon' Geordie wasn't "feeling the sub. So he got in there and we put in all sort of sub-basses to make it come up, but nothing was working, so he ended up picking up a bass and Andy had gone to Italy by then, so I was in charge, so we pumped up the bass with live bass and Geordie played that final real low bass line on that tune. So yeah he did play bass on that album."

Andrew Alekel worked as an engineer in the LA drum sessions with Dave Grohl. "I knew of KJ from when I was a kid and the song 'Eighties' was on the radio in Southern California (the legendary KROQ). Later in the 90s I realised who Youth was due to the success of The Verve's *Urban Hymns*, which he did production work on. I tended to memorise and research the credits on the albums I liked back then. The analogue internet, AKA: THE LIBRARY. HAHAHAHA.

"I managed and worked out of Grandmaster from late 1998 to mid 2013. After that, I did various things there until late 2015.

"I became involved in the recording due to Dave Grohl being asked to play drums. He loved the Grandmaster drum room and the studio had multiple spaces that could be used. Everything from super dry to massive ambient sounds.

"Nick Raskulinecz was Dave's go to guy at the time and I had assisted him on a ton of projects at Grandmaster BEFORE he became a big Grammy winning producer and engineer. So we had a good working relationship, figuring out how to make happen whatever crazy idea he might have as far as sounds were concerned.

"I was stoked to be involved because working with those two was always super fun and killer sounding. I mean, watching Dave play even 5 notes was very powerful and pretty magical, let alone when he unleash the beast. Dave is as good as any session player, but he has that rare thing where as soon as he hits a kick, snare and hat you know it's him. There are very few players that have such a sonic signature.

"The wildcard in our little equation was I had never worked with Andy Gill. Nick hadn't and I don't think Dave had either."

The drums were recorded last at Grandmaster Recorders on North Cahuenga Boulevard in Los Angeles. As Andrew describes: "It was located on Cahuenga Blvd and Sunset Blvd. Right smack dab in the heart of Hollywood. It was active from 1972 to 2016 when the owner passed away.

"I only remember Jaz being there from the band. We were working in Logic, as opposed to tape or Pro Tools. The session files were massive even before the drums were put on. There were temp tracks so Dave could learn the songs, or at least hear the ideas before coming into the studio. So, Andy ran the computer, Nick dialled in the sounds and I took care of headphones (cue mix) for Dave. Nick and I would set up the microphones and whatever else... the setup was pretty big. More on that in a minute.

"We had a drum tech there as well. His name is Gersh and has worked with Dave on a zillion different projects. He brought in a very cool DW kit that was made from 200 year old wood that sounded great. He also has a great snare collection, so we had the options covered for the core sound."

The sessions lasted for 5 days in March 2003.

"When you've got professionals like Andy, Dave and Nick, things are going to be focused and expertly done. But, if you're not having fun, then why are any of us doing this? Nothing was ever stressful. It was more about finding the proper plan of attack for each song and going for it. These songs were difficult and intricate. Dave would often comment on it and was excited for the challenge...ONLY TO MAKE IT MORE CHALLENGING. Here's why: the way Dave played on Queens of the Stone Age's *Songs For The Deaf* had become popular. He had played the drums and cymbals separately. Jaz and Andy were into that and Dave, Nick and Andy wanted to go further. We got even more separate. Not only did we go very micro, layering drums that would make Freddie Mercury jealous, parts were layered in different rooms

162

with all kinds of different kits and percussive stuff (any object you could bang on and mic up). It started to become about how we could make the next song crazier. Jaz was very into it.

"We had a range of perfect vintage drums to broken stuff to sound...um...broken. Nothing was out of bounds or dismissed. If Dave wanted to try it, we tried it. He would build the track starting with whatever he felt would be the best foundation. Sometimes hi hat, sometimes kick & snare. It depended.

"As you might imagine, once a foundation was laid, Dave would do a more wild take just to see what could work. Some of that might get used, it might not. Since the rest of the song was already there, you could really tell what was working. It's why McCartney recorded bass last on Beatles songs. He could figure out where all that melody could go and not interfere with other important parts of the arrangement.

"We would usually start around noon and go until early evening. Why? Andy's plan as a producer and a British person in Los Angeles was 'I want to have a nice dinner every night I'm here.' HAHAHAHA. So, he wanted to be out of there before places closed. But also, drumming is physical as hell. You can only go playing this type of music for so long before fatigue sets in. If you go too long, it will affect the next day's performance for sure. So that was the plan... basically focus on 3-4 songs per day, I think."

Andrew doesn't recall recording any drummers other than Dave Grohl.

"I didn't, but I think there might have been an attempt with someone else for a few days that didn't work out. I remember this because Andy said they went to a studio 3x the cost of Grandmaster and didn't get results. I remember Andy lamenting how much money they could have saved if they never did it and how Grandmaster sounded infinitely better to him."

Andrew wasn't sure how Dave got involved on the album, but "he was definitely a fan of the band though.

"We used the drum room a lot on this, but we also used the warehouse/garage (1000s sq feet) and the wood room. One thing that got a TON of action was the hallway that connected the drum room and the garage. Typically I would put a bass cabinet or combo amps in there. Dave did a lot of low tuned overdubs in this small, narrow spade that would be really dry and punchy. BUT, you open the door to the garage and/or drum room, put mics in there...instant echo chambers that you

163

could control the dampening by how much the doors were open! These kinds of ideas would typically start with Nick exclaiming, 'DUUUDE!' When that would happen, I knew we would be going for it!

"Andy Gill was an amazing person. One of the nicest people I've ever worked with. The ultimate in kindness. We kept in touch for years and years. Any normal person would always react with, 'You're working with Dave? No way!' But everyone in the know would react with 'You're working with Andy Gill? Do you even understand the level on which that guy operates? LEGEND, MATE!'

"I've worked with Nick on tons of stuff, Dave on a lot of stuff and Andy on this one project. They made a fucking formidable team. Jaz was always excited with the results we got and it sounded MASSIVE. Amazing players, rooms, engineers and producers will do that, you know?"

Working on the 2003 self-titled album proved to a very important project for Andrew and would be a reference point later on in his career.

"When I worked on Nine Inch Nails' *With Teeth* (with Dave on drums), the KJ record was a reference point. They wanted that drum sound. Trent and Atticus kept saying as I was setting up, 'What's the trick? You gotta tell us the trick!' I just kept saying, 'It's the room and Dave.' They kept thinking I was hiding something. When James Brown, the engineer, pulled up the faders of two medium distanced mics that he brought with him and they heard Dave hit the snare, Trent said, 'Holy Shit' and James said, 'It's all right there isn't it?' My reply was, 'I told you, no tricks!'"

Jaz Coleman was extremely proud of the album upon its release in mid-2003 when he spoke to online heavy metal site *Blistering*: "I see this as being the band's most powerful work to date, because of the fact that I'm still playing the album. Even though I perform on it, I'm still playing it myself. I've never had that before." He wasn't too bothered about the financial success of the brand new platter at the time. "You know what? I don't give a shit about how it will do! I lose money doing Killing Joke because there are so many paid jobs I should be doing."

On 22nd of July Jaz Coleman and Geordie guested on BBC radio's *Freak Show* premiering 'The Death and Resurrection Show' from the upcoming album. Jaz talked about working with violinist Nigel Kennedy, as well as composing the new national anthem for New Zealand, which is now sung in Maori thanks to Coleman. The songs that the pair chose for the show were Public Image Limited's 'Public

164

Image', Adam Ant's 'Xerox Machine', Abba's 'Winner Takes It All', the Sex Pistols' 'God Save the Queen' and 999's 'Emergency'.

The album was originally meant to come out in mid-June 2003 through their own Malicious Damage label and be distributed via Sony, but the band ended up releasing it on 28th of July through Zuma Records. This was an unknown company that would not end up paying the band. At one point according to Jaz the album had sold nearly half a million copies according to the label, but they wouldn't be paying the band and they had to sue the company. Zuma seemed only to have made a few releases outside of the ones relating to the 2003 Killing Joke album, their other main artist being an English rock band called Shining, formed in 2000, who had their 2002 album *True Skies* released on the label - not to be confused with the Swedish black metal outfit or the Norwegian hard rock act of the same name.

At the time of writing the album is not available on compact disc and was only issued on vinyl in January 2008.

All the songs were credited to Jaz, Geordie and Youth as well as producer Andy Gill, which is the only instance of someone from outside the band receiving credits for composing their songs.

The album opens with a nearly 7 minute 'The Death and Resurrection Show' anthem, which starts off with just Geordie's jittering guitar and Jaz's celebrational lyrics in great anticipation. 'Total Invasion' is an anti-authoritarian cry for action with Jaz whispering the lyrics to a great effect. 'Asteroid' is an apocalyptic vision about the renewing energies of nature through fire. 'Implant' is a song inspired by the experiments of microchip implantations on humans, which took place in China among other countries, during the writing of the album. 'Blood On Your Hands' is about the corporate takeover of the world. 'Loose Cannon' is the finest moment of the album thanks to the Geordie's rumbling subliminal bass and Jaz's menacing vocal delivery, in which he refers to himself as being "one step from a cannibal." 'You'll Never Get to Me' is a beautiful balladesque track on the celebration of life and the joy of friendship and survival. 'Seeing Red' and 'Dark Forces' are about warmongering, and the same goes for the 'Inferno' bonus track. The closing track 'The House That Pain Built' is about questioning one's faith and the need of catharsis.

The critical reception of the album was mostly favourable. *Billboard* gave it an 80 out of 100, noting that "Grohl's furious playing fits perfectly with the wall of rage erected by Joke vocalist Jaz Coleman and fellow founders Geordie Walker on guitar and Youth on bass." John Robb of *Playlouder* wrote that the album "may well be the best rock record you'll hear all year." *Alternative Press* gave full 5 stars while *Mojo* gave 4.5 out of 5 and *Uncut* as well as *AllMusic* awarded the album 4 out of 5.

Rolling Stone gave the album a negative review, awarding the album only 2 stars out of 5, and wrote that "all the humorless gloom and doom feels oppressive after a while." The same goes for *Q* magazine, which also gave a score of 2 out of 5, saying that the album was "patchy." In 2005 the second self-titled album was ranked at number 355 in *Rock Hard* magazine's book of *The 500 Greatest Rock & Metal Albums of All Time*. "This album is Killing Joke at their best, a must for every fan and a good introduction for those who don't know them yet," complimented *Bass Inside* in September 2003.

Raven told Joel Gausten in *Pandemonium: Inside Killing Joke* that along with *Extremities* the second self-titled album was "the definitive Killing Joke album." This was due to the albums being more focused and pointed in their vibe.

Two music videos were released to promote the album. The first was for the lead single 'Loose Cannon', directed by Crooked, which featured a muscled man body popping on his own. It has similar vibe to music videos done by Jonas Åkerlund, who became famous for controversial music videos such as 'Smack My Bitch Up' for the Prodigy song. A very simple video, with flashy editing and a dark vibe, it's perfect for the context of the song, and very much a product of its era, as the case often is with music videos.

The single was released as a compact disc featuring the full album version and radio edit as well as a special B-side of 'Wardance (the ultimate version)', which was a re-recording of the classic track with Grohl on drums, which also appeared as the bonus track on the US version of the album. A 7" vinyl in clown shape was released with the album track backed with the ultimate version of 'Wardance'. As a novelty the single was also released as a DVD, which featured the music video, demo version of the song and B-side 'Zennon' as well as a short behind the scenes look at the recording of the drum sessions in Los Angeles. The 2 minute clip features Jaz drinking whiskey out of a bottle and saying how the band has recorded 11 albums and not done one love song. Dave Grohl describes how he first met up with Jaz, who had turned up to the hotel bar dressed in a priest uniform. Strangely enough it states at the end 'To be continued...' although no further footage has since appeared apart from similar shots briefly in *The Death and Resurrection Show* documentary.

The second single was 'Seeing Red'. The single featured the full album version at 5 and half minutes, radio edit, which was a minute and a half shorter, and a Jagz Kooner remix and instrumental both clocking around 7 and half minutes. A cheap 3D animation music video was released, showing an oil refinery and its pipelines, men digging the ground and Jaz going mad; a prime example of computer animation gone horribly wrong.

On 1 August 2003 the band would finally return to the stage for the first time since 1996, starting with appearance at Przystanek Woodstock Festival in Zary, Poland. The over 300,000 thousand strong festival was organised by anti-racist Never Again Association. The tour promoting the second self-titled album would take the band around the world from Europe to the States and Australia, and would last until the end of November.

The band announced the world tour with Jaz having the following to say to online music magazine *Logo*: "We're going to play a hundred and forty shows around the world this year, and every single one will be a life changing experience for whoever is there. It's a ritual, a religious ceremony. It will be as intense as it's ever been. I can't wait to feel the hackles rising that old shiver down the back. When we play live, there's nothing on earth to touch it.."

Ted Parson joined the band to play on the tour supporting the second self-titled album. Paul Raven asked Ted Parson to join Killing Joke full time after Prong had dismantled and he had moved to Norway. Ted had previously had friends in and out of the band, such as bassist Troy Gregory whom he holds in high regard.

Ted Parson: "I heard the band when I was 16 years old, when I was in high school living in Massachusetts, and that's when all that the Post Punk music came in and it was Killing Joke for me. Killing Joke, Gang of Four, Joy Division all that stuff from England, but Killing Joke was one of my favourites and I went to go see them in Boston and they just blew me away and I thought they were just stood the best band ever and still do, but yeah I heard them when I was still in high school, after all that old Hard Rock stuff I started listening all this Punk and Post Punk stuff, cuz it had to be like 1979 or 80.

"When I was living in New York and became friends with Big Paul, the drummer, cuz he was a friend of my other friend and then one thing led to another we became really good friends that I was kind of nagging about his drumming style and how his life was and Killing Joke and how much I really admired his style and we just became friends over the years and then when I was in Prong, we asked Paul Raven to come in and play bass, which we were very excited about cuz Prong were huge Killing Joke fans so when Paul Raven came in and joined Prong we made that bond. Became really good friends, almost like a brother and he asked me after Prong broke up and he and I left from Prong still going he asked me if I wanted to join Killing Joke and I thought he was joking, no pun intended, and I said of course I will, but meanwhile so I said yeah I'm definitely in.

"We start rehearsals in Prague and we're getting ready for a 3 month world tour. It was a good dream gig for me, it really was."

Apart from finding Jaz a bit intimidating as he "had heard a lot of stories about him", Ted Parson felt that he fit into the band pretty well. When Prong dismantled he moved to Norway and got married, but Paul Raven, who had also been in Prong, got in touch and asked if Ted wanted to join Killing Joke full-time. He said of course he would.

"I try to play the same beats Big Paul played which I knew that you know front and backwards. I knew those songs inside and out so wasn't a lot of practice for actually playing with the band and you know, I knew every song and I just, you know, I just tried to play the best I could with my own style. The first rehearsal we played at this rehearsal space outside of Prague. [It was] a big place where we stayed as well. Jaz and Geordie got into this big fight, and I don't know what it was about you guys, they fight like brothers those guys, and Geordie left it, went to the bar and we could we got back together again and then there was another episode I think later that day, or the next day, where I was concentrating on playing drums for the band, playing the songs, and I had my eyes shut and Jaz said 'ho ho ho hold on hold on we gotta stop. Why do you have your eyes closed? We don't have our eyes closed in Killing Joke when we're playing our music' and I said 'Well sorry Jaz', you know when I was kind of intimidated by mister Coleman and I said sorry, because that's the way I play and focus on music and it was a big deal and I said okay I'll try to keep my eyes open and then later on Geordie said don't be intimidated by Jaz he can be a bully sometimes. He is quite a theatrical person indeed. On tours he'd get really drunk and attack us with like plastic forks and things and and I'm thinking oh my God this guy is a nutcase, but he is brilliant but he's an absolute nut job."

Ted got on particularly well with Geordie, who is one of his favourite guitar players as well.

"Raven on tour was kind of like in his own world. With Jaz we didn't really hang out that much but he was a nice guy you know, depends on what day it was." Overall Ted felt that being in the band had been a great experience even though some of the road crew at times weren't at the top of their game.

Apparently the money Ted was played for drumming wasn't all that great and getting paid sometimes required some hassle. Also parts of the tours didn't go too well either.

"Europe was was okay, but we went to the States and like some of the gigs weren't promoted right, or the attendance level was really bad. You know if you were like in the middle of Kansas so there's maybe 30 people there you know. It's like that touring with any band really unless you were like the Rolling Stones. That's what you have to do in the States, you have to pick up the little gigs along the way. New York and LA, those are the big gigs, but you don't have to play like New Jersey, and this place and that place, along the way so it's kind of like what the hell am I out here doing this? Even Big Paul was telling me this when I first met him in New York, 'You know what, I don't think I want to play drums anymore' and I said 'What do you mean?', but he was playing in all those other bands like Warrior Soul, and I said 'You can't quit playing drums because you're great.'" Paul was telling Ted stories about Jaz and telling him he'd never get into the band again in the late 1980s, but fortunately the original line up reunited in 2010.

The band still had a contract, which sometimes caused problems as Jaz and Geordie weren't too keen to play to just 20 people, which contradicted Ted's own views since he was used to honouring the contract and playing the show regardless of the size of the crowd.

"Those 20 people are die hard fans, you have to play for them. You know you drove like a million miles you can't cancel. So some of the gigs were kind of disappointing, but you know every night I played my best. I played my heart out for those guys, you know.

"There were a couple of gigs we had to cancel because Jaz had a bad throat. And I think it was because he was drinking too much. It was kind of a shame because every gig to me is precious."

One of Ted's finest moments in the band was the session the band did for BBC 1's *Rock Show,* where they played new songs from the latest album such as 'Total Invasion', but also older material like 'Requiem'. Afterwards Geordie commented to him that now he is actually playing really well, after about 50 gigs.

He found being away from his family and children for months at a time difficult. He also didn't find it financially very viable to carry on with the band, but is delighted to see the original line up reformed.

"I did a month and a half in Europe and month and a half in the States and I only got paid for half of that, which was kind of a drag." The band were having financial difficulties, but Ted had a contract, so he was meant to get paid for every gig.

Also, after returning from his last stint with Killing Joke, Ted was diagnosed with brain cancer. Some doctors had given him only months to live. He still plays drums locally, but no longer tours with bands. The next drummer would be young Benny Calvert, who Ted thinks was a good choice for the band.

October 2003 saw the release of the second and final single from the album, 'Seeing Red', which was released with four versions, including a Jagz Kooner remix. Kooner is an English record producer who is known for his work with Radio 4, Manic Street Preachers and Primal Scream.

In 2005, with the new drummer Benny Calver, the band performed shows around Europe from February to October. Most notably there were two shows to commemorate their 25th anniversary on the 24th and 25th February at London's Shepherd's Bush Empire, resulting in the excellent *The Band That Plays Together Stays Together* DVD and live CD.

Reza Udhin joined the band in 2005. Reza is known in goth circles from fronting the UK band Inertia. With him on board the band then began work on their next album in Prague.

"My friend Nick Walker was the keyboard player in the band from around 1994. He asked me around that time if I would consider being the back up keyboard player, if for some reason he couldn't do a show. I said yes. But it wasn't until 2005 that he was unable to do shows anymore and left the band. I naturally took over, as I had been in the wings for quite some time."

There wasn't any direction given by Jaz or anyone else regarding how he should be playing the keyboards. "At the time, I just recreated the keyboards from the albums using the original master tapes that I acquired from Abbey Road studios in London. I got them transferred to

170

a Hard Drive, then painstakingly went through all the synth sounds on the tapes and resampled the sounds and effects for each song from all the albums to that point!

"My first show was supporting Motley Crue at The Glasgow SECC on 14th June 2005. By that time, I had already spent about 4 months living in Prague with the band, rehearsing and recording the *Hosannas* album. Now, that was an experience! We were mainly all drunk around that period. Living above the recording studio and rehearsing in the dark and dingy basement, hence *Basement of Hell*."

2006 – Hosannas From The Basement of Hell

Recorded using the engineer from their first EP, a minimalistic approach and recording equipment from the 1970s, the band sounds rawer than before. While songs like the title track and 'Tribal Antidote' are definite Killing Joke many songs tend to suffer due to excessive length. The Killing Joke symphony to the Gathering if you will.

UK Album Chart #72

Jerry Kandiah: "Killing Joke asked me directly if I'd want to go to Prague with them to get the next album done. This was *Hosannas From The Basement of Hell*, which really was basement of hell. I was there for 8 to 9 months, but it was supposed to be 3 months. That was a quite big one for me. I got to know them pretty well after that.

"They said I'd only have to come out for 3 months and said they had the songs written and it was all going to be easy. But nothing is ever easy with those guys. So got there. Three months turn into four, five, six, seven, eight months. 'Coz they say Geordie has some guitar ideas. We were putting the studio together at the same time as getting the ideas for the songs together. I was in there for a long haul. Things started to get a bit darker, but I stuck in because I had started it and I was going to stay there 'til the end no matter what, and I'm happy we got that album finished and mixed and went out there. It was a bit of a tough one. Turned out real cool. It has a real vibe.

"And I never forget a few moments."

When Jerry arrived in Prague to work on the album Raven met him "and he had a case of beer, bag of weed and a porno mag and he goes 'Welcome to Prague! There you go!' Classic Raven. He is the most rock & roll person I've ever known and I do miss that guy. We had some great nights out on the tequila in Prague causing all sorts of mayhem. It was brilliant."

The album was recorded in Faust Studios in Prague, which were owned by a "jolly old fella who goes around with a big smile on his

172

face" according to Jerry Kandiah, who worked as the studio engineer on the album. The owner used to play in bands back in the communist days of the Czech Republic. "He owns a big block of flats and in the basement he started a studio. It basically had no equipment. Had his old speakers and literally I'd get to start with my laptop, which I luckily bought with me and finally got a computer, so we moved onto that. Then he got some decent speakers and then he got a mixer and by the end of it he had a fully functional studio on the proceeds of the Killing Joke album recording.

"We built it up to a pretty professional studio by the end of it, but at the beginning there was nothing, so I literally had to work on what I had. Get some ideas together and work with the guys and just pull that album together in the chaos of Prague. Every night we'd go out very late and then start work mid-day every day including Sundays. It was hardcore. I managed to just about keep my sanity."

Jerry Kandiah and the new drummer Ben Calvert lived together for the most part of the recording sessions and apparently Ben fitted in to the band really well. "He was loving it. And the guys loved him. He is a great guy. Haven't seen him since though.

"He is a very solid drummer. We didn't really need him until towards the end of the album when he came in and just smashed the drums out. Apart from that he was watching *Family Guy*, smoking a lot of weed and having some Stellas. As I was working every day he was just chilling out and having a laugh.

"There was once in the studio when Jaz had this more orchestrally type song and they were having a bit of a fight whether it should be on the album or not. They were having a bit of a fight in the middle of the studio. It started getting a bit much and it got to a stage where Jaz was literally on his hands and knees like a dog with Geordie's leg in his mouth biting on his skin until he was bleeding and that's when I went in and had to pull them apart and Geordie just walked out of the studio. I was like, 'what's going on now?', so I thought ok, we've lost Geordie and we kind of carried on with a bit of stuff and literally two hours later Geordie walks back into the studio looks at Jaz and he goes 'should we go out for a pint?' and Jaz goes 'Alright then' and off they went! So I was like now I got no one to record, so I just took the rest of the day off.

"They're kind of like a dysfunctional family that come together. I got used to it by the end of it."

According to Jerry Kandiah there are a few songs left over from those sessions which didn't make it on the album. "There is always a few. It's never like that's it, those are the songs, that's the album. Few ideas or even more substantial ideas that are left off from the album, which are not really working with the flow of the album."

A couple of songs cropped up on the singles. The 'Hosannas From the Basements of Hell' 7 inch single had an alternative version of 'Afterburner' while the normal version of the song appeared on the CD single along with 'Universe B'.

"I'd been to an all night rave. Taken some LSD. I was just getting back at 8 o'clock in the morning to go to the studio for 9 o'clock and I was just creeping back in hoping that no one would notice. I'd been out all night and as I get to the studio these cars are pulling up. It has got Killing Joke and the managers and the record company all there. I was just thinking 'oh fuck, I've just been busted' and I had to kind of pull myself together, get into the studio, but luckily all they wanted to do was that the record company wanted to hear the songs. So all I had to do was load up a song, press play and let them vibe it out amongst themselves. I sat back and they got single malt whiskey out and I was like 'I'll have some of that' and it took the edge off. I managed to pull through and I don't think anyone noticed apart from Raven that I hadn't even been to bed yet. Quite a few nights like that in Prague. Then we obviously went out with all the management afterwards. They are quite funny, [David] Bianchi after 9 or 10 pm he basically forgets about the business side of it and we start drinking and it doesn't matter anymore."

There was immense pressure from the record company to get the album finished and the budget ran out. "We had some quite serious issues. Some people ran away, but I didn't, I stayed and stuck it out and we got that album finished and I'm proud of it. Whatever happens with the business side of things who cares, it's water under the bridge. We did a great album that has a real vibe and it feels like the basements of hell, because that's where we were. It's no joke, it's not fantasy, it's reality."

This period for the band was rather dark and it turned out that Raven had picked up his old heroin habit while the making the album.

Raven left the group after recording the album to go on tour with Ministry. He asked Killing Joke's keyboard player to go along with him on the tour rather than carry on with Killing Joke, which Jaz was none too pleased about.

Former keyboard player Dave Kovacevic recalls "My worst memory

174

was hearing that Paul Raven had passed over. I had seen him a bit before in Camden London. He was always the most 'alive' man I knew."

The cover artwork for the album is from a painting by Russian surrealist painter Victor Safonkin entitled *Inhuman Rearing*. The inside booklet is taken from *Society of Good Inventions and Hidden Aims* also by Safonkin. He has described his work as Eurosurrealism or European classic surrealism and symbolism.

According the Jaz this was most likely the darkest period of his life. He told Eugene Butcher of *Vive Le Rock* in the summer of 2013 that when the band got a new recording deal and relocated to Prague they dragged on the recording process as long as they could as now at least they would have their rent covered. Drug and alcohol problems plagued the band as well. Raven had got more involved with heroin, which he had always flirted with, and both Jaz and Geordie were drinking heavily. Times were violent. Jaz would live with a Czech girl for four years, but then had no real recollection of who she really was.

'Hosannas From the Basements of Hell' was the first single from the album, reaching number 72 in the UK Singles Chart. 'Invocation' and 'Implosion' were also released on a promo CD-R, resulting in limited radio play.

The track listing on the album is 'This Tribal Antidote', 'Hosannas from the Basements of Hell', 'Invocation', 'Implosion', 'Majestic', 'Walking with Gods', 'The Lightbringer', 'Judas Goat' and 'Gratitude'. The songs are credited to Jaz Coleman, Geordie Walker and Paul Raven. 'Invocation' marks the second and so far the last time Killing Joke has incorporated components of classical music. The album tends to suffer from the excessive length of the songs. The majority of the album is not very memorable apart from maybe the opening track along with the title track.

The Japan CD bonus track was 'Universe B', which had appeared as a B-side to the 'Hosannas from the Basement of Hell' single. Another B-side, which didn't appear on the finished album, was 'Afterburner'.

The album was released on 3 April 2006 and was met with a warm reception in the press. Paul Brannigan in *Kerrang!* magazine claimed "Out of step with the world they might well be, but Killing Joke's righteous frenzy still feels horribly necessary." He awarded the album 4 out of 5 stars. The album peaked at number 72 in the UK Albums Chart and number 173 in France.

The band went on world tour to promote the album, starting in

Belgium in April with someone called Kniel replacing Raven on bass. The earlier shows prior to this had been either cancelled or postponed. Original tour dates were rescheduled due to mental health problems. I had the chance to witness the band live at the Corporation in Sheffield on 7 May, and I have to admit it was one of the worst shows I've ever seen in my life. In the review I wrote at the time I stated how their earlier show at the Shepherd's Bush Empire for their 25th anniversary had been purely magical and even their first song 'Are You Receiving' sounded fresh. This was a whole other affair. The band took to the stage 45 minutes late with a couple of hired hands to fill the line-up for Jaz and Geordie. The show was littered with problems with the sound and you could tell the whole thing was very off. Jaz told the audience "You're fucking depressing, you make me depressed. Fuck off!", which I certainly did. At the time the band was a shadow of its former self. Physically Jaz wasn't in the best of shape either. He had put on weight and was clearly bloated. The set at that point had heavily relied on material from their debut album. I only managed to catch 'Gratitude' from the album they were promoting, which was a good indication of the lack of classic tunes from that album.

The last show to promote the album was played at the Beautiful Days Festival in Devon, UK, in late August, while the remaining dates in autumn were cancelled due to Jaz's back problems.

PART FIVE

Reunion Of The Original Line Up

2010 - Absolute Dissent

Reunited with the original line up the band makes a contemporary album with retro flavours. The 1980s synth pop of 'European Super State' contrasts well with the sledgehammers such as 'This World Hell' and proves that they still possess the original magic. Glorious and epic return.

UK Album Chart #71

Paul Raven's funeral in Geneva, Switzerland, in 31 October 2007, was what set the wheels in motion regarding the regrouping of the original line up of the band. Paul Ferguson recalls how the seeds of the reunion were sown. "In 2007, my dear friend and colleague Paul Raven died suddenly, and to my surprise. It was upon attending his funeral that I reconnected with Jaz and we made amends. The hatchet had been buried, so to speak, and the idea planted to reform the original lineup."

In 2008 the band would release their first music together back with the original line up, in the form of a live in the studio compilation album *Duende: the Spanish Sessions* recorded at Youth's studio in Granada, Spain. In the liner notes Jaz says that the original line up have not been in the same room since February 1982, but the pieces of the puzzles locked back together, as he points out that while the band has had multiple line ups over the years "the original line up bears no comparison to later line ups, neither socially or musically." Jaz is keen on writing new music with the band which is as reactionary and revolutionary as what they've done in the past. On top of learning two different sets, roughly five hours' worth of music, they start working on new songs to be performed on their upcoming reunion tour and he would tease an album for January 2009.

The album, which can be seen as their typical set of the time, was first released by the band themselves, to be sold at the shows, but was also later released by Eastworld Recordings in November 2009. The majority of the songs consisted of older material the band had written together back in the late 70s and early 80s, but also included a couple of newer tracks with the track list being 'Requiem', 'The Wait', 'Tomorrow's World', 'Bloodsport, 'Psyche', '$,O,36', 'Millennium', 'Tension', 'Primitive', 'Are You Receiving', 'Whiteout', 'Pandemonium', 'Eighties' and 'Love Like Blood'.

The first show with Paul back on the drums would take place in Club Quattro in Tokyo, Japan on 13 September, followed by dates around Europe. At most venues the band would play two consecutive evenings, the first night dedicated to their earlier material and the second one for the later.

In October the band would play their first live shows in London with the original line up for two decades. On 3 October the band played material from the first two albums, while the second night, on 4 October, they concentrated on *Pandemonium* and the early singles from 1979 and 1980. Both of the gigs were released as an exclusive limited edition 3 disc live CD. 1500 CDs were produced of each night and made available straight after the gig. Both sets came with an exclusive 3rd photo disc, which included 30 professional instant photos including some taken backstage. These were later re-released together as a box set as well. It's worth noting that the second night featured the new track 'Time Wave', which was recorded during the *Absolute Dissent* sessions, but didn't make it onto the album and would only surface years later in the *Singles Collection*.

The last two shows were in Los Angeles and New York in mid-October before the band got busy with their first album back together.

"Quite a few of those songs were started off with jamming sessions at Youth's studio in Spain," says Reza, who played keyboards on the album. "From memory, we then took the songs to Youth's shed studio at the back of the garden of his home in London and worked on them there for a while, before we headed to Britannia Row Studios in London where we did the final recordings and mixing."

Dante Bonutto was asked to start the UK offices for Finnish heavy metal label Spinefarm and on top of wanting to bring back catalogue from artists such as Children of Bodom and Nightwish he also wanted to sign new acts to the label. The band moved to Spinefarm in 2009, roughly a year before they released their first new material on the label. "Chris Ingham, a friend of mine, who was working in publishing, mentioned to me by the way Killing Joke don't have a record deal at the moment. I wasn't aware of that, so I owe that to Chris. I knew the management and met the band and got the conversation going. And eventually signed the deal and got the band making their first record with the original line up back together again. I hadn't heard any new music at the time. I think it was basically done on the fact that this was an amazing band, amazing reputation and the original line up is back together again. What a great opportunity to work with these seminal artists." Dante reckons that in hindsight it has been a new phase in the band's career and the impact of the original group returning together has been monumental.

Comparing them to the other artists on Spinefarm he reckons "they are a different beast. We really want to make sure with them is that what they feel, what they believe in, what they say, what they do comes across directly to the fans as much as humanly possible. We just want to give them that platform to do it from and hopefully a secure kind of family environment to do it from. I'd hate to think that anyone would think that Killing Joke's vision was in anyway altered or certainly not diluted by what we do. Killing Joke is one of our most important bands. If you have Killing Joke on your label it will attract other artists to the label. It's a huge piece of branding for Spinefarm, because you can't find credibility. It's not possible. If you try, you're not credible automatically. They have that intrinsically. People know if you're working with Killing Joke you must be doing something right."

Dante has a background in music journalism in the 1980s and knew the band due to its influence in both rock and metal circles. "One thing that did became clear from early on was how many bands existed in rock and metal loved Killing Joke and were influenced by Killing Joke. This went right through the alternative scene – and the independent scene. Killing Joke never sat in one particular category. Their appeal is so broad and their appeal is much more than just their music. Now that they are back with the original line up there are four very different spirits involved in the band. When you got someone like Jaz fronting the band who was so many views on world matters, which I find interesting and very educational reading his lyrics."

In March 2010 an interesting Killing Joke collaboration found its way to the opening track of *Classic Rock* magazine's compilation. *With a Little Help from Their Friends* featured 14 songs, and 'I Buy' was an exclusive song for the compilation, featuring Killing Joke without Jaz. The vocals are delivered by Tim Burgess, who is best known as the lead singer of the alternative rock band The Charlatans. There is no shadow of doubt that the Charlatans were influenced by Killing Joke and Tim is a self-confessed fan of the band.

The new album was recorded during October and November 2009, which also marked the band's 30th anniversary. The album was recorded in various studios: Britannia Row Studios and The Dreaming Cave in London, Youth's Space Mountain Studio in Granada, Spain and Studio Faust in Prague, Czech Republic.

Dante: "When I started hearing the record, I was really amazed how great it was. I knew it was going to be good, because they are a band of great quality, but it was really good. For a band that's been around for quite a long time at that point already. Had a very successful career. Sometimes with those artists it's more about touring – not about the new music because the creative spark isn't always the strongest after a number of years or the chemistry isn't what it was back in the early days. Clearly that wasn't the case with Killing Joke at all. I think some of their best music of their career has been made in the last three Killing Joke albums. It was really heavy. It was really nasty. It was really relevant. It was really on the edge. It was really powerful. It was very vibrant. It was never easy listening. Killing Joke should never be easy listening. It was challenging, the lyrics were challenging.

"The first time we heard it we went down to the studio. I think it was Britannia Road Studios in London where Youth was in at the time working on bits and pieces. I brought the press guy we were using at the time with us as well. It was me, him and some other people as well and Youth just played us a track from the record. The track was 'The Great Cull', which is a very, very timely lyric looking at it now – and we all started headbanging in the studio like idiots. It's one of my favourite Killing Joke tracks still. It was so heavy, you know. I knew when I heard it that this was going to be amazing because they were making this kind of music and the album turned out great and we got great response and great reviews. And [they are] always entertaining in interviews. One of the things that came for me from that record was when I read the lyrics Jaz had written - I was more proofreading them, to check the spelling and things like that, but obviously when you read lyrics you absorb them – was how interesting they were. I took away some of the things he wrote and I googled them and researched them more, because I wasn't aware of some of the things and reference points he was making in the lyrics. A lot of what he wrote on that record is what you can relate exactly what is happening today. I think in the course of that record to today I think Jaz Coleman a lot of people

181

massively respected him – he has become some sort of a prophet. A lot what he has been saying, actually from the beginning, particularly in the last few years has been spot on. You know what's actually going on. He is actually at a very elevated position at the minute. When we do the next interviews with Jaz people will listen and listen very carefully to what he is going to say about the next ten years."

"We did over twenty songs and then we've been arguing over which ones go on the fucking record for the last six months!" Jaz told to Rob Haynes of *The Quietus* in August 2010. The album had the working title 'Feast of Fools', but eventually that song didn't even make it on to the album, but would surface in 2012 in the *Singles Collection*.

Michael Rendell, who was responsible for the additional engineering on *Absolute Dissent*, recalls in the *Youth: Sketch, Drugs & Rock n Roll* documentary directed by Paul Elliott Sean Lamberth that the first sessions he did with the band were traumatic. Rendell has worked with Youth on multiple projects and is used to Youth being the producer and at the helm of the recording sessions, but back with Killing Joke the band all reverted back to their adolescent insecurities, and he apparently spent most of the sessions being abused, from being called a cunt to having his chair kicked. Happily it seems it worked out well at the end as he has since worked on the subsequent albums the band has done.

In March 2010 the band announces on their 30th anniversary that 24 of the shows slated to begin in the UK on 15 April are now postponed. Paul describes the decision on the website as having happened because "unforeseen circumstances have made meeting deadlines impossible and have led to this extremely hard decision." At the time of the news the album was carrying the title 'XIII: Feast of Fools' and the release was due to be April, but it was moved to September.

Prior to the album the band released the 'In Excelsis' EP in June 2010. It featured the title track 'In Excelsis', 'Endgame', 'Kali Yuga', 'Ghost Of Ladbroke Grove' and 'Ghost Of Ladbroke Grove (Dub)'. This would mark the first new material from the original line up in decades. It is worth noting 'Kali Yuga' was exclusive to this release and is a completely different track to 'Kaliyuga' from the *Extremities* album. It only shares the same title. The dub version of 'Ghost Of Ladbroke Grove' wasn't on the album either, but the rest appeared as the same versions in *Absolute Dissent*.

Ladbroke Grove is a road in West London in the Royal Borough of Kensington and Chelsea, but also a name given to the close surrounding area of Notting Hill and Kensal Green. Ladbroke Grove has a special meaning to Jaz as he told Eugene Butcher of *Vive Le Rock* in the summer of 2013. It has always been a magnet for artists, and there were a lot of rehearsal and recording studios back in the 60s and 70s that would house bands such as Pink Floyd and Jimi Hendrix. Jaz's long time dream when he was younger was to move to the area and start a band. Nowadays the place is very different.

"We got amazing response to it right at the beginning," says Dante Bonutto regarding the EP. "We knew at that point that there was going to be great interest in the album – and there was." Over the years Youth's dub versions had become an important part of the singles. "Youth's fantastic. When he does those dub mixes, or different versions of the songs, fans love that. Particularly the dub stuff I believe. People absolutely love what he does. He is a talented guy."

The track listing on the comeback album was 'Absolute Dissent', 'The Great Cull', 'Fresh Fever from the Skies', 'In Excelsis', 'European Super State', 'This World Hell', 'Endgame', 'The Raven King', 'Honour the Fire', 'Depthcharge', 'Here Comes the Singularity' and 'Ghosts of Ladbroke Grove'. The songs are credited to the original line up - Jaz Coleman, Paul Ferguson, Martin 'Youth' Glover and Kevin 'Geordie' Walker. Additional keyboards on top of Jaz's were provided by the band's touring member Reza Udhin. There are some absolutely essential Killing Joke songs in the form of 'European Super State', 'The Raven King' and 'Ghosts of Ladbroke Grove'.

Unreleased songs 'Sixth Sun', 'Time Wave' and 'Feast of Fools' surfaced on the super-deluxe version of *The Singles Collection*, only available from Pledge Music in 2012.

"I think the album ended up being voted in many people's best-ofs of that particular year," recalls Dante. "A lot of musicians really related to that record. That record has got a very kind of nasty sound to it. It's really great. Very punk in a way. I suppose it kind of had that metallic edge to it as well. I loved it. I thought the artwork was really interesting as well. At that point we knew that we were off running in a brand-new phase of their career and that relationship with the band continues to this day and I hope we have another record out next year."

Respected music magazines such as *Q* and *Mojo* awarded the album 4 out of 5 stars while *BBC Music* found the album very favourable with John Doran saying that "They easily manage to step out from the long shadow cast by their own first two albums on this close-to-genius release." Dom Gourlay of *Drowned in Sound* calls the album "a remarkable achievement for a band whose creative zenith appeared to have been locked in the annals many moons ago." He gives it 8 out of 10 and is pleased that the band has come back in such a great shape. *Kerrang* and *Alternative Press* gave the album 3 out of 5.

Spinefarm as a label wasn't influencing the band's direction or decisions, as Dante explains: "There are certain artists, especially established artists and sometimes new artists too, who have a particular creative vision and a particular way of working and have a reputation for independent thinking and that's what fans love about the group. I think when you have bands like that I think you interfere at your peril really with that. Certainly, with Killing Joke fans don't want to think the music is in anyway manipulated or manufactured or overly marketed. It's not what the band is about at all. What I think the Killing Joke fans want to know, and this is obviously absolutely true, that whatever the band delivers is straight from them to the fans. We are the releasing platform. We can advise, we can offer help, support, any financial support when required, but the vision remains intact. Our aim with Killing Joke is focus their vision and put a spotlight onto their vision. Not diluting it by any size, shape or form. So, the A&R of Killing Joke is: sign the band, put them in a studio and listen to the records. If it's more than that you're getting it wrong with Killing Joke. Killing Joke is a unique entity and mustn't be tampered with. Obviously as time goes on our relationship is built on trust, so they'll probably come to us more for certain bits of advice more to do with the release strategy I think really. The music, the visuals that's their domain. They are the creative force there, so I want fans to know that's untampered with."

The two CD Deluxe Edition had a bonus disc, *Absolute Respect*, with 11 cover songs from everyone from Foo Fighters to Metallica. This was later also released as a standalone release. The decision to do the tribute album was from a conversation the label had with their management. "They were so many artists that really respected Killing Joke and had done covers of theirs over the years and had done remixes," says Dante Bonutto. "We thought it was a good idea to bring all these assets together and create some bonus content – and just to show where the band was in the marketplace in terms of the level of respect that they got from other artists. I think the only new thing we might have had was a new version of 'Love Like Blood', which was done by Dead By April

184

I think on that particular record, because we felt that having something new was probably a good idea. I was working with Dead By April at the time anyway, so I think they actually recorded that song specifically to be used on the album. I think the other tracks had probably already existed, but they weren't pulled together."

The album was supported by a extensive tour starting in Edinburgh in mid-April and lasting until July the following year, with a couple of months off during the early part of the year.

2012 – MMXII

Following in the footsteps of the previous album their second offering with the original line up is their most dense ever. 'In Cythera' is a heartfelt ode to friendship and supporting those suffering from addictions and takes us back to their mid-80s recordings while funky 'Trance' nods to their early days and 'Corporate Elect' reflects 21st century Killing Joke at its best. A fitting soundtrack to the new dawn.

UK Album Chart #44

The first taste of the upcoming album came in February 2012, when 'Rapture' was uploaded to YouTube. Jaz would describe the inspiration behind the song to Gregory Adams of *Exclaim!* magazine upon the release saying the song is about the way he perceives a Killing Joke concert. "It's a spiritual experience for myself to get into that state of grace... music is the theme of mantra. I'm not into organised religion at all, but I've always liked what Fela Kuti did in Nigeria, playing music like it was a temple. Maybe we will evolve into a time where we will be performing for ritualistic and spiritual reasons alone and not for monetary reasons?"

'In Cythera' was the first single from the album, and the music video by Mike Coles was uploaded to their YouTube channel on 6 March. The video incorporated elements from the then unreleased Killing Joke documentary by Shaun Pettigrew, *The Death and Resurrection Show*. The single itself was released on 19 March as a limited and numbered 12" coloured vinyl, and as a compact disc. The CD version featured 'Penny Drops' as an exclusive B-side. 'Corporate Elect' was the second single, released on iTunes on 1 December accompanied by an extended version of 'On All Hallow's Eve' as the B-side of the single.

'In Cythera' is at the time of writing the last song in which Jaz sings about the Island. At this stage it is also about friendship, longing and surviving addiction. The island Kythira, which is also transliterated as Cythera, Kythera and Kithira, is an island in Greece situated opposite

186

the south-eastern tip of the Peloponnese peninsula. This particular island is a distant one from the seven main Ionian Islands. Cythera has a rich and varied history with archaeological remains from the Helladic period, which are contemporary with the Minoans. There is archaeological evidence of trade as far as Egypt and Mesopotamia. In Ancient Greek mythology Cythera was seen to be the island of celestial Aphrodite, the Goddess of love. Parts of the song originate from 'Golden Lane', which was written in Prague in 2007, but remains unreleased. The lyrics share the same lines about dishonesty, breaking down inside and not having expressed enough love.

The album was recorded in 2011, mainly in The Doghouse Studio in Oxfordshire, England, with some work done at Studio Faust in Prague, Czech Republic. Apparently, the band had worked on as many as 26 songs.

"We recorded this at quite a few studios around the world, lots of remote recordings, where we sent each other parts that we were doing at our own studios, then they were assembled together," explains Reza. "I flew out to Prague for a few weeks and shared an apartment with Jaz, whilst I recorded lot of Jaz's vocals and Geordie's guitars for the album."

Youth: "Some of the tracks are more kind of densely produced, but we did a lot of overdubs on guitars on *Absolute Dissent* and did not do any on this album. Live guitar stage really. We did a conscious decision of keeping it quite raw, but nevertheless there are a lot more keyboards on this album and that makes it a bit dense, but I think there is still space there I think. It is a valid point I think that is because our production criteria is to make it modern as well as timeless. The way we mixed it and the way we balance things with a little bit of a more modern perspective."

Jaz and Paul shared the lyric writing on the album and the drummer describes his inspiration as follows: "The inspiration is still what I see around me. It's political discontent. I'm not content with the way the world is. I'm not content with us being manipulated. Not content with genetically modified crops. I'm not content with the air that we breathe. I'm not content with corporate takeover of the world and that's inspiration enough."

Paul: "Young and inexperienced on the first two records, but still open to try to forge a new sound for ourselves. Something different we thought. Something that was unique and trying to carve our own identity and I think we have that sound with whatever we do now. We got a few years under our belts, so we can afford to dabble in whatever we want and make it ours."

The song 'Trance' shares some similarities with their early song and live staple 'Pssyche' to which Youth comments that "It's a big nod to that. I'm surprised that got on actually." Having heard about the excess amount of recordings they've been doing I ask Youth about the songs that were left off the album. He replies saying that "There is this one 'Fukushima', which is the best anthem we have done since 'Love Like Blood'. Geordie didn't like it. Geordie's fault. Might put that out on a solo album or something."

Jaz: "If someone in the band doesn't really like something I normally support them on it, because I don't want anyone in the band putting out a song that they don't like. So we always do an excess amount of music and start throwing stuff out. Some of the stuff we turn out with people are really shocked with and horrified in many cases."

Regarding the guitar overdubs on the album Jaz says "Most of the time it's just one guitar. He won't do any more than that. I got him do a feedback track on 'Fema Camp' and beyond that he wouldn't do it. To the point where the engineer would have to take a single track and bump it up. Take an aspect of the single track and double it. He wouldn't double it. He records everything in stereo, so it sounds fucking double from the beginning anyway, sounds fucking quadruple!

"Geordie insisted you recorded everything again live. So whatever you recorded he wanted you to do it again to get this live feel. He doesn't want it perfect. (Geordie's ultimate record is *The Who Live at Leeds*). When Youth is more studio pro, produced sound. You got this conflict going on with the two at any time of the production."

"I try not to [do overdubs]," says Geordie. "We have a legendary chemistry." And he mentions about his different approach to recording and the whole band acting as producers who "had to watch that Youth chopping it all up if you're not careful."

Paul: "I think it's a great record. I'm very proud of it. I think it is distinctly a Killing Joke record. Everybody has given their finest performance on this record."

Lyrically there is a shift toward more global issues such as corporate power and greed expressed in songs like 'Corporate Elect', but Jaz insists it wasn't a conscious decision to go in that direction.

Jaz: "Nothing is a conscious decision in Killing Joke. We don't plan

188

anything. We just bloody get in the room and play and it lands like that. Really nothing – and there is no writing process. We just make our lives colourful and get in a room together and it all comes out."

One of the unreleased songs, or at least unused lyrics, is 'Suicide Tribe', which is a song about political control and destruction of the planet and namechecks the Rockefellers whom Jaz claims a member of the band has been working for.

When the album was about to be released Youth had been talking about the possibility of recording the band's greatest hits as acoustic versions, but this never went beyond the idea stage.

The album was released on 2 April 2012 having been recorded in The Doghouse Studio in Oxfordshire, England and Studio Faust in Prague, Czech Republic the previous year. The ten tracks that made it onto the album were 'Pole Shift', 'Fema Camp', 'Rapture', 'Colony Collapse', 'Corporate Elect', 'In Cythera', 'Primobile', 'Glitch', 'Trance' and 'On All Hallow's Eve'. The iTunes exclusive bonus track was 'New Uprising'. All tracks are credited to the original line up Jaz Coleman, Paul Ferguson, Youth, and Geordie Walker. Two of the best latter-day Killing Joke compositions are fierce and corrupt 'Corporate Elect' and the touching ode to friendship and struggles with addiction in the form of 'In Cythera'.

Classic Rock gave the album 9 out of 10 with *Rolling Stone, Terrorizer, Mojo* and *Kerrang* all awarding the album 4 out of 5 stars. In *Classic Rock* the review said that it was "the end of the world as we know it. But what a way to go." "Not bad, as a one word review," describes Mick Middles in *The Quietus,* who believes the album will silence all those in doubt. "For all its doom-laden prophecies, this is music that gladdens the heart," he adds.

Prior to the release of the album the band embarked on a UK tour in March, followed by a European tour. Although around half of the songs on the set were from the new album, they hadn't been heard by the audiences yet at the time, which sometimes resulted in a more lukewarm response from the Gatherers. The album was released by Finnish label Spinefarm Records, and the distribution was handled worldwide by Universal Music Group. *MMXII* reached number 44 in the UK Albums Chart and also charted at number 9 in the Finnish Album Chart, as well as number 134 in the French Albums Chart.

On 9 May an anti-consumerist music video for 'Corporate Elect' directed by Mikee W. Goodman was released on YouTube to promote the new album.

Dante: "I think at that point as we'd done the first album our relationship had grown and blossomed. I knew more about the band and the personalities. My memory of that [album] was that it was pretty much left to them to deliver the music and Mike Coles I believe on that record on the artwork. He has worked with them from early in the career. Mike knows how to work with Killing Joke. How to work with four different personalities and used to doing that as well. I think that's the thing with Killing Joke it is working with four individuals who come together and create this great music together, but they think in their own space I think. You got to find some way of working with them, but with that record I'm sure we had some discussions about track listing and what should go on and formats, but essentially the music was delivered by the band."

The album got a good response from the press and the fans and not too unsurprisingly took the top spot in my top 5 albums of the year for *Vive Le Rock* magazine.

In late July Killing Joke announced on Facebook that Jaz Coleman had gone missing. This later turned out was a publicity stunt created due to the band pulling out of a downsized UK tour with The Cult and The Mission scheduled for September. The dates were originally planned to be stadium dates, but were moved to smaller venues due to the lack of ticket sales.

On 6 May 2013 the band released *The Singles Collection 1979-2012* in a collaboration between Spinefarm and Universal Records. The compilation was the first truly great collection of their whole career and was released to universal acclaim. I awarded the magnificent collection the full 10 out of 10 in *Vive Le Rock* magazine with the headline "The pure magic of the most amazing post-punk outfit to ever walk the planet." The review I submitted read as follows: "The mighty Joke release a chronologically arranged career spanning compilation showing the full power and colourful musical journey through the decades. Opening by the mesmerising vibes of 'Nervous System' followed by their most defining moment 'Wardance'. The first disc covers the glorious 'Eighties' including their shiniest star 'Love Like Blood'. Second disc takes us to the industrialisation and modern day 'Corporate Elect' with latter day gems like hateful 'Hosannas from the Basements of Hell' and anti-technology 'Loose Cannon' and prove to us how these originators never went stale and while evolving with the times never lost their unique sound. Excellent selection omitting only the funk madness of 'Pssyche'. For the gatherer the most exciting part is the last 10 track rarities disc featuring B-sides and soundtrack cuts as well as three unreleased songs from *Absolute Dissent* sessions along with the captivating *Democracy*-era 'Four Stations of the Sun'. The absolute highlight is 'Time Wave', which made an appearance on their set during the reunion tour. Regrettably the demo version of the song does not reach its full potential, but does pound to the consciousness like their best sledgehammers. Unfortunately the recently recorded anthem 'Fukushima', which Youth talked about in our cover feature, does not appear on this compilation. The sound of the Earth vomiting is perfectly captured on these pieces of plastic and remind us how the sickness carries on, but as long as it comes across like this may it never heal."

The compilation was released as a 2 CD, 3 CD limited edition with the third disc being dedicated to rarities as well as a mind-blowing 33 CD single deluxe box set, which came with a hand-numbered hinge lid cigar container made from black lined rigid board finished with matt print retrospective artwork, 33 career spanning CD singles plus select B-sides in full colour card wallets featuring original artwork, a rarities disc including previously unreleased studio tracks, a 32 page book including rare photos, archive notes, band commentary, and a poster designed and hand signed by long time Killing Joke artist, Mike Coles, printed on 250gsm silk art along with an aluminium screw top branded cigar tube containing original wrappers of cigars smoked by Jaz Coleman and Paul Raven during the recording of *Hosannas From The Basements Of Hell*.

On Saturday 8 September the band planned on playing at Metropolis Studios in London with a staggering £195 ticket price. The event, with complimentary drinks and meet and greet opportunities with the band, would also be filmed for television and DVD, but the event was cancelled. Needless to say the fans didn't appreciate the cost of the tickets.

November 16 saw the release of Shaun Pettigrew's *The Death and Resurrection Show*. "It's been an incredible journey that really started back in the 70s, when I was hanging out in a squat called the Apocalypse Hotel, close by to where the band were living in Ladbroke Grove. Years later I got to know Jaz more closely when we were both living and working in New Zealand and eventually we got to talking about making a film exploring some of Jaz's experiences and thoughts on things like spirituality and the politics of the Western world around us. Jaz wrote to me and outlined his own ritualistic journey from 1982 onwards and this became the essential ribcage structure of completed shots in the order that they appear in both of the film's storylines.

"We had lots of conversations about what would work, a study of the profane and ritual history of Killing Joke through the eyes of a journalist; the effect of Killing Joke music on fans; the ability to change your external and internal reality; to achieve a true joining of one's God-spirit, and to understand your own destiny, by using ritual magic to achieve success or your own self-worth.

"In the initial film - LSBYP - *Let Success be Your Proof*, produced and co-directed by Jaz and ILC Productions, is about pilgrimage, multiple coincidences and the search for a mythical Island called 'Cythera'. This was the original concept for the film and a parallel story to Jaz's book *Letters From Cythera*.

"In the final main film - TDARS -*The Death and Resurrection Show*, produced and directed by ILC Productions became the main Killing Joke chronological story.

"We actually completed both of these two film storyline ideas and produced the Pal DVD with both on but which I have to say 'hand on heart', I endeavoured to make the first work into the second but it became too hard to connect the two together and ultimately sell."

In 2013 the band would play a couple of dates in the UK and Europe starting with an intimate warm up show at Zombie Hut in Corbyn. From April to June the band would be touring the US. In 2014 the band would only play on 14 August at The Picturedrome in Holmfirth and the following day at the Fleece in Bristol.

192

2015 - Pylon

Latter day Killing Joke masterpiece from the pulse of 'Autonomous Zone' to the depths of 'Into the Unknown'. New Cold War themed album where the reunited original line up is closing a successful comeback trilogy.

UK Album Chart #16

The album was recorded in multiple studios: in Vada Studios in Worcestershire, The Lair in Bath, The Doghouse Studio in Oxfordshire and The Hive in Prague, Czech Republic. Prior to the release of the album, the 'I Am the Virus' and 'Euphoria' music videos had appeared online and the songs were released as digital singles.

The album was produced by the band with the help of English record producer and audio engineer Tom Dalgety. Tom is best known for his work with Pixies, Ghost and Royal Blood. He had also worked on the band's previous album. "We knew Tom," explains Dante Bonutto, "so there was a slight change in the personnel they were working with, but then essentially again the record was delivered by the band and my memory of that mainly is that how amazing the record was and every time I was hearing another track it was just incredible. There were so many great choices of singles and tracks that could lead the way like 'I Am the Virus', which is now again a very relevant song and it's getting huge hits on YouTube now."

The first taste of the album came on none other than 11 September coinciding with one of the worst terrorist attacks on American soil. The thought provoking 'I Am the Virus' was released as a lyric music video done by the band's favourite graphic designer Mike Coles.

Reza: "Recorded all over the place again, but a lot of work was done at a few studios in Prague. I flew over to Prague to help out on this album too, together with Jaz and Geordie."

Jaz Coleman didn't really see the chart success of the album as something spectacular. He says: "You know I've never given that much consideration. It's always the same when we release a record. It was a nice surprise that it went to number one in the UK, but the main thing is as long as I'm passionate about it and the guys are passionate about it and we love the result it doesn't matter how well it does on the charts.

"What do you say after 37 years in the same band with the same people you started when you were teenagers. It has been a great journey. As we get older we're even more passionate about it. I want to do more of Killing Joke. This is our third record since 2010, so we're really creative. We're not revelling in the past. We always think we haven't reached our best yet. This album is something else."

When asked about whether the current political climate has influenced the album: "It always does. Although saying that I don't really see politics as an answer to anything. Revolutions never work. Revelations would work. A spiritual revelation would work. I'm very concerned about things. We've walking into fascism. Benito Mussolini said corporatism is fascism and that's what we're living.

"The TTIP agreement and the Trans-Pacific Partnership. The nation state will be finished. I don't know any legal recourse. They won't even be able to sue these multinationals once this is signed. It just goes to show no ordinary person has had a choice in this and there is nothing democratic about these agreements. We're in the final stages of moving into a unipolar world. There is this one problem. Mr. Putin doesn't agree! And that's where we are in a new Cold War. And you are on the frontline!

"We've done a new Cold War album. This is really sounding like a new Cold War to us. I spend most of my time in Russia, I'm working in St. Peterborough State Symphony Orchestra for two years now. So I get a very different perspective to the BBC and CNN narrative. Very different perspective the Russians have. Mr Putin has 85 per cent popularity over there and he said to the G20 people that he'll never accept a unipolar world.

"The way these big financial powers behind central banks work is that they normally get rid of like [Libyan revolutionary Muammar] Gaddafi and Saddam Hussein. Putin knows he is in the firing line. It's very unstable at the moment. Very very unstable. The thing is Nato policies are being dictated by neocons. The godfather of neocons is [Polish-American diplomat and political scientist Zbigniew] Brzezinski and he is [Barak] Obama's foreign policy chief. He is the guy who fucking cooked up 9/11. He said we need a new Pearl Harbour. He is the guy who created the Taliban back in the day when he worked for

Jimmy Carter. Incredible. So he is the guy pulling the strings now. All these colour coded revolutions we've been having; the Orange revolution etc. It's all instigated. Since 94 we've had an agreement that we wouldn't circle them and we wouldn't expand. What's the interest close the Russian border? Well, you can see that's not happening. The Russians are very jumpy. And of course it is stupid now we push Russia into economic alignment with the Bric nations and the US dollar won't be used in the way it was used before. America is doomed in a long term. It can't survive. Before it was using dollar in all petroleum dealings. Well now of course oil is so cheap. It's just not a problem anymore, so they won't be trading in US dollars anymore. In the end the US can't survive, but by then maybe this New World Order thing would've already kicked in. We're in the last stages of it.

"Three British prime ministers have talked about the New World Order. What are they talking about? The only reference we have is Mr. David Rockefeller said, this guy that they all kneel before. It's funny someone really really close to Killing Joke goes regularly to the Rockefeller jet. It's funny. Of course they knew before. They had to stage 9/11 because they'd never get American foreign policy behind Iraq and Afghanistan. They'd never be able to do the expansion unless they had the public behind them fighting an enemy that has been essentially created. When you think who funds Isis it all goes through Saudi Arabia, but I'm sure it's British tax payers' money. Amongst other things you know. Because at the end we need an enemy. We need to keep this tension up, because Dr. Kurt Lewin, a great psychiatrist, who is this inventor of this shock thesis, said that by perpetual shocks on society mankind stays in a child like state where he is easier to control he is more malleable. These think tanks they advise we fund these very evil terrorists as it opens up budgets for the military industry complex etcetera and keeps every one in a general state of fear, which is when people are easier to push around. That's what has happened really. We're now there. Here we are in Europe, who is making these decisions, you ask yourself. Who decides we are going to war with Russia? It looks like Mrs. Merkel is told what to do and the rest of them are all kind of stooges most often politicians, aren't they? Let's face it, when you sell off all the wealth of a nation, what do you have left? Nothing. You have a protectorate. They're just protectorates for a global empire and that's what you have now. And a fragmented society. That's all on their little gadgets all the time. On their little gadgets wanking

195

off! I say that because 70 percent of Internet traffic is porn. So most of the world now is choking the chicken!"

Youth: "The last album was quite progressive dare I say it. It has got a track 10 minutes long and lot of synths. 'Corporate Elect' is fierce as well. Previous two albums have been covering a lot of places we've been to before. This is, dare I say it, our metal album really. It's very very heavy and quite fast some of it. It's great. Couple of big end of the world anthems and a few funky bass lines. Not too much disco going on on this one."

Paul told *Vive Le Rock*'s Paul Hagen in 2015: "I think it's a thoroughly intense album. It was a bit of a challenge for me to record some of these tracks. I mean not technically but physically. They're kind of fast. It's a bit difficult technically to be doing a rushed hi-hat, snare, tom tom, fill, snare, all at the same time. So they're intense from a playing point of view for me and they were a bit of a challenge. So far - knock on wood - the guitars are right in your face as well which to me is so really, really good. Geordie played some amazing guitar stuff on this. It's pretty intense."

"In fact, I played the new album to Alex Paterson from The Orb, who's an old associate of ours, and I said 'what do you think?' and I showed him the sleeve and he goes 'oh yeah, a lot of metal, not enough disco.' Which helped actually on the running order we had. We made sure there were a couple of disco ones in there. Actually, the running order now has made it less heavy heavy, metal heavy but we could have done like seven, eight tracks just that were all kind of very metal. At one point I was calling it our 'black' album, you know. But we kind of balanced that out a little bit now but it's still one of the heaviest albums we've done I think," Youth told *Vive Le Rock*'s Paul Hagen.

As for the tracks that didn't make it onto the final version of *Pylon*, Youth explains to *Vive Le Rock*'s Paul Hagen the difficulties of pleasing everyone in the band. "It's frustrating because one of the strongest tracks from *MMXII* was a track called 'Fukushima' that both me and Jaz absolutely loved. I thought it was one of our big anthems in the vein of 'Love Like Blood' and Geordie just got a bit vinegar on it and didn't like it so we never used it. I'm still pinching myself about that. On this album there was a track we did called 'Love is a Law,' which again is in a similar sort of vein. Geordie did finally agree to it but we never got around to doing it and both could have been the big trailblazer tracks for the albums. We have a history of doing, you know, self-sabotage.

From putting 'Change' on as a B-side to whatever. So I suppose it's in tradition of that, we're still doing that."

Dante: "One thing I remember on that record and we discussed with the band was during the course of our relationship working together there was almost like a three-album plan and that was the last part of the triptych, if we can call it that. I don't know why that was thought about, but it seems like that's what it was. There were these three great albums that were coming out that were taking the band forward in a really dramatic sense and increasing their profile, their live business and connecting them more to the media. All sorts of things were kind of going on. I think there was a thread that ran through those three records linking them together. In terms of the visuals, in terms of the sonics and the intent of making them. And obviously we haven't kind of closed the chapter as we got more to come, but I think those three records are going to be seen as [a whole]. Maybe at some point we're going to release them as a box, or as a body of work, so I think they're all done very much in the same spirit. Certainly, the same people, apart from the producer shift on *Pylon*. Same team apart from that pretty much and I'm very proud to be involved in those records. Three amazing records and *Pylon* probably being the best and the heaviest. What was exciting with that was, again, the band were in such a creative form. Recorded about 16 tracks I think and where we kind of spoke up was how to use the extra material in terms of creating two CD formats. We did a special release for the Record Store Day. We had a lot of flexibility because of the amount of tracks they've recorded and also how good they all were. How long of them actually were as well. Lots of music we could really work with too. It was great. It was really good. I think when someone delivers a record like that and even the title was really interesting."

In 2016 long time keyboard player Reza Uhdin parted ways with the band. "I couldn't do the full European Tour in 2016, as I was touring the USA with my own band Inertia. So I got a friend of mine to replace me. It was also probably the right time to leave. I had done 11 years with the band by then. No hard feelings, I still speak to them all. Best was playing the shows, always a great vibe. Worst, probably band arguments on tour. Particularly around 2005. Lots of crazy and fun memories... including being driven from Beijing in China to a festival site, which we were told was just outside of Beijing. We reached there 14 hours later, whilst baking in the hot sun in a small minivan. Also, doing a show in Glasgow where half way through the set we somehow

197

knocked out the power in the venue, the audience had to be evacuated in the dark. Later on we found out we had knocked out the power for the entire block of clubs and venues where we were at, not just our venue!"

Reza's friend Roi Robertson took his place, describing some of his most memorable experiences here: "One of the worst was playing in Belgium on the last date of the 2016 tour, and that dodgy laptop I was given to use on stage decided to fucking crash, yet again, during a song. I had to reboot it, so I signalled to the band that it was fucked and we had to stop for a moment whilst I sorted it out, and then had to endure Jaz standing next to me calling me all sorts of things as I calmly tried to explain to him what was happening. That was a very long two minutes or so, let me tell you. So now, I play with two identical keyboard set-ups running simultaneously on stage in case one goes down. There are many good memories of course... apart from anything else, it's such a privilege to travel the world with them, and experience the different ways of life, people, clubs, restaurants and food, in so many countries and cities. I mean, for example, I loved going to Mexico City and partying at the top of the hotel in their open roofed bar, re-visiting South America and discovering the wonders of Ceviche and Pisco Sours, hanging out in some of my favourite cities, like Berlin, Hamburg, Paris and Prague. Also, getting to DJ in Brooklyn along with Youth, supporting The Prodigy at a festival in Valencia, playing with Guns N' Roses to 70,000 people in Germany, playing a synth-solo on stage with Tool most nights of our US support tour with them, the list goes on and on... but the best thing has to be meeting the wonderful woman who is now my fiancee on that tour, so I have much to be thankful to them for indeed."

Dante says getting to know the band and Jaz Coleman in particular has been particularly fascinating. They worked together on *Magna Invocatio*, which came out in 2019, in which he rearranged Killing Joke's music for a classical orchestra. The project had been in the making for a number of years and was received the much critical acclaim. "It is quite well known that Jaz used to drink quite a bit in the old days of Killing Joke," says Dante, "I didn't know him in that era. He is a force of nature now. It might've been amplified even more at that point. I've only met him more recently, but I find him absolutely fascinating. He is such a deeply intelligent man. What he keeps pointing out about Killing Joke is that they don't have a lot of academic qualifications as a band, but they are really smart people. That's an interesting point. What do qualifications really mean? It's about what's up here and how you use it," Dante says, pointing to his head. He points out how well Jaz is respected among academics and intellectuals. "The power of music, but it's really more than music it is what it represents to people. It's the whole package of it. It's the message as well. One of the things I've really enjoyed working with Killing Joke, and is very memorable, is the loyalty and support of the fans – the Gatherers. With all the bands I've worked with it's rare to find a group of people who are so involved with an artist and back them all the time. Interested in what they do and support them so much. So ingrained in the world and the detail of Killing Joke and what they represent. Sometimes people who aren't involved in music, or perhaps the arts in general, they sometimes undervalue the power that music has in people's lives and undervalue the music as a cultural force. And a force that can be of great good and comfort – and solace to people in difficult times as well. That's what I take from Killing Joke. Just how much that band and their music means to the fans and people that love them, so we have to take it very, very seriously because of that. The band certainly takes that very seriously indeed. I think it just reinforces the impact the music has in all of our lives and how it informs our lives. Defines us really as people. The things that we think and the things that we do. Killing Joke is the perfect soundtrack to the whole of your life. It can hit every aspect of what you do. To headbanging to what you're really thinking and that's a very hard place to occupy as a band and such a long period of time. So I think that they are unique."

The album was released on 23 October 2015. The track listing was 'Autonomous Zone', 'Dawn of the Hive', 'New Cold War', 'Euphoria', 'New Jerusalem', 'War on Freedom', 'Big Buzz', 'Delete', 'I Am the Virus' and 'Into the Unknown'. A limited deluxe edition bonus disc contained the following on a second CD: 'Apotheosis', 'Plague', 'Star Spangled', 'Panopticon' and 'Snakedance (Youth 'Rattlesnake Dub' Remix)'. The regular version of 'Snakedance' would surface on the Record Store Day vinyl release. As on the previous albums all the tracks were credited to Killing Joke: Jaz Coleman, Paul Ferguson, Youth, and Geordie Walker. Whilst finishing this book in 2020 songs such as 'Autonomous Zone', 'New Cold War' and 'I Am the Virus' have never felt more relevant. Truly classic Killing Joke.

The album did extremely well in the press and was chosen as the album of the year in *Vive Le Rock* magazine, and as one might guess it was also my number 1 album for the writer's top 5 of the year. Miles Picard awarded the album 9 out of 10 in *Vive Le Rock*, stating that the album is the band's "most sonically abrasive collection of songs for some time, with lyrics addressing the brutal injustices of capitalist hegemony and the inability of the world leaders to curtail the uncontrollable excesses of global monetarism." The album was at number 10 in The 20 Best Metal Albums of 2015 in *Rolling Stone.* John Robb concludes in his 9 out of 10 review in *Louder Than War* that "*Pylon* is yet another instalment in this engaging and strange story and a place to get truly lost in." However, Sean Barry of *Consequence of Sounds* says the album is "strong and consistent, to be sure, but with the lack of variety, *Pylon* is likely to be remembered as an album that just kept a constant rhythm for 56 minutes."

The album would be promoted with extensive touring, starting from Eurorock Festival in Belgium in mid-May and ending with supporting none other than hard rock legends Guns N' Roses at the arena shows in June the following year. Paul damaged his leg during rehearsals a day before the band was due to play at Sideways Festival in the capital Helsinki and was quickly replaced by Jason Bowld from Pitchshifter.

Jaz: "Paul broke his leg yesterday, so we had to switch drummers very quickly, but these things kinda happen. He'll heal up I know that. Everything is really good with the summer festivals. After 37 years you do these things over and over again.

"I love Finland. We generally come here during the summer, but I always think it'd be great to come here with Geordie and get a house in the North and do some fishing and go crazy in the woods. There are quite a lot of bands that we like from Finland."

Bowld did a fantastic job of filling in and plays in a style similar to the powerhouse drumming Big Paul is known for in his absentia for a couple of shows during the summer. Bowld's skills can be witnessed in the excellent live television broadcast from Hellfest festival in France from 20 July. One of the notable shows was the show at Brixton Academy in London on 4 November 2016 labelled as 'the Great Gathering', which resulted in a live album, but was also filmed. This is yet to be released.

Jason Bowld tells in the *Sex, Wax and Rock n Roll* documentary by Mont Sherar how Paul had sent him an email afterwards thanking him for filling in when he couldn't do it. "That's really rare," he states sincerely, "for someone with such a great success with such a ground-breaking band." Bowld would go on to describe the band as "industrial James Brown" as it is "all about the groove". In the documentary it becomes apparent how drummers from Dave Grohl to Martin Atkins highly value Paul's unique and integral drumming.

Youth told *Vive Le Rock*'s Paul Hagen how working with Jaz became easier when he gave up drinking: "Much easier. If he carried on drinking we wouldn't be working together and the drinking stopped me working with him before. I wouldn't tour in 2004 because of the drinking, and Geordie's. Because then the work becomes meaningless and pointless and it's not about the work, it's about the next drink. It's avoidance on a grand scale. I'm not interested in that with them, or with anyone else really. So if they're not serious about what they're doing, I'm not really serious about being a part of it." Drinking had been a big low in the band's career. "Not just the drinking, pills and stuff like that. There's been times where I've had to... he [Jaz] has turned blue on the tour bus in America and I've had to pull his tongue out and put a spoon down his throat to stop him dying. Pick him up and walk him down the road and take him to hospital. I've got many friends who have become victims and battered by alcoholism and addictions of all kinds and Jaz's was one of the most traumatic. All praise to him for having the courage and the ability to sort of knock that on the head and get through it. I know 100% he's so much happier for it, a much greater person for it and his work is much better. I think *Hosannas from the Basements of Hell*, which was at the peak of the alcoholism, is probably the worst album. If he hadn't of stopped drinking, it just would have just got worse and that would have been very sad."

Jaz explained his new life to *Vive Le Rock*'s Paul Hagen: "My partner is a fitness trainer and I'm into boxing and I do quite a lot of physical stuff. Pretty much six days out of the week I do it," Jaz says. The clean living appears to have led to him living a more orderly life, which is perhaps unsurprising giving his former situation. "I mean I didn't sleep for 25 years. I had like a sleeping disorder. Of course, as soon as I stopped booze everything was fine. I did have a tablet addiction. I got on these tablets that are meant to calm you down from panic attacks and of course three years after I started taking them I was in a taxi reading about how they'd taken them off the market because there were people who were murdering people. So I thought I'd better get myself checked in pretty soon because I was so addicted to these things. I tried to give

201

up these fucking anti-anxiety tablets. I went to New Zealand and I didn't sleep for 11 days and I went absolutely mental. They took me back to Europe and the doctors in Europe said 'you were so heavily addicted to this stuff, we're surprised you didn't kill yourself when you came off this stuff'. Then I had to over a two-year period come off 0.5 at a time every six months. Once I dealt with that, then I dealt with the alcohol. The system I use with alcohol is not this 12-step rubbish that makes you into a really boring person that no one wants to hang out with anymore. The system I use is after a full moon, once you're in the waning moon it's simple. You take a vow that you'll never fucking drink again and to break that vow is death. It's not an option anymore. It means it's forever. It means it's not an option anymore. I've got loads of people off booze with this. You know they're never going to drink again because to drink is death."

In May 2020 the 'Turn To Red' EP was released as a limited edition of 1,000 copies on red 12" vinyl by Cadiz Music. The release was originally planned for Record Store Day 2020, but subsequently released for general sale as the event was postponed due to the Covid-19 pandemic.

Dante also states that now, especially with streaming, you try to categorise bands, "but with some bands there is no other point of reference, apart from them, Killing Joke, they occupy that very rare position where they are the market leader. I can't even think of a band who is number two. They are unique."

The future of Killing Joke? Apparently, a new album is planned for the autumn of 2021. "If there is any group that is going to be interesting after this [Covid pandemic of 2020] or in the aftermath of this, it's going to be Killing Joke. Their views on so much of this has been going on for so long," stated Dante from Spinefarm Records.

About the author

Jyrki "Spider" Hämäläinen is a long-time contributing writer for UK's number 1 music magazine *Vive Le Rock* and a former full-time editor one of Finland's biggest magazines *Seiska*. He is one of the Gatherers, Killing Joke's loyal supporters, and has covered the band extensively over the past decades. He graduated with a 2:1 in BA(Hons) Media and Popular Culture from Leeds Metropolitan University and studied MA Cultural and Critical Studies at Birkbeck University of London.

https://jyrkihamalainen.wordpress.com/